# AMERICAN
# STONEWARE

HENRY HOLT AND COMPANY

*New York*

# AMERICAN STONEWARE

## William C. Ketchum, Jr.

Published by Henry Holt and Company, Inc.,
115 West 18th Street, New York, New York 10011.
Published in Canada by Fitzhenry & Whiteside Limited,
195 Allstate Parkway, Markham, Ontario L3R 4T8.

Library of Congress Cataloging-in-Publication Data
Ketchum, William C.
American stoneware / William C. Ketchum, Jr.
p.   cm.
Includes bibliographical references (p.165) and index.
ISBN 0-8050-1263-X
1. Stoneware—United States.   I. Title.
NK4364.K48   1991                           90-27437
738.3'0973—dc20                              CIP

Henry Holt books are available at special discounts for bulk
purchases for sales promotions, premiums, fund-raising,
or educational use. Special editions or book excerpts
can also be created to specification.
For details contact:
Special Sales Director, Henry Holt and Company, Inc.,
115 West 18th Street, New York, New York 10011.

First Edition

DESIGNED BY LUCY ALBANESE

Printed in the United States of America
Recognizing the importance of preserving the written word,
Henry Holt and Company, Inc., by policy, prints all of its
first editions on acid-free paper.∞

1   3   5   7   9   10   8   6   4   2

# CONTENTS

# INTRODUCTION

DURING THE PAST twenty years American collectors, always seeking new frontiers, have turned their interest to a variety of antiques and collectibles. Few of these, however, have received the sustained attention devoted to stoneware. That these simple, utilitarian pots, jugs, and jars, often undecorated and originally designed to serve the most basic functions, should have so captured public attention is a reflection of several factors.

By far the most important of these is availability. From the 1630s to the present day, American potters have made stoneware. Moreover, unlike porcelain and the various earthenwares, it has been produced from one end of the United States to the other. Stoneware kilns existed throughout New England, New York, and Pennsylvania, down along the Atlantic Coast in Maryland, Virginia, and the Carolinas, across most of the South, throughout the Midwest and Southwest, reaching even to the Pacific at California.

And, particularly appealing from the collector's point of view, much of this ware bears the mark of a potter or pottery. That is not to say, of course, that the majority of these durable vessels were so identified. In fact, probably not one in ten was. However, marked ware is so widely distributed that it is often possible for enthusiasts to recognize and to collect pieces associated exclusively with a particular pottery, community, or state.

This historical interest has been greatly furthered by the publication of scholarly works narrowly focused on the kilns of a single region or state. These books, which include Lura Woodside Watkins's *Early New England Potters and their Wares*, M. Lelyn Branin's *The Early Potters and Potteries of Maine* and *The Early Makers of Handcrafted Earthenware and Stoneware in Central and Southern New Jersey*, as well as my own *Potters and Potteries of New York State, 1650–1900*, have allowed serious collectors to learn a great deal about the craftsmen whose work they own.

There have also been a substantial number of monographs focusing on an individual pottery, the shops of a particular community or area, or a certain form of decoration. These are set forth in the bibliography.

What is lacking, though, is an overall view of the American stoneware industry. There have, in fact, been only two attempts at a general survey of the American ceramics industry: John Ramsay's *American Potters and Pottery*, published in 1939, and my *Pottery & Porcelain Collector's Handbook*, issued in 1971; both are now out of date.

The goal of *American Stoneware* is to provide the general collector with a ready historical reference to the stoneware produced in our nation from the seventeenth through the twentieth century. Admittedly, this cannot be all-inclusive. Some states, such as New York, Virginia, and Ohio, had so many potteries that selectivity has been dictated by space limitations. Certain areas of the South and Midwest have not yet been thoroughly researched. Nevertheless, most collectors in most localities should find their favorite potters and kilns amply covered as well as discovering a few of whose existence they were unaware.

Those familiar with the companion book in this series, *American Redware*, will note that this volume does not contain an appendix of marks. This is due to the fact that the number of known stoneware potters' marks is so large (that included with my *Potters and Potteries of New York State* alone ran to fifty-four pages!) that they would require a text of impractical size. What I have chosen to do is to refer throughout the book to known marks whenever discussing a given pottery.

As with *American Redware* I have selected as illustrations pieces which, while not always common, may become available to the average collector. Many of these are either marked or otherwise identified with a specific maker, making it possible for the reader to see the form and decoration associated with an individual or locality. However, as always, I caution against the indiscriminate assigning of provenance to unmarked pieces, an abuse particularly prevalent in this field where some dealers and auctioneers are quick to attribute a piece to Clarkson Crolius or Thomas Chandler, for example, since this would greatly enhance its value.

A finely turned pot or one showing sophisticated decoration is a joy in itself, regardless of maker; and collectors should be encouraged to seek beauty rather than mere identification. A related factor is form. While it is generally true that stoneware was made in a more limited number of vessel types than redware, it is also true that crocks, jugs, pots, churns, pitchers, and cuspidors do not tell the whole story. All sorts of odd items, from funnels to toy whistles, were made in stoneware, and many of these are illustrated here. A broadly based collection will reflect the total production of the American craftsman.

# AMERICAN STONEWARE

# 1

# STONEWARE POTTERY MANUFACTURE

STONEWARE, technically, is a ceramic body composed of certain clays, which when fired at about 1200 C., becomes vitrified or glasslike, being both nonporous and nonabsorbent and having a hardness approaching that of steel. The clay or clays (for a stoneware body is frequently composed of a mixture of earths) suitable for its manufacture are found in widely scattered locations across the United States; New York, New Jersey, Pennsylvania, Virginia, the Carolinas, and other areas of the South, Ohio, Illinois, Missouri, and Minnesota, Texas, Arkansas, and California, among others.

On the other hand, large sections of the country do not have any native stoneware clays, most notably the New England states. Thus, stoneware manufacture has often taken a different course than that associated with redware, the other traditional American utilitarian ceramic.

Frequently faced with the expense of importing suitable clay and also with the need to build kilns that could withstand higher temperatures than were required to bake an earthenware body, stoneware makers turned relatively early to the building of larger manufactories, the association with local businessmen who could supply an infusion of much needed cash, and the widespread shipment of ware.

That is not to say that there were not one-man or family shops. These existed in substantial number throughout much of the South into the twentieth century, and similar nineteenth-century examples could be found from Maine to Missouri. However, at an early date small factories appeared in such places as Edgefield, South Carolina; Clay County, Indiana; and the Amboys area of New Jersey. Some of these, by the late 1800s, had become large businesses. For example, in 1880 the Caire Pottery at Poughkeepsie, New York, had thirty-six employees and covered an entire city block; while the Portland (Maine) Stoneware Company had by 1867 a stated capital of $100,000, and in 1873 its output had reached $120,000 per annum.

Edwin Bennett

The Pioneer Pottery of East Liverpool, Ohio.

*Postcard view of the mid-nineteenth-century Bennett Pottery at East Liverpool, Ohio, providing a good idea of the relationship among the important buildings: kiln, pot house, drying shed, which made up an early factory.*

## THE CLAY AND ITS PREPARATION

Regardless of size, a stoneware pottery operated in much the same basic way. Suitable clay was a necessity, and if not available locally it had to be shipped in, often at substantial cost and inconvenience. Fortunate were those who controlled a rich deposit. The famous claybank owned by the Morgan family of Cheesequake, New Jersey, supplied material for dozens of kilns up and down the Eastern Seaboard for over a hundred years—at substantial profit to its owners.

Until the advent of railways, clay was either wagoned or shipped by river flatboat. The earth used at the well-known Bennington, Vermont, pottery went both ways: by water from New Jersey or Long Island to Troy, New York, and then by team the twenty miles or so (all uphill) to Bennington.

These clays were of no particular color; they might be an off-white, yellow, buff, brown, or bluish gray, depending upon the organic matter and the iron present (the latter producing a darker shade). And they could fire to anything from a near white to a brown or even a red body as with certain English stonewares. Presence of the latter color has led some to the rather pedantic conclusion that American redwares should not be called "redware" since there are stonewares of the same color. What this argument overlooks, of course, is that while there are very few pieces of American stoneware with a true red body, practically all our redware shows some variation of this characteristic hue.

Stoneware clay was usually excavated in the spring or fall and stored in a cellar or hole in the ground where it was left to "season" for several months to improve its plasticity. Then the earth was washed and screened to remove particles of grass, rock, and wood. This process involved pouring water over it until the clay was reduced to a creamy mass or "slip," then passing this through a series of screens that would catch the foreign matter. The newly cleaned clay next flowed into a vat where it was allowed to dry out.

Once dry, the earth was cut into blocks and stored until needed when it would be run through a pug mill that consisted of a cylindrical vat with a central rotating shaft armed with wood or metal rods set in a spiral pattern. Clay was poured into the mill, and as it rotated, driven by horse, mule, water, or even manpower, the earth was crushed and mixed, emerging as a soft homogeneous mass about the consistency of bread dough. This was then formed into long tubes, or "bolts," ready for the wheel.

## MAKING THE WARE

Stoneware clay when prepared in this way had a uniform consistency and plasticity, allowing it to be formed in several ways. Most common prior to the late 1800s was turning, or "throwing," on a potter's wheel, an ancient tool consisting in its most simple form of two horizontally mounted wooden disks joined by a vertical shaft. Though later water- or steam-powered and today electrified, this was initially driven by the potter who rhythmically kicked a treadle attached to the lower shaft causing the disks to rotate.

A block or ball of clay, measured by weight to provide a certain vessel type, was placed on the upper disk or "wheel head," and as it turned the potter raised and formed it with the use of various shaping tools. Handles and spouts, made separately, sometimes with use of an extruder, were applied; and wooden ribs or smoothers obliterated the characteristic ridges left on the surface by the craftsman's fingers (these, however, may often be found on the interior of earlier stoneware vessels). A wet sponge was used to polish the outside of the pot; and, finally, it was cut from the wheel head with a piece of looped wire, leaving the elongated concentric circles so often seen on the bases of stoneware vessels.

The mid-nineteenth-century introduction of the jigger or jolly, a revolving base that accommodates various sized plaster molds, greatly simplified pottery turning as well as causing the output to be much more uniform in size and capacity, an important factor in a craft where employees were customarily paid by the number of gallons produced on a piecework basis.

Molding ultimately became the way most American stoneware was manufactured. Press molding, forcing a glob of clay into an open mold, was used in this country as early as the eighteenth century, usually in the making of decorative elements (faces, figures, and floral motifs), which were then applied to a piece before firing, a technique termed "sprigging."

Drape molding, the manufacture of pie plates and platters by draping a slab of clay over a wooden form and then trimming off the excess, was occasionally used in stoneware manufacture but was far more popular among redware makers.

It was slip casting that came eventually to dominate industrial stoneware production. As early as the 1820s New Jersey craftsmen were pouring liquid clay or slip into plaster molds, which might be made of one to four pieces. As the water in the slip was absorbed by the plaster, a layer of clay would adhere to the in-

*A circa 1845 engraving of Washington Smith's Greenwich Pottery in New York City. Factories such as this, which were located in large cities, were more compact than those located in rural areas.*

*Blue-decorated, salt-glazed stoneware beer stein with pewter cover made 1890–1905 by the White Pottery, Utica, New York. Molded ware like this replaced earlier, traditional hand-thrown stoneware.*

terior of the mold, and when this had dried and hardened the mold was opened and the vessel removed.

By 1880 this molding technique, which was both fast and accurate, was widely employed at the major industrial kilns. Since such ware could be manufactured less expensively than turned pottery, its producers undersold and destroyed the traditional stoneware factories. Only in isolated areas, such as the mountains of the South, did the local potter survive.

## DECORATION

Stoneware has been decorated in several ways. One of the earliest to be employed was incising, whereby a stylus was used to scratch designs in the rubber-hard body of a vessel prior to firing. Customarily, the decoration was then filled with cobalt blue or manganese brown (the two coloring agents that could stand the heat of a stoneware oven). Most incised decoration dates to before 1840. However, extremely well-executed examples from Illinois, New York, and North Carolina can be traced to the 1870s and '80s.

Floral patterns are most common among incised designs; though humans, animals, birds, houses, sailing ships, and even entire vignettes may be found. Among the most remarkable is a cartoon depicting the British greasing a flagpole in New York City to prevent Washington's victorious troops from raising the flag of the new nation. It appears on a jug in the collection of the Museum of the City of New York. The collector will certainly encounter incised names, dates, and even "poems," such as those inscribed by the South Carolina slave potter Dave. Later examples are often on a background of Albany slip rather than being scratched directly into the clay body.

Sometimes confused with incised decoration is impressed decoration. This consists of designs either stamped into the soft clay of unfired vessels by means of a cookie cutter–like device or impressed with a roulette wheel that leaves a band of decoration about the vessel. Relatively uncommon, impressed decoration was used by pre-1830 potteries in New Jersey, Manhattan, and, particularly Boston, where the Edmands kiln in Charlestown employed a variety of devices, including eagles, cannon, hearts, shields, stars, circles, squares, and triangles. It is also sometimes found in other areas, including Virginia, South Carolina, Ohio, and Maine, where during the 1880s the Gardiner Stoneware Manufactory regularly embellished its rather ordi-

*Salt-glazed stoneware preserve jar with impressed coggle decoration of alternating fish and berries; attributed to Old Bridge, New Jersey, 1805–15.*

nary salt-glazed crocks, jugs, and churns with stamps depicting an eagle, cow, or swan.

Applied decoration involved attaching to the rubber-hard vessel decorative elements that had been hand shaped or formed in a press mold. Though time consuming and in some cases requiring expensive molds, this technique was widely practiced; it was, though, almost always for pieces made to order rather than for regular production.

One of the most spectacular examples is a jar attributed to the Georgia potter James Long, which is embellished with faces of Thomas Jef-

ferson and Andrew Jackson framed within floral cartouches surmounted by eagle and banner. But equally remarkable pieces from Ohio, Massachusetts, and Vermont could be named, as well as the ubiquitous Southern face jugs that customarily combine wheel-turned bodies with applied, hand-shaped elements. It should also be noted that decorative elements might be cut into a mold, so that cast stoneware would also be decorated. A good example would be the "Indian" flasks produced by the Athens, New York, pottery during the 1830s.

Freehand slip decoration, applied either with a brush or by means of a slip cup, is familiar to all collectors of American stoneware. The customary coloring agent in New England, the

*Salt-glazed stoneware jug with incised, blue-filled, decoration and marked by Nathan Clark & Company, Mount Morris, New York, 1835–46. Incised decoration was usually highlighted in cobalt or, rarely, manganese.*

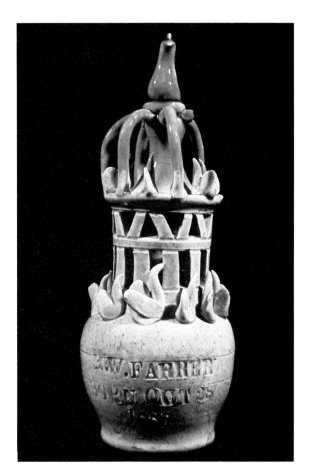

*Fanciful display piece, or "whimsey," made by R. W. Farrer (Farrar) in 1887; stoneware, partially glazed in brown mineral slip. Potters of the Farrar family worked in Vermont and New York as well as in Canada.*

interesting abstractions of the federal swag-and-tassel motif.

However, with the introduction of Spencerian script at midcentury, decorators, many of them women and children, began to turn out sophisticated, though often stylized, representations of birds, animals, humans, houses, ships, and genre scenes. The best of these, such as the circus and beach vignettes from the Fulper Pottery of New Jersey and the bizarre pointillistic birds from the Rochester, New York, kilns are true folk art. Much of the rest is hackneyed and derivative, reflecting a knowledge of and reliance upon English pearlware decoration.

The decline in artistic inspiration is particularly evident in stencil decoration, which became

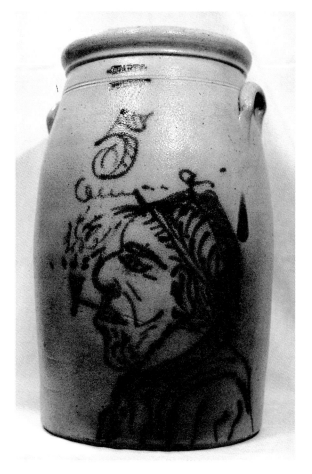

Midwest, and as far south as North Carolina was cobalt. However, early Northeastern potters also employed manganese to achieve a purple, brown, or black; and Southern craftsmen such as Thomas Chandler of South Carolina favored locally available kaolin or pipe clay that produced a brilliant white.

Before 1850 most such decoration was quite ordinary: squiggles, a floppy tulip derived from European designs, vague floral patterns which optimistic collectors have seen as "pine trees," "butterflies," or even "tornados"; and a few

*Salt-glazed stoneware apple butter jar with simple banding and stenciling in blue. Pennsylvania, 1860–90.*

popular in western Pennsylvania, Virginia, and West Virginia after 1870. Brushing blue over a cardboard or metal stencil required only the most minimal skill and could be done quickly, so it saved pottery owners money. Often combining floral and figural decoration with the name of the pottery or the customer for whom a piece was made, the stencil favored mass production. The technique spread as far west as Missouri and down into Texas at the close of the nineteenth century.

Around 1900 a few advanced potteries, relying heavily on craftsmen who had been trained in Germany, combined several techniques to produce stoneware that was wheel turned, molded, often bore impressed decoration and, due to advances in kiln technology, might be decorated in green or red as well as the customary blue. The ware of these shops—the Robinson Clay Products Company of Akron, Ohio, the White Pottery of Utica, New York, and Wingender Brothers of Haddonfield, New Jersey—reflects a happy combination of technical advance with individual craftsmanship.

## GLAZING

Since it is vitrified and nonporous, stoneware does not really require a sealing glaze. However, a piece of unglazed stoneware looks something like concrete, so as early as the fifteenth century Germanic craftsmen inparted a smooth glasslike finish to their wares by throwing crude salt into

◄ *Salt-glazed stoneware churn with elaborate freehand decoration in cobalt blue, marked HART'S/FULTON. Made by Samuel Hart, Fulton, New York, 1840–76.*

*Molded salt-glazed stoneware pitcher, mug, and mustard pot, all from the White Pottery, Utica, New York, 1890–1904.*

the kiln when the fires were at maximum intensity. This salt would instantly vaporize and the sodium in it would combine with silica and alumina compounds in the clay body to create a transparent soda glass glaze with a shiny, pebbled surface commonly referred to among collectors as "orange peel."

Salt glazing was the norm in the Northeastern and Midwestern United States throughout the nineteenth century, and examples will also be found from as far south as Georgia and as far west as Texas. More important, however, from the collector's point of view, a salt glaze was customarily combined with the incised, impressed, or slip decoration found on those pots regarded as desirable by most collectors. Indeed, salt-glazed, blue-decorated examples are re-garded by many as synonymous with American stoneware.

There were, however, other important finishes. By 1800 glazes made by mixing naturally occurring clays with water were also being employed. Best known of these is the Albany slip mined from the Hudson River at Albany, New York. However, similar clays, which will, during baking, melt and cover the stoneware body with a smooth, opaque, colored glaze, were found in California, Michigan, Indiana, and Texas. Most fire to a shade of brown, though the slip from Leon, Texas, may range in hue from green to gold.

Initially, most craftsmen probably used these clay slips primarily to coat the interiors of vessels (a surface not open to the air could not be affected by the salt thrown into the kiln), or to glaze small items such as soap dishes, inks, and mugs that were often stacked within or under other vessels. However, after 1850 many shops began to employ commercially prepared varia-

*Salt-glazed stoneware jar, marked* TRUMAN SMITH. *Made by Truman Smith, Clay City, Indiana, 1846–65. Smith was born in and probably trained in New York State, and his ware reflects a style popular there 1820–40.*

and west into Texas and Arkansas. The basic glaze composition was wood ash, clay, and sand, which produced a drippy olive or brown finish. The addition to this mixture of slaked lime resulted in a smoother and more uniform finish characterized by a gray-green or yellowish hue; while adjustments in the proportions of these ingredients or the addition of ground glass, iron foundry cinders, or even salt caused the glaze to assume a different color or texture.

The alkaline glaze was durable, often extremely attractive, and inexpensive, using elements readily available to the potter rather than salt or commercial clay slips that might be costly or hard to obtain. Interestingly, it was not part of the European tradition from which most of the South's primarily British and German pot-

tions of Albany slip to finish most of their ware. This was particularly true in the South where salt was sometimes expensive or hard to obtain and preparation of the native alkaline glazes was time consuming.

As important as they were to the trade, natural clay glazes are of little interest to collectors, at least outside the South and Southwest where they often constitute much of the ware available. This is unfortunate, not only because of the role they played in the history of American stoneware but also because so many interesting forms are found primarily in these surfaces.

A third, extremely important, finish was the alkaline glaze developed around 1820 in the Edgefield, South Carolina, district from where it spread throughout most of the Deep South

*Albany-slip-glazed watercooler made by and bearing the stenciled mark of the* CANNELTON STONEWARE CO./ CANNELTON, IND. *This Indiana piece dates 1872–90.*

◀ *Alkaline-glazed stoneware jar incised "Feb. 11, 1844/ Mr. L. Miles/Dave." Made at the Lewis Miles Pottery, Edgefield District, South Carolina, by a black potter known only as Dave.*

ters had come. The only counterpart is found in Asia, and some have speculated that the glaze was introduced by men familiar with certain glaze recipes obtained from Chinese sources. Whatever the case, alkaline glazes are the most important distinguishing characteristic of Southern stoneware, and there is a substantial and growing body of collectors attracted to this pottery.

The last stoneware glaze to be developed is a white, opaque finish referred to as Bristol glaze, after the chemists of that English city who developed it in the late nineteenth century. Bristol is a combination of ingredients, primarily feldspar, kaolin, zinc oxide, and whiting, rather than a naturally occurring earth. It was created to mimic desirable but costly porcelain and white earthenwares and satisfy the Victorian preference for a clean, sanitary appearance.

Introduced into this country during the 1880s, the Bristol glaze was adopted by industrial potteries throughout the Midwest, West, and South, often combined with Albany slip in the brown-white ware still made today. It also served as a base for spongeware, covering the coarse stoneware surface with a smooth canvas upon which sponging in blue, green, brown, or yellow could be applied. Major sources of such ware during the early twentieth century were the Red Wing, Minnesota, Stoneware Company and the Western Stoneware Company, which had several factories in the midlands.

## FIRING

The final critical step in stoneware manufacture was the baking or firing of the ware in a brick or stone structure called a kiln or oven. This was composed of one or more fireboxes in which wood or coal was burned, a "firing chamber" in which the ware was stacked, and a series of vents or flues to carry heat from the firebox through the firing chamber and, eventually, out through chimneys.

Kilns are usually either round or oblong in shape, the former often called "beehive" kilns. In ovens of the updraft type, the fireboxes are below the firing chamber and heat passes up through it and out. More modern downdraft kilns do not have chimneys in the roof, so rising heat is forced to circulate down again through the stacked ware (a more efficient method of heat distribution) and out flues at the base of the oven.

The oblong or rectangular kiln has the firebox at the front of the oven, the firing chamber in

*Molded figure of a dog in the Staffordshire manner, stoneware with a Bristol-slip glaze sponged in blue and brown. Ohio, 1870–90.*

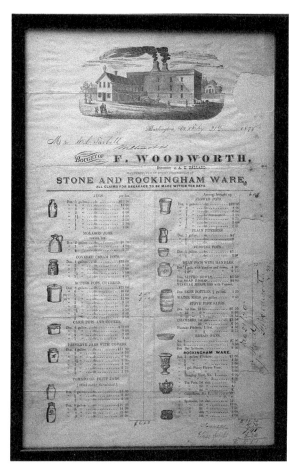

wise would stick together in the firing process. The larger the kiln the more ware it could hold, and industrial ovens of the late nineteenth century often accommodated over a thousand gallons.

The firing period varied by kiln size, ware type, fuel, and other factors and might range from twelve to thirty-six hours. During this time the potter would insert and withdraw small bits of ware called draw trials that helped him to determine the proper time to put salt in the kiln or the state of the glaze. Once the maximum suitable firing time had elapsed, the craftsman would shut down the fires and after a two or three day cooling-off period unload the kiln.

Ware of good quality was either sold at the kiln or, in most cases, shipped by wagon, rail, or boat to wholesalers, many of whom were hundreds of miles away. Even in the eighteenth century, Virginia potters were selling in New England, and the Crolius and Remmey families of New York regularly shipped wares not only along the South Atlantic coast but to the West Indies. And, with the development of transcontinental railways, Ohio, Indiana, and Illinois manufactories flooded the Far West with their products. As a consequence, marked American stoneware is likely to show up almost anywhere in this country or in Canada.

the center, and the chimney or flue at the rear so that heat passes across the pottery from front to back. The best-known American example is the low "groundhog" kiln still used by some Southern craftsmen.

Whatever the type, the kiln is filled or "stacked" by the potter using various pieces of baked clay "kiln furniture"—rings, rolls, disks, and triangles—to separate pieces which other-

# 2

## PRODUCTS OF THE STONEWARE FACTORIES

UNLIKE THEIR BRETHREN who turned red earthenware, stoneware potters made a fairly limited number of items. An 1809 price list printed by the Clarkson Crolius Pottery in Manhattan (the earliest known such document) listed jugs, jars, pots, pitchers, mugs, churns, spout pots (which are now termed batter jugs), kegs or watercoolers, inkwells or stands, and chamber pots.

The Phoenix Stone Ware Factory at Edgefield, South Carolina, offered in an 1840 advertisement (*Edgefield Advertiser*, April 2, 1840) only the following items: jugs, jars, pots, churns, bowls, or pans and pitchers, while the Erie City (Pennsylvania) Stone-Ware Manufactory price list of August 1867 contained jugs, jars, pots, churns, pitchers, milk pans, flower- and chamber pots.

Little changed over the years. However, the items described were all standard production pieces made in quantity to meet a more or less constant demand. Stoneware makers also turned out a surprisingly large number of other pieces either in response to regional taste or reflecting individual orders. Since many of these latter objects were small they were often Albany-slip glazed and have fallen within the general collector prejudice against such wares. However, they represent an important aspect of stoneware production.

### STORAGE VESSELS

Because of its great durability, stoneware was particularly suited for the manufacture of jugs, jars, pots, crocks, and similar items used in the preservation and storage of foodstuffs. Indeed, the great majority of pieces found today in this medium served such a purpose.

*Missouri potters produced a variety of storage and dairying vessels. Seen here are two jars, a churn, and a jug in various glazes, all dating 1870–1900. The churn is by J. M. Hummel of Florence, the jug by Kemp & Stine of Dresden, the jar at left by Joseph Bayer of Washington, and the one in mixed clays by W. Wessel of Deepwater, Missouri.*

## Jugs

Jugs, which might range in capacity from a tiny half-pint whiskey "taster" to a great twenty-gallon vessel suitable for storage of water, wine, cider, vinegar, or cooking oil, were a product of every stoneware manufactory. Early examples were ovoid or egg shaped (a style that persisted in the South late into the nineteenth century), gradually becoming squat during the 1830–50 period and straight sided after 1860. By 1890 large Midwestern firms were producing molded or jiggered examples with shoulders tapering at a 45-degree angle and covered with a brown-and-white glaze, as well as pieces, such as the Bristol-finished "Weeks Patent Jug" from Akron, Ohio, with an offset spout and wire bail handle. Most earlier examples were salt glazed or covered with some variation of an Albany-type slip, except in the South, where alkaline finishes were often preferred.

Prices varied greatly over time and geographic area. Early Eastern and Southern potters sold by item. Thus, Benjamin DuVal of Richmond, Virginia, in 1812 offered five-gallon jugs at $10 per dozen, while J. Park Alexander of Akron, Ohio, was in 1865 selling a similar item for 7 cents a gallon, reflecting a trend to sales by the gallon, which was widespread in the South, Southwest, and Midwest after 1840.

*Molasses Jugs*   Squat, straight-sided vessels with a pouring spout pulled from the lip opposite the handle were used to store the sweetener used throughout much of the country. They are a late form, appearing after 1850. Most were given an Albany-slip or other dark, mineral glaze. The Albany (New York) Stoneware Factory offered three sizes during the 1850s and 1860s: one-half, one, and two gallon at $2.75 to $6.50 per dozen.

*Syrup Jugs*   Southern potters were more likely to produce what they termed a "syrup jug," a bulbous vessel with two handles, one on each side of a central orifice, which lacked a pouring spout. A similar form was occasionally made in the North where, in five- to eight-gallon capacity, it was used for liquid storage. Southern examples are found in alkaline glaze, most others in a salt glaze.

*Extremely rare salt-glazed stoneware jar made and*   ▶
*marked by Jonathan Fenton, Boston, Massachusetts, 1793–96. Impressed rose on one side, fish and cartouche "JF" on other.*

*Late, straight-sided, salt-glazed stoneware jug stenciled* CENTENNIAL/1876/MYERS & HALL/AKRON,OHIO. *Though they marked their ware "Akron," this firm was actually located in Mogadore, Ohio.*

*Harvest Jugs* Squat ovoid vessels with a strap handle across the top, a funnel-like aperture through which they are filled, and a tapering tube from which to drink or pour were made in both the North and the South. The form is distinctly European, appearing in seventeenth-century genre paintings; although Southern examples, which often incorporate a face, are termed "monkey jugs," and are claimed to have an African origin. Northern pieces are customarily salt- or Albany-slip glazed, while Southern jugs have an alkaline finish.

*Leach Jugs* Looking like an ordinary jug but having a body punctured with many drain holes, these rare pieces were used in making lye from wood ashes. The lye, in turn, was employed in the production of soap. A marked example from a Fort Edward, New York, pottery is known.

*Fountain Jugs* The same double-handled form, with the addition of a bunghole at the base into which a wooden or pewter faucet could be inserted, served as a form of watercooler, usually prior to 1870. Perhaps the most spectacularly decorated example is that made by Gordon Purdy at Atwater, Ohio, in the 1850s. Alkaline-glazed versions were made during the same period by Thomas Chandler of Edgefield, South Carolina.

### Jars

Made in great quantity and variety for use in the storage and preservation of food, these are among the earliest American stoneware forms. Ovoid examples were found at the site of the Yorktown Pottery (1720–45); and both these and straight-sided ones are illustrated in the Crolius price list of 1809. Ranging in capacity from one-eighth to four gallons, they cost the same regardless of shape.

*Stoneware field jug in a mineral slip with cobalt handles, probably a presentation piece. Attributed to A. H. Rhodenbaugh, Middlebury, Ohio, 1855–70.*

*Salt-glazed stoneware preserve jar with manganese decoration in a reddish brown, made and marked 1831–54 by Henry Glazier of Huntingdon, Pennsylvania. Manganese is rarely used on stoneware.*

*Salt-glazed stoneware preserve jar with cobalt vase of flowers decoration, Pennsylvania, 1860–90. Jars like this were designed to receive a tin lid sealed with wax, hence the term "wax sealers."*

Most earlier stoneware jars had a wide, flaring collar to hold in place an oilcloth or waxed paper covering or an inner rim on which a lid sat. However, late-nineteenth-century examples, particularly from Pennsylvania and the Midwest, offered several variations in the closure. Some, referred to as "wax sealers," had a double rim to accommodate a tin cover held in place by candle wax; others, termed tomato jars or "corkers," had a narrow throat that was plugged with a cork. More complex closures included various screw tops and the Weir Jar, patented in 1892, which was originally made at Monmouth, Illinois. Its top was fastened down by an iron clamp similar to those found on glass canning jars.

## Pots

These semiovoid storage vessels may be distinguished from jars by their much wider mouths and the more frequent presence of opposing handles. They did not have matching tops. They are often called cream pots due to their use in separating cream from fresh milk. Though sometimes referred to as "jars," many of the massive vessels turned by the slave potter Dave at the Miles Pottery in South Carolina were technically pots. Cream pots ranging in size from one to four gallons were sold by the Woodworth Pottery of Burlington, Vermont, during the 1870s. The smallest size cost $4.50 per dozen; the largest, $12.

*Blue-decorated, salt-glazed pot marked WEBB & KELLOGG/ERIE, PA. The firm of Webb & Kellogg made stoneware at Erie, 1861–63. Its ware is uncommon.*

## Tobacco Humidors

A variation on the crock form is the humidor. Examples made in the mid-nineteenth century by Edmands & Co. of Charlestown, Massachusetts, had fluted sides and an Albany-slip glaze. Much more elaborate were the blue-washed salt-glazed examples produced at the Utica (New York) pottery of White & Son, 1890–1900. These were embellished with applied rams' heads, embossed human faces, and coggled banding.

## Crocks

Though the term crock is of relatively recent origin, the form—straight-sided vessel, usually with small horizontal ear handles—is not. Examples were found at Yorktown (1720–45). By the 1850s Eastern potteries offered two variations of what we now refer to as crocks: squat, wide ones with a capacity of one to four gallons termed "cake pots" and taller examples, holding one-half to six gallons, which were called "butter pots." Both were customarily purchased with matching stoneware covers.

To add a bit of confusion, very large examples of the form, often fifty gallons in capacity, were described as "meat tubs" in an 1899 advertisement of an Akron, Ohio, stoneware consortium. These containers, which were used not only for salting down meat but for the storage of such items as cracked corn and oats, were widely made throughout the Midwest and South during the late nineteenth century.

*Blue-decorated, salt-glazed crock with whimsical design marked SEYMOUR & BOSWORTH/HARTFORD, CONN. Made at Hartford 1871–90.*

*A group of three rundlets or small watercoolers:* left to right, *New England, 1820–40 in tan mineral slip; Ohio, 1830–60 in salt glaze, and New York City, stamped* C.CROLIUS/STONEWARE/MANUFACTURER/MANHATTAN WELLS,N.Y., *in blue-decorated salt glaze, 1800–14.*

*Blue-decorated, salt-glazed stoneware water keg mounted on legs, Pennsylvania, 1840–60. These colorful vessels were often referred to as "Blind Pigs."*

### Watercoolers

Referred to variously as kegs, coolers, or fountain jars and in pint and half-pint sizes as rundlets or swiglers, these semiovoid or barrel-shaped vessels had a bunghole at the base and open tops or, if covered, a filling hole. Later examples were straight sided. Some, with charcoal purification systems, were designed for water storage. However, earlier specimens, up to ten gallons, were frequently filled with hard cider, beer, wine, or in the rundlet size, hard liquor. Often made as gifts, coolers and rundlets were sometimes elaborately decorated. Norton & Fenton of Bennington, Vermont, in 1847 sold standard coolers for 25 cents per gallon but charged twice that for "ornamented" ones.

An interesting variation is the "blind pig," a quart keg that rests on its side upon three or four stub feet. Though I know of no marked examples, these pieces, which are richly decorated in blue, are attributed to mid-nineteenth-century Pennsylvania.

### BOTTLES

Earlier examples resembled the green glass sack bottles of the eighteenth and early nineteenth century, with long necks and semiovoid bodies. By the 1860s shops throughout the country were producing half pint, pint, and quart bottles with straight sides, short necks, and bulbous rims. These were used for real or ginger beer and various soft drinks and are usually impressed with the name of the bottler, not the manufacturer. Most were hand thrown, though some, such as the well-known Dr. Kronk's root beer, were cast. All were modestly priced. In the 1850s the

*Three nineteenth-century salt-glazed stoneware "pop," or beer, bottles. Though most of these vessels bore the name of the merchant for whom they were made, the twelve-sided molded example at right also includes the date, 1849, and the manufacturer's stamp, PATENT/PRESSED/W.SMITH for Washington Smith of New York City.*

Gardiner (Maine) Pottery offered the quart size at $1 per dozen.

An unusual version was the gemel bottle, two vessels formed together with a central lift handle. Earlier examples, such as those made and marked by Absalom Stedman in New Haven, Connecticut, during the 1830s, were designed as castor bottles for vinegar and oil. However, there are larger and later forms (including one with four bottles conjoined)—the purpose of which is unclear.

### Ring Bottles

These circular vessels of doughnut form, sometimes mounted on stubby feet, are said to have been hooked over the saddle pommel when traveling on horseback or carried into the fields around a worker's arm. In either case they might contain water, cider, or something stronger. They are thought of as typically Southern and were produced there until the early 1900s, though the Indiana craftsman J. B. Rhodes of Harmony made and signed one in the 1880s.

*Two early stoneware bottles:* right, *in Albany slip, marked* C.CROLIUS/MANUFACTURER/NEW-YORK, *Manhattan 1835–49;* left, *salt glazed and impressed with name of the Hartford, Connecticut, merchant,* I.W.GILBERT, *1820–40.*

### Flasks

Flattened ovoid receptacles used for carrying water or alcoholic beverages were widely manufactured until the 1850s, when they were replaced by more practical glass hip flasks. The usual capacity was pint or half pint. The Richmond (Virginia) Stone Ware Manufactory sold them for a dollar a dozen in 1812 and called them "ticklers," a quaint expression that perhaps refers to the effect produced by their contents.

### Canteens

Flattened wheel- or disk-shaped vessels, often with a wire handle and heavily embossed in blue-filled designs, were made in pint and quart sizes both by Whites and by the Robinson Clay Products Company of Ohio around 1900. Many were advertising items, such as one stamped "G. A. Stiff/Saloon/McKinney, Tex."

## TABLE AND COOKING WARES

Few tablewares were made in stoneware, perhaps due to its greater weight. By far the most important form was the mug, though the pitcher was the most common. Outside the South, where various bowl types remained in production throughout the 1800s, serving and eating utensils in this medium must be counted rare. Vessels used in cooking are more common.

### Mugs

Straight-sided tavern mugs slipped in brown oxide and impressed "WR" for William III of England were made at Yorktown, Virginia, 1720–45; while a century and a half later ornate turned examples in salt glaze with applied and molded decoration were being produced at the White Pottery in Utica, New York, and the Win-

*Two salt-glazed stoneware flasks, both 1820–50 and from New England or New York. Note how the mineral slip used to line the example at left has run down the body.*

*Two salt-glazed stoneware mugs with cobalt blue banding within scribed lines; New York or Pennsylvania, 1820–40.*

gender shop in Haddonfield, New Jersey. In both cases they were the most elaborately decorated pieces of their period with the later Germanic forms often having pewter lids. On the other hand, simple mugs in salt glaze or Albany slip were made by almost all pre-1850 stoneware factories. A rare marked example by Daniel Ack of Mooresburg, Pennsylvania, 1857–82, has no decoration. Pint and half pint were standard sizes, the quart (sold by Crolius in 1809 at 9 shillings per dozen) far less common.

Variations included large steins of quart and quart and a half capacity, richly embossed and blue decorated and made by both Whites and Wingenders at the turn of the century. There were also the rare, novelty mugs in the bottom of which the potter had placed a replica of a frog (or something nastier!) as a surprise for the drinker. Quite a few of these were turned out by the Loogootee, Indiana, Pottery, 1890–1900.

The addition of a small soap pocket to the side of the vessel made a shaving mug such as the ones produced about 1900 by Beryl Griffith of Clay City, Indiana. The form is much more common in redware.

### Goblets and Glasses

Though seemingly impractical, drinking vessels were sometimes made of stoneware. Alkaline-glazed footed goblets and tumblers are attributed to the Sterrett family of Shelby County, Alabama, about 1870; and the White Pottery of Utica, New York, made tall, blue-decorated lager glasses, 1880–1907.

### Pitchers

Early pitchers were thrown on the wheel, but by the 1820s New Jersey firms were turning out molded examples patterned after English designs and usually covered with a dark, mineral slip. Throughout the nineteenth century Eastern and Western firms offered two types: "Plain Pitchers" and "Fancy Pressed Ware." Sizes varied from pint to two gallon with a substantial price difference. For example, Plaisted & Co. of Gardiner, Maine, sold gallon plain pitchers at $3 a dozen, while molded examples of the same size brought twice that much. Alkaline-glazed Southern wares, such as those impressed TL by Thaddeus Leopard of Winston County, Mississippi (about 1880), often resembled eighteenth-century Liverpool jugs in form. An interesting variation was the beer pitcher, which had a hooded spout to prevent ice or foam from exiting.

### Punch Bowls

Though the White Pottery at Utica, New York, made a substantial number of turned, footed punch bowls embellished with coggled, impressed, and embossed blue-filled decoration, 1890–1905, the earliest known example (attributed to New York or New Jersey, 1790–1810) has incised floral patterns filled in cobalt. In 1990 it sold for $200,000, a record for a piece of stoneware.

### Sugar Bowls

Though not a production item, covered and usually footed sugar bowls were made during the early 1800s. Pennsylvania and Virginia pieces were elaborately decorated in cobalt slip, while an example made in Utica, New York, 1832–39, for a member of the Nash family of potters was covered with dark Albany slip. Like most nonstandard wares, sugar bowls were seldom marked. A rare exception is impressed A. COFFMAN/ROCKINGHAM CO.,VA. (1855–65).

---

*Cobalt-decorated, salt-glazed pitcher, Pennsylvania, 1850–80. A form popular with collectors.*  ▶

## Salts

Small, footed receptacles found in the South and Midwest are thought to be open salt stands, though they are of a size in some cases to have also served as egg cups. Most are in a dark, mineral slip. An alkaline-glazed master (larger) salt is attributed to the Phoenix Factory, Edgefield District, South Carolina, about 1840. Much more interesting from the collector's point of view are salt shakers or casters in figural form. Several in the shape of a hen or duck and of blue-decorated salt glaze are attributed to Pennsylvania, mid-nineteenth century.

## Bowls

Bowls for use in the preparation, serving, or eating of food were made in great quantity throughout the South during the nineteenth century. An extraordinary example, in a green alkaline glaze with abstract and floral design in brown, bears the stamp TRAPP & /CHANDLER and was made at Kirksey's Crossroads, South Carolina, around 1845 by master potter Thomas

Chandler. The Phoenix Stone Ware Factory, active in the same area of the state about 1840, advertised "Bowls or pans of all sizes from ½ gallon to 5 gallon" (*Edgefield Advertiser*, April 2, 1840).

Both the form and the terminology applied to these vessels varied greatly from place to place and time to time. Most of what we think of as "bowls" (or mixing bowls, a term which appeared in the Northeast about 1870) had rounded sides and molded rims. A similar form but with straight sides set at an angle of 60 degrees or so was called a cream riser in the South and a pudding pot in the North where it was used for cooking and was available at $3 per dozen in the gallon size from the Woodworth Pottery of Burlington, Vermont, during the 1870s.

## Pans

Shallow vessels with sloping sides were referred to as pans or bread pans and resembled the form called a nappy in yellowware or Rockingham finish. Later examples (about 1900) had a heavy, collared rim and were given a dark Albany-slip

*Blue-decorated, salt-glazed mixing bowl made and marked by SIPE, NICHOLS & CO./WILLIAMSPORT, PA., 1875–77. A rare form and a rare maker's mark.*

or white Bristol finish. The addition of a wire bail handle turned the latter into a stew pan of the sort made by the Red Wing Union Stoneware Company of Red Wing, Minnesota, from 1900 into the 1930s.

### Bean Pots

Squat ovoid covered vessels with one, two, or no handles in sizes ranging from one-half to two gallons were used in baking and serving beans. They first appeared in stoneware price lists during the 1850s and are still being made. Most date from the late nineteenth or early twentieth century (such as the variation with an added wire bail handle made by Minnesota's North Star Stoneware Company, 1892–96). The customary glaze is brown or brown and white.

### Pipkins

Less often encountered is the ancient pipkin, the body of which resembles a bean pot except that it often has a pouring spout and always has a long, hollow handle through which steam escapes. Shards of these were found at the Yorktown, Virginia, pottery site (1720–45).

### Colanders

Also sometimes used as cheese strainers, these were bowls perforated across the lower half. One made at the Lewistown, Pennsylvania, Pottery, 1872–97, bears the incised signature of Anna Margretta Dipple who ran the shop after her husband's death. Colanders are often confused with brown-glazed, handled, straight-sided stoneware dipping baskets used in the chemical industry.

### Pie Plates

The pie plate, so common in redware, was not usually made in stoneware, no doubt due to its

*Molded bean pot, blue-decorated, salt-glazed stoneware made at the White Pottery, Utica, New York, 1890–1904.*

weight. Late examples in a dark brown slip exist (in about an 8-inch size), and the Hart Brothers Pottery of Fulton, New York, offered them in an 1879 advertisement.

### Cake Molds

Though common in redware, American stoneware cake molds are exceedingly rare. Brown-glazed examples are thought to have been made at the Whately, Massachusetts, pottery, and a New York or Pennsylvania example, salt glazed with cobalt decoration, is illustrated in *Early American Folk Pottery* by Harold F. Guilland.

### Batter Jugs

These hybrid pieces, also referred to in pottery advertisements as batter pails and pancake pitchers, consisted of an ovoid body with tubular pouring spout, open top, wire bail handle, and a small lug handle at the rear base to serve as a lift. Both top and spout were usually given fitted

*Blue-decorated, salt-glazed stoneware batter jug made and marked by* EVAN B. JONES/PITTSTOWN, PA., *1870–87.*

tin covers. They were used to mix and store pancake batter. Most examples date to the second half of the nineteenth century; though an essentially identical form made at Manhattan's Crolius Pottery in the eighteenth century may be what was termed in the firm's 1809 price list a "spout pot."

## Coffeepots

Never a popular form in stoneware, these do appear occasionally. Most are Midwestern, seem to date about 1900, are unglazed and sometimes bound in tin. Less often seen are salt glaze or Southern pieces in alkaline glaze. Cogburn & Massey of Washington County, Georgia, called a similar form a "coffee boiler" in an 1820 advertisement. Most elaborate are the molded, pewter-hinged pots made by White's of Utica, New York, 1890–1907, as advertising pieces for Faust Blend Drip Coffee.

## Teapots

Squat, ovoid teapots were made at many Eastern and Midwestern factories. Usually mold formed, they were given a dark brown glaze described (incorrectly) in advertisements as "Rockingham." The firm of A. J. & J. L. Russell at West Troy, New York, made two sizes, offered at $6.50 and $7.50 per dozen.

## Meat Tenderizers

Round or square blocks of stoneware with a knobby surface and a hole in which to place a handle were used widely enough in butcher shops and homes that a substantial number have survived. Many are embossed PAT'D DEC 25, 1877, and most are attributed to Ohio potteries.

## Rolling Pins

Bristol-slip-glazed stoneware rolling pins with blue transfer decoration and wooden handles are common. They are pictured in catalogs of the Western Stoneware Company, Monmouth, Illinois, as late as 1935.

## Vinegar Funnels

Once made at many potteries, these are rarely found today. A large, handled one appears in a photograph of the Keystone Pottery, Washington County, Tennessee (1870–1910), and they were offered around 1900 by the Hilfinger Pottery of Fort Edward, New York, and by a pottery in Denton, Texas. From Hilfinger one could get a set in three sizes for $2.

## Sauerkraut or Pickle Presses

These unusual objects looked like large stoneware churn tops and were designed to hold sauerkraut or pickles beneath the surface of the brine in which they were being steeped. They were made in sufficient quantity that one Texas manufacturer, William Saenger of Elmendorf (about 1900), marked his.

## HOUSEHOLD AND DAIRY VESSELS

Stoneware was employed in the manufacture of an interesting variety of items for the home and farm. For such items as hot water bottles and cuspidors, it was an ideal medium, used well into the twentieth century. For others, like thread holders, it proved ill suited and was quickly replaced by other materials.

### Washboards

Whitmore, Robinson & Company of Akron, Ohio, advertised "Improved Stone Washboards" in 1871, but only a few examples, usually in a Rockingham-type glaze or in cobalt on a Bristol finish, have survived.

### Soap Dishes

Made in some quantity, usually with a brown mineral finish, these were sold in two sizes by the Albany Stoneware Factory during the 1850s; prices were 12 and 17 cents apiece. Most soap receptacles were oblong, resembling more common examples in Rockingham, but there are also some circular ones with pedestal bases. In either case, the shallow dished top was perforated so that soapy water might run down into a lower chamber.

### Washbowls

Massive stoneware washbowls or basins in a light tan salt glaze were made at Zoar, Ohio, in the first half of the nineteenth century. Washbowls in two sizes were manufactured 1829–38 by the Athens, New York, firm of Clark & Fox. It is likely that matching pitchers were also produced.

### Milk Pans

Somewhat similar are milk pans used in cooling fresh milk. Early nineteenth-century examples were quite large (16 to 20 inches in diameter) with sides canted at a 45-degree angle and rolled rims. They were customarily given a brown mineral glaze. By 1900 the Monmouth (Illinois) Pottery Company was turning out two-gallon

*Three small stoneware objects in a brown mineral slip:* left to right, *penny bank, soap dish, and creamer, all New York or New England, 1840–70.*

versions with thick collars, curved sides, and heavily Albany-slip-glazed bodies.

### Churns

Stoneware was ideally suited to the rough treatment churning entailed and was easily cleaned, so churns were made over a long period of time. The Phoenix Stone Ware Factory at Pottersville, South Carolina, offered "churns of all sizes" in 1840; and by 1910 the Star Pottery Works at Elmendorf, Texas, was producing a Bristol-glazed example with a cast-iron dasher mechanism. Eastern examples were semiovoid with small horizontal lifts. Southern ones often had two ear handles opposite a single lift. Later Midwestern churns were straight sided.

### Mortars

The same durability that recommended its use in churns encouraged the manufacture of stoneware mortars and pestles. Early examples, like the one inscribed "For Dr. L.L. Painter, made by B.R.L. Coffman, August 18th 1860" and by a Mt. Herman, Virginia, potter, are hard to find. However, many larger mortars were made around 1900 for the pharmaceutical industry.

### Chicken Waterers

Also known as poultry fountains, these are dome shaped with an aperture at the base from which the bird may drink. Early examples like those made and marked at the Haig Pottery in Philadelphia in the 1850s are elaborately embellished in blue. More common are those in Bristol glaze or the greenish yellow Leon-slip finish employed in the early twentieth century by the Meyer Pottery of Atascosa, Texas. The form is still produced.

### Umbrella Holders

Many large commercial potteries in the East and Midwest made cylindrical umbrella holders during the late nineteenth and early twentieth century. These were sometimes given a varicolored glaze, in other cases left unglazed so that they might be decorated by Victorian "Sunday painters."

### Twine Containers

An unusual and seemingly unsatisfactory form is the beehive-shaped string or twine container.

---

*Blue-decorated, salt-glazed churn with rare jockey's head design marked T. HARRINGTON/LYONS. Made by Thompson Harrington, Lyons, New York, 1852–72.*

and pedestal base have been found. They are brown glazed and probably from Pennsylvania or the Midwest.

### Match Holders

Match holders or safes are relatively late, reflecting the development of the modern match. At the turn of the century the White Pottery at Utica, New York, made many conical salt-glazed ones, often with advertising logos in blue. Much rarer are their cobalt-decorated wall match "pockets," though one marked and dated 1889 is known.

### Inkwells

Round inkwells with a central reservoir and one or more holes for quill pens were made by most early stoneware shops. Less common were elaborate oblong "fountain ink stands," which combined two wells (for red and black ink) with pen holders. The smaller size was sold for 50 cents per dozen in 1847 by Norton & Fenton of Bennington, Vermont; in 1812 Benjamin DuVal of Richmond, Virginia, asked $1 per dozen for fountain inks.

### Ink Sanders

Despite their important role in writing, sanders appear to have seldom been made in stoneware. Most examples seen are pedestal shaped in a brown slip, though a few blue-decorated, salt-glazed specimens are known. All have numerous, tiny holes in the top for the absorbent sand to pass through.

The only known example with blue foliate decoration was made, probably as a gift, by Alexander V. Boughner of Greensboro, Pennsylvania (1861–68). Later ones in brown-and-white slip were produced in Texas.

### Candlesticks

Candlesticks in stoneware are exceedingly uncommon. One pair known were made 1852–54 by James Carr of South Amboy, New Jersey. Their baluster form and yellow-brown glaze were clearly designed to mimic then-popular Rockingham examples.

### Grease Lamps

A few footed grease lamps resembling in form the ancient betty lamp mounted upon a saucer

*Two salt-glazed stoneware inkwells, New York or New Jersey, 1830–50. These pieces were described as "common inks" in manufacturers' price lists.*

### Ink Bottles

Though made in quantity by many nineteenth-century potteries, these conical, shouldered storage bottles were rarely marked or even mentioned in price lists.

### Chamber Pots

Before indoor plumbing, manufacturers produced various "necessaries." One of the most ancient is the chamber pot or chamber, a bowl with a handle and flattened rim. A salt-glazed example with the initials AD in cartouche was made by Anthony Duche, Sr., of Philadelphia, 1730–50. They were still being produced two hundred years later by the Red Wing Union Stoneware Company of Minnesota.

### Bedpans

Less often seen in stoneware are bedpans. Midwestern salt-glazed examples from the late nineteenth century were cast in an ovoid, flattened at one end with vertical emptying spout. The same form is found in Bristol slip.

### Spittoons and Cuspidors

Once commonplace and a necessity of tobacco chewers, these vessels have passed from use. The spittoon is round and its top slopes inward

*Three pieces of Albany-slip-decorated stoneware:* left, *a preserve jar stamped* FARRAR & WAIT *(Fairfax, Vermont);* center, *flowerpot with attached saucer;* right, *spittoon. All 1860–80.*

to a central hole. It also has an emptying aperture high on the side. Cuspidors, on the other hand, have narrow waists and are emptied through the top. They first appear in pottery price lists during the mid-nineteenth century and were still found in Western Stoneware Company (Monmouth, Illinois) catalogs in 1926. Earlier salt-glazed examples might be elaborately blue decorated, while brown and white or blue sponged on white was customary after 1890.

### Hot Water Bottles

These generally sausage-shaped receptacles do not appear in catalogs until late in the nineteenth century. Early examples, such as those made by the Dorchester, Massachusetts, and Bangor, Maine, potteries, are in salt glaze and may be wheel thrown. Ones made at Red Wing, Minnesota, in the 1920s were cast and round with embossed decoration shaded in blue or brown. These had metal screw tops, while their predecessors were corked.

### Flowerpots and Urns

From the 1860s on, every large stoneware manufactory turned out quantities of flowerpots, some with attached saucers, as well as decorative hanging pots, vases, two-piece calla lily pots, urns, and even the unusual perforated bulb kasse used in Pennsylvania German families to grow onions for seasoning. Many of these were given a dark "Rockingham" slip. Salt-glazed, blue-decorated examples were less common as are the matte-finished "tanware" pieces from Pennsylvania and West Virginia. Much the same forms were made in redware and sold for half the price.

*Molded salt-glazed stoneware doll head with cobalt and manganese decoration, attributed to the Fulper Pottery, Flemington, New Jersey, 1870–1900. Imitating European forms made in porcelain, these are extremely rare.*

## TOYS AND FIGURAL PIECES

Though such things are more often associated with the redware potter, a surprisingly large number of toys, miniatures, and figurals were made in stoneware, the more durable medium.

### Banks

Perhaps the most common of these are penny banks or "money jugs." These small receptacles came in a variety of forms, all with a slot large enough to receive the large nineteenth-century coin. Some banks were indeed jug shaped; others took the form of an onion, an urn, or even a log cabin, such as the remarkable blue-decorated salt-glazed ones produced in 1852 by the Philadelphia potter Thomas Haig.

### Dolls and Doll Heads

Though extremely rare, these occasionally appear on the market. Usually the form is a bust

designed to be attached to a cloth body. These imitate (but not very well) the porcelain examples widely imported during the nineteenth century.

### Water Whistles

These charming toys, usually in the form of a salt-glazed, blue-decorated bird, animal, or human, are generally attributed to Pennsylvania, where more common examples in redware are also found. All are extremely hard to come by.

### Marbles

In 1889 the making of "American Agate Marbles" was introduced in Akron, Ohio, by A. L. Dyke, and during the next decade several competing manufacturers made Akron the "marble capital of the world." However, most children preferred glass, and stoneware marbles are rarely encountered today.

### Miniatures

Small-scale versions of jugs, crocks, pitchers, pots, flasks, and churns were made either as toys or, possibly, as salesmen's samples. Some are blue decorated and salt glazed, but most are unadorned. Perhaps the best known are the tiny jugs in Albany slip with incised decoration produced during the last quarter of the nineteenth century. Some, with slogans such as Centennial/ Augt.16th/1877 (Centennial of the Battle of Bennington), are known to have been made at the Bennington, Vermont, pottery. A second group advertising saloons and liquor dealers is thought to have been made in the Lexington, Kentucky, area.

Another unusual form is the whiskey flask, or "taster," in the guise of a pig, usually with a map of the Illinois railway system inscribed upon its back, which was produced by the Anna (Illinois) Pottery in the 1870s and 1880s.

*Two cast stoneware Staffordshire-type mantel figures ▶ in a tan mineral slip attributed to the Lyons, New York, pottery, 1870–75.*

### FIGURAL PIECES

A large number of figural forms in stoneware are known. Some, such as the grotesque but marvelous jugs embellished with snakes and human forms, were usually made to order as gifts or presentation pieces. Typical are 1870–1900 examples from the Anna, Illinois, pottery and from smaller kilns in Calhoun, Boonville, Clinton, Pilot Grove, and California, Missouri. On the other hand, anthropomorphic face jugs were and are made in great quantity at many Southern factories.

A more traditional category are mantelpiece figures and doorstops—usually in the form of dogs, though human and other animal figures appear—based on English Staffordshire figures. New England and New York examples were usually given a brown mineral slip, but Ohio lions might be salt glazed and blue decorated, and dogs were finished in Bristol slip splashed with brown manganese.

Most figurals date from the second half of the nineteenth century, though the Monmouth Pottery Co. of Monmouth, Illinois, was turning out pigs, dogs, cows, and chickens in the early 1900s; while at the same time Minnesota's Red Wing Union Stoneware Company made such unlikely things as small traveling bags in brown slip, as well as shoes, bulldogs, footballs, and advertising figures.

### MISCELLANEOUS PIECES

A large number of specialized forms made in stoneware are known. Some are so odd and of so little concern to most collectors as to rate only

passing notice here. A few, however, are both interesting and rare.

### Grave Markers

Several nineteenth-century Southern potters made blue-decorated, salt-glazed tombstones, usually on special order. Known manufacturers include John D. Heatwole, J. Coffman, and G. N. Fulton of Virginia's Shenandoah Valley, the Falkner family of Sterrett, Alabama, and Charles Decker of Tennessee's Nolichucky Valley. The Bell family of Strasburg, Virginia, also produced molded stoneware lambs of the sort traditionally used as footstones on children's graves. Neither of these items should ever be considered as collectibles. There are also mineral-glazed cone-form vases that taper to a sharp end and were used to contain flowers at a grave site.

The Saenger Pottery of Bexar County, Texas, made these about 1890–1900.

### Sundials

At least two blue-washed, salt-glazed sundials are known. Both were special orders and are thought to be from a Philadelphia pottery, probably either Haig or Remmey. No marked examples have been found.

### Fence Posts

Square fence posts of unglazed stoneware are seen in the South and Midwest. Though sometimes mistakenly called grave markers, these can be readily recognized by the holes through which strands of barbed wire passed.

### Water Pumps

Perhaps one of the oddest items to be made in stoneware, the water pump was extremely practical, being subject neither to rust nor rot. They looked much like cast-iron examples, and must have been reasonably popular since the firm of Weaver & Cordery at Brazil Township, Indiana, specialized in their manufacture from 1873 until around 1910. A related form is the water bucket made in Bexar County, Texas, in the early twentieth century. It resembles a rimless churn and has a wire bail handle. The obvious impracticability of this form assured its limited distribution.

### Stills

Looking like a handleless large watercooler with a bunghole and two vertical tubes extending from the top, early stills, like that made and marked about 1837–39 by Henry Nash of Utica, New York, were used in whiskey making. Later examples were employed in the chemical industry.

### Horse Feed Boxes

Square, unglazed stoneware boxes for use in stables were advertised in 1879 by the Hart Brothers Pottery of Utica, New York. They do not appear to have caught on, and I have never heard of an example being found.

### Birdhouses

A cylindrical example with tapering roof surmounted by a turned finial, a door, and a hole for a wooden perch is attributed to A. E. Smith & Sons Pottery of Norwalk, Connecticut (1865–75). Other similar pieces were made in Pennsylvania, the Midwest, and the South.

*Price list of Price & Bachelder's Erie City Stone-Ware Manufactory dated 1867. This Pennsylvania pottery made a typical line of stoneware products.*

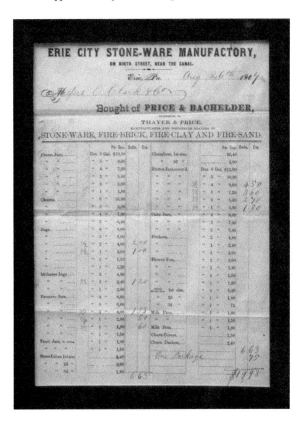

### Stove Tubes

Looking like unglazed crocks that lack both top and bottom, these were employed to protect surrounding wooden surfaces from the heat of metal stove pipes. They were made everywhere. Cowden & Company of Harrisburg, Pennsylvania, sold them in a dozen sizes around 1900. The largest, 6″ x 12″, cost $2.16 for a dozen.

### Portable Furnaces

An earlier version of the barbecue grill, these bucket-shaped heaters had an inset perforated top and a lower ash receptacle reached through a small door. They burned charcoal or twigs for cooking and space heating. First advertised in New York and Pennsylvania in the 1820s, they were still being made in the South and Southwest in the early twentieth century at shops such as the McDade Pottery of Bastrop County, Texas.

### Smoking Pipes

Since their manufacture required only molds and a very small oven, smoking pipes were widely made, often by individuals who did not otherwise engage in the pottery business. Some were alkaline glazed, like those of the Falkner family of Sterrett, Alabama, others unglazed or salt glazed like the remarkable sixty-seven different forms found in excavation of the Point Pleasant, Ohio, pottery (1849–80). Perhaps the most unusual was a novel six-bowl pipe made in the late 1800s by William Decker of the Nolichucky Valley, Tennessee.

### Hunting Horns

At least two of these exist. One is a long tube tapering to a flaring mouth and was also made at the Decker family's Keystone Pottery in Tennessee during the late nineteenth century. A second example, shorter but of a similar form, was also turned in this state, by William Grindstaff of Knox County.

### Ant Traps

And a final oddity, the ant trap, which looked like a pan with an inner ring. Table or pie safe legs would be set inside this ring and the outer "moat" was filled with water to prevent the passage of ants, roaches, and similar pests. Made in Pennsylvania of redware, they were still being produced in Albany-slip-glazed stoneware at the Richter Pottery in Bexar County, Texas, 1890–1910.

# 3

## MAINE AND NEW HAMPSHIRE

THE LIMITED NUMBER of stoneware factories that were established in these northern New England states reflects some of the economic realities faced by manufacturers of salt-glazed wares. Both Maine and New Hampshire were far removed from sources of stoneware clay. Their small populations were for the most part confined to coastal areas, where they were readily served by seaborne traders carrying wares made in Boston, New York, or even New Jersey. The isolated inland communities had a thriving redware industry that survived into the late 1800s.

Few were willing to invest in a stoneware business that would have to import clay at a high premium and trade in a small and very competitive local market (higher production costs made it unlikely that Maine or New Hampshire craftsmen could sell at a profit in Massachusetts or Connecticut). Nevertheless, there were those who ventured and some, particularly in Maine where the Canadian markets of New Brunswick and Nova Scotia could be exploited, who succeeded.

### MAINE

Portland, Maine's largest city and an important seaport, was also the site of the state's first stoneware works. In January 1834 Martin Crafts, a potter from Whately, Massachusetts, arrived in the city and about a year later was joined by Eleazer Orcutt, also of Whately and a seasoned craftsman who had been employed during the years 1833–34 at the stoneware works of Israel Seymour in Troy, New York.

In February 1835 Crafts bought an old distillery on Green Street near the Portland waterfront and converted it to a pottery. The partnership, to which salt-glazed crocks and jugs impressed ORCUTT & CRAFTS/PORTLAND may be traced, was active by June when *The Yankee Farmer* noted that stoneware was being made in

Portland and urged "all who have occasion to use vessels for domestic purposes, as they value health and money, and as they regard comfort and neatness, to try at least some of this ware and judge its utility."

Such local boosterism notwithstanding, the heavily mortgaged pottery did not prosper. Orcutt sold his interest to Crafts in September 1836; and by April of the following year Martin's uncle, Caleb Crafts, also of Whately, had arrived to take over the business.

In partnership with a local man, William Fives, Caleb Crafts ran the shop from 1837 until 1841, producing a substantial number of bulbous jugs and jars stamped C.CRAFTS & CO./PORTLAND. However, the property was sold to satisfy tax and mortgage liens in 1843, passing into the hands of Thomas Seal & Company (1844–46) and then Clough, Calhoun & Co. One of the very few known examples of Maine stoneware with incised decoration—a jug with a crudely picked-out flower—bears the mark CLOUGH CALHOUN/ & CO./PORTLAND,ME.

A local merchant, John T. Winslow, taken into the Clough firm in 1847, assumed full control the following year, moving the business to the suburb of Westbrook and managing it successfully until 1867. That year a relative, James N. Winslow, took over the shop and incorporated it as the Portland Stoneware Company.

The company prospered throughout the nineteenth and well into the twentieth century, though after World War II the manufacture of stoneware was discontinued in favor of selling clay products and other raw materials. The business was finally terminated in 1969.

Portland's other stoneware works, Lamson & Swasey, started as an earthenware pottery in 1875. Three years later the firm, now called the Portland Pottery Works, began to make utilitarian stoneware. One of the original proprietors, Rufus Lamson, withdrew in 1883. Eben Swasey continued with a new partner, L. Frank Jones, until Lamson returned in 1886.

The pottery remained active until at least 1891 (as late as 1905 it described itself in bills submitted for goods sold as a "pottery manufacturer"), leaving behind a great number of straight-sided crocks, jugs, and jars, many stenciled E.SWASEY & CO./PORTLAND,ME. (sometimes with the addition of a U.S.A.). Unlike the wares produced by other Maine stoneware works, these were often glazed in brown and white, a style described in a contemporary price list as "Half Light and Dark Swasey Stoneware." Less often seen are salt-glazed, blue-decorated pieces impressed LAMSON & SWASEY/PORTLAND,ME.

Maine's third stoneware works was built at Gardiner, a sizable inland community on the Kennebec River northeast of Portland. In 1837 Alanson Potter Lyman, a lawyer from Bennington, Vermont, and later a partner of Christopher Webber Fenton in the United States Pottery there, bought the site upon which the pottery was erected. It was run by Decius W. Clark, a practical potter born in Vermont and trained at West Troy, New York.

Clark was a remarkable craftsman as may be seen from the lovely ovoid jugs and jars decorated in cobalt or manganese and bearing the impression LYMAN & CLARK/GARDINER. Apparently, talent wasn't enough. In May 1839, Lyman sold the manufactory to Robert Thompson and Charles W. Tarbell, and by the following year Clark was in Bennington, Vermont, working at the Norton stoneware kiln.

Both Thompson and Tarbell were businessmen. The stoneware marked THOMPSON & CO/GARDINER,ME or R.THOMPSON & CO./GARDINER, sold from 1839 to 1854, was made by hired potters. The output was substantial: $6,500 worth in 1850 alone.

Another change in management occurred in 1854 when Thompson (Tarbell had died in 1844) transferred the shop to the potters Orrin L., Alfred K., and Hiram N. Ballard of Burlington, Vermont. Though ware stamped BALLARD &

BROTHERS/GARDINER, ME. is fairly common, the Ballards were not long in Gardiner. In June 1855 they sold the manufactory, and by the next year Orrin and Alfred were again making stoneware in Burlington.

The new owners, Francis A. and William Plaisted and William H. Wiles, marked their wares F.A. PLAISTED & CO./GARDINER ME., reflecting Francis's dominant position. He soon bought out his brother and in 1863 purchased Wiles's interest. The latter, incidentally, was the only potter among them, the Plaisted brothers being local entrepreneurs.

Despite the financial panic of 1858 and a fire that destroyed the plant in 1866, the firm prospered under the guidance of Francis Plaisted. Following the fire the pottery was rebuilt on a new site in neighboring Farmingdale, and a son, Frank C., joined the management, a change reflected in ware impressed MANUFACTURED BY/F.A. PLAISTED & SON/GARDINER, ME.

However, in 1876 the Plaisteds retired from business in favor of Charles Swift and William M. Wood of Gardiner who titled their shop the Gardiner Stoneware Manufactory, the name it bore through various changes of management until production ceased sometime between 1890 and 1892.

During this last period wares were stamped with variations of the cipher GARDINER STONEWARE/MANUFACTORY/GARDINER, ME. and often impressed with small blue-filled designs of an eagle, swan, or cow or various combinations thereof. To my knowledge this is the only use of impressed decoration on Maine stoneware, and so distinctive are the stamps that unmarked pieces bearing such impressions are readily identified as being from Gardiner.

The last Maine stoneware works was established in 1880 at Bangor on the Penobscot River. The owner, Anders Perrson, was a potter who previously had an interest in the Gardiner-Farmingdale works and who moved east to capture the growing Canadian trade. He built a factory on Patten Street in Bangor, a portion of which still stands, and by 1890 was selling $33,000 worth of stoneware annually and was shipping five or six carloads of stoneware to St. John, New Brunswick, alone.

Buoyed by Canadian trade and somewhat insulated from the competition of mechanized Midwestern factories which was devastating the New York and New Jersey potteries, the Bangor works remained active until around 1918. Large quantities of salt-glazed or Albany-slip-finished ware, marked variously BANGOR, BANGOR/MAINE, or BANGOR STONE WARE CO./BANGOR, MAINE, may still be found in eastern Maine and the Maritime Provinces of Canada.

*Salt-glazed stoneware crock with impressed, blue-filled image of a cow; made and marked by the GARDINER STONEWARE/MANUFACTORY/GARDINER, ME., 1880–90. This Maine firm was one of the last to employ impressed decoration.*

*Salt-glazed stoneware hot water bottle or foot warmer made and marked by the* BANGOR STONEWARE CO./ BANGOR MAINE 1880–1915.

## NEW HAMPSHIRE

New Hampshire had only three stoneware manufactories. The first of these, at Nashua on the Merrimack River in the southern part of the state, was built in 1838 by the Crafts family, potters from Whately, Massachusetts. Thomas Crafts, the father, had been shipping ware to wholesalers in Nashua for some years when he decided to establish a local branch.

The first manager was a son, James M., then only twenty-one, and the extremely rare mark T.CRAFTS & CO./NASHUA dates to this period. However, in the summer of 1838 an older son, Martin Crafts, who had been running the stoneware works at Portland, Maine, came to Nashua to take over the business. Yet another member of the clan, Uncle Caleb, who also had run the Portland works, was in Nashua about 1843–45.

These close family connections are mirrored in an existent 1845 price list, which is titled simply "Crafts & Co." Nevertheless, Martin's dominance in the business is reflected in the fact that ware made from 1839 until the business was shut down in 1852 is marked simply MARTIN CRAFTS/ NASHUA, N.H.

There were two much later factories at Keene in southwestern New Hampshire. In July 1871, James Scholly Taft and his uncle James Burnap bought a woodenware factory there and converted it into an earthenware pottery. The building promptly burned to the ground, but the partners (neither of whom was a potter) rebuilt, adding stoneware to their list of products.

In the same year another manufactory opened in Keene, this one owned by the firm of Starkey & Howard and also manufacturing both red earthenware and stoneware. The rival works stood within sight of each other, and competition for the local market must have been intense. In 1872 the *New Hampshire Gazette* valued the total output of both firms at $35,000.

Something had to give and it was Starkey & Howard. In June of the same year they sold out to W. P. Chamberlain and E. C. Baker. The shop continued, however, under the guidance of Abner S. Wight, a skilled potter from West Sterling, Massachusetts. But there just wasn't room for two potteries in Keene, and in 1874 J. S. Taft & Co. acquired its competitor, using the buildings for redware production while continuing to produce stoneware at its original site.

The Keene Stone & Earthenware Manufactory, as it was styled, remained active late into the nineteenth century. Traditional forms, sometimes with simple blue decoration, are impressed J.S. TAFT/KEENE, N.H. or J.S. TAFT & CO./ KEENE, N.H. No marked ware seems to have survived the brief life of its competitor.

# 4

# VERMONT

THOUGH ISOLATED both from major population centers and sources of clay suitable for making stoneware, Vermont became one of the most important centers of the trade. Indeed, the Norton factory at Bennington symbolizes for many collectors the very nature of blue-decorated salt-glazed stoneware.

The history of the state's several kilns is closely bound up with that of two families—the Nortons and the Farrars. About the first much is known, about the latter, very little.

But Vermont's first stoneware potter was of another family equally well known. In 1800 Jonathan Fenton, who had been trained in a shop at New Haven, Connecticut, and who had been a partner in a Boston firm from 1793 until 1796, arrived in Dorset, Vermont, a small community on the present State Route 30 in southwestern Vermont.

It was an odd place for a "big city" stoneware maker; but perhaps the Fentons were early adherents of the "back to the land movement."

Jonathan's brother, Jacob, left his New Haven business in the same year for Burlington, New York, which was even smaller than Dorset.

In any case, Jonathan Fenton built a small kiln in the area known as Dorset Hollow, where from 1801 until 1810 he made both redware and stoneware. None appears to have been marked, though a salt-glazed jar with incised fish in the Boston manner has been attributed to the site due to its similarity in form to a shard found at the Dorset Hollow location.

In 1810 Fenton bought land a few miles away in East Dorset, where he erected a new kiln for the manufacture of both stoneware and redware that appears to have operated continuously until 1835. Two sons, Richard Lucas Fenton and Christopher Webber Fenton, shared in the business at various times resulting in several marks, none of which are common: J.FENTON/EAST DORSET, R.L.FENTON & CO./EAST DORSET, and R. & C. FENTON/DORSET, VT., among others. There is also a remarkable "face jug," impressed

J. FENTON, which may be by Jonathan Fenton. It is in the collection of the San Diego Museum of Art.

The longevity of this tiny shop is remarkable both in light of its isolated location and the fact that between it and its source of stoneware clay lay a larger factory, that established about 1793 in Bennington near the New York border by Captain John Norton.

The Norton pottery lasted a century, finally closing its doors in 1894. Several writers have considered its history, the most recent, *The Jug and Related Stoneware of Bennington* by Cornelius Osgood.

John Norton, the founder of this potting dynasty, was born at Goshen, Connecticut, in 1758. It is likely that he also learned his craft there, for the redware potter John Kettle was established in the community by 1776. In 1785 Norton and his wife moved north to Bennington, which was situated on an important road from Troy, New York (now Route 7), and was in a position to command the trade of three states, New York, Vermont, and New Hampshire.

Norton initially was both a farmer and potter, working a two-hundred-acre grant about one and a half miles south of Bennington center. According to tradition he built a kiln on this site in 1793 for the production of redware that was manufactured exclusively until around 1804. That stoneware production was established by that date is evident from recent research done by Cathy Zusy, former curator of the Bennington Museum and author of an important monograph on the history of the Bennington Stoneware Pottery.

On October 23, 1810, a local diarist, Hiram Harwood, recorded that his father's wagons had drawn several loads of stoneware clay from Troy (where barges from New Jersey would have unloaded) to Bennington. Thereafter, the diary makes frequent references to stoneware production at the Norton kiln.

And despite the evident problems involved in operating a stoneware shop at a location both remote from a suitable clay supply and also with the most limited distribution facilities (there was neither canal nor, for many years, a railroad at Bennington), the Norton business thrived.

The founder took his son Luman into the business around 1811 or 1812 and in 1815 another offspring, John Norton, Jr., joined the firm. Then, in 1823 John Norton withdrew into retirement; and by 1828 John Norton, Jr., had transferred his interest to his brother. If marked at all, wares from 1804–1823 are thought to have

*Blue-decorated, salt-glazed watercooler, or "fountain," made and marked by J. & E. NORTON/BENNINGTON, VT., 1850–59. The ware made at the Bennington works under the guidance of Julius and Edward Norton is often exceptionally decorative.*

*Blue-decorated, salt-glazed churn made and marked, 1850–59, by J. & E. NORTON/BENNINGTON, VT. The lion decoration is rare.*

borne the now rare impression, BENNINGTON FACTORY; while from 1823 until 1828 the mark was L.NORTON & CO./BENNINGTON.

From 1828 until 1833 Luman Norton (who had moved the pottery a half mile down Route 7 to his own farm in 1823) controlled the business, stamping his products simply L.NORTON/BENNINGTON.

In 1833 he shifted the shop again, this time two miles north into the rapidly growing center known as East Bennington to distinguish it from the original community, now called "Old Bennington." In the same year Luman took his son, Julius Norton, into the business; the ware now bore the logo L. NORTON & SON/BENNINGTON or L.NORTON & SON/EAST BENNINGTON.

By this time Luman, who was born in 1785, was looking forward to retirement. By 1838 ware with Julius's imprint, J.NORTON/EAST BENNINGTON,VT., was being produced, and by 1841 advertisements of the firm's products bore his name alone.

Three years later Julius Norton entered into a partnership with his brother-in-law, Christopher Webber Fenton, second son of Jonathan Fenton of Dorset. It was not the first contact between the families. Christopher's older brother, Richard, had worked for Luman Norton about 1828–30; and it is possible that Jonathan Fenton was the one who introduced John Norton to the art of stoneware manufacture.

Christopher's arrival on the scene shook up the staid Bennington works. Ware that had previously been of the traditional ovoid form with sparse decoration in cobalt or manganese (a color used more often here than at most early-nineteenth-century shops) suddenly became straight sided with more complex blue floral pat-

terns; and molds were used, apparently for the first time, to produce pitchers in a brown glaze, referred to as "dark lustre." Such ware often bore some variation of the mark NORTON & FENTON/BENNINGTON,VT.

Fenton was an innovator and clearly too much of a risk taker for Julius Norton. The partnership was dissolved in 1847. Christopher Webber Fenton went on to found the United States Pottery at Bennington, specializing in finer wares such as porcelain and Rockingham; and Norton returned to traditional stoneware.

In 1850 he took a cousin, Edward Norton, into the firm, and in 1859 his own son, Luman

*Blue-decorated, salt-glazed four-gallon jug made by Julius and Edward Norton, 1850–59, and bearing their mark, J. & E. NORTON/BENNINGTON, VT.*  ▶

Preston Norton. Vessels from the prior period are stamped J. & E. NORTON/BENNINGTON, VT. and the latter J. NORTON & CO./BENNINGTON, VT.

Upon the death of Julius in 1861 the company mark became E. & L.P. NORTON/BENNINGTON, VT., an impression that was to endure for twenty years and is found upon some of the most highly decorated stoneware produced in this country. Everything from floral bouquets and birds to deer, lions, castles, and complete village scenes adorned the crocks, jugs, jars, and churns turned out in vast numbers by this highly successful firm.

Yet the variety of vessels made during this period actually decreased. Where price lists from earlier periods listed such relatively uncommon objects as mugs, inkwells, and soap dishes, an 1865 E. & L. P. Norton listing revealed little but pots, jugs, and jars.

Luman Preston Norton left the business in 1881 to follow a new career as president of a local bank, and Edward carried on until his death in 1885. His son, Edward Lincoln Norton, guided the firm through its final years. It was shut down in 1894. Ware from this period is rarely decorated with any elaboration, and the latest examples (1886–94) often bear only the stenciled mark THE EDWARD NORTON CO./BEN-NINGTON,VT. and a capacity number, also printed.

However, an interesting specialty of the era, one which had been made at least as early as 1876, were the little brown jugs. These minia-ture Albany-slip-glazed jugs were incised with such messages as "Merry Christmas, 1877," "Centennial/July 4th/1876," and, rarest of all, "E. Norton & CO./BENN-Vermont/1793–1893" in honor of the centennial of the pottery.

Far to the north of Bennington was yet an-other early stoneware shop, this one founded by members of the Farrar family. In 1798 Isaac Brown Farrar of New Ipswich, New Hamp-shire, brought his family to Enosburg in the northwestern corner of Vermont. It is not known if he did any potting here; but by 1805, when his son Stephen Hammon Farrar was born, Isaac was in Fairfax, a farming community on the Black River some twenty miles northeast of Burlington. Sometime early in the nineteenth century he established a pottery there.

The location was an unlikely one. Fairfax was not on a main road or waterway. And, yet, Far-rar made redware and, at some undetermined date, also introduced the manufacture of stone-ware. In 1831 Hiram Harwood noted in his diary at Bennington the passage of one Jason Merrill, a young potter who was heading to Fairfax to work for a "gentleman potter."

Merrill was apparently often on the move (in 1824 he had absconded from his apprenticeship with the venerable potter Absalom Day of Nor-walk, Connecticut), but he was also a trained stoneware man. So it is likely that by this date salt-glazed wares were being produced at Fairfax despite the great difficulty in obtaining suitable clay. A few pots stamped I.B. FARRAR/FAIRFAX remain to commemorate this era. As sons ma-tured they were admitted to the business, as re-flected in wares impressed I.B. FARRAR & SON and I.B. FARRAR & SONS.

Isaac Brown Farrar died in 1838, and by 1840 the firm was in the hands of his son George Whitfield Farrar and a J. H. Farrar, also probably a son. A price list of this year bears their names and describes the customary basic stoneware forms.

By 1851 when the next existent price list ap-pears the shop was titled the Fairfax Stone Ware Pottery, and was run by Farrar & Stearns. The Farrar was almost certainly a son, and quite pos-sibly it was either George W. or Stephen Ham-mon Farrar who was running the Fairfax works in 1857.

For several reasons the chain of ownership is hard to decipher. There were many Farrar off-spring, most of whom became potters, who were either named for ancestors or were given closely similar names. Moreover, unlike other

Northern craftsmen (but very like their Southern brethren), the Farrars preferred to use initials instead of fully spelling out their first and middle names.

Finally, the Farrar family did not confine its efforts to the state of Vermont. Members of the family were also active in New York and, particularly, in Canada. In fact, the family appears to have run potteries in the St. Johns (St. Jean)-Iberville area, south of Montreal, at the same time they were active in both Fairfax and Burlington, Vermont.

Moses Farrar (who had worked in Troy, New York, 1835–36) had a pottery at St. Johns by 1840 and a few years later his partner was Ebenezer Lewis Farrar, a son of Isaac, who had built the first stoneware kiln at Burlington, Vermont. Since there is also stoneware marked E.L. & G.W. FARRAR/FAIRFAX, VT., it is evident that Ebenezer was associated with George in that venture as well.

Things got sorted out a bit in 1857 when Ebenezer L. and Stephen Hammond Farrar took an ill-fated trip on the steamboat *Montreal*. The ship burned, and both were lost. George W. Farrar continued the St. John factory alone, and it is quite likely that at this point the Farrars ceased to work in Fairfax.

There is other, as yet unidentified, Fairfax stoneware. There is a price list from 1856 for the firm of Lewis, Bostwick & Cady; and the mark LEWIS & CADY/FAIRFAX, VT. dates to the same era, both probably reflecting the attempts of others to revive an industry already doomed by close proximity to the larger stoneware manufactories at Burlington and Bennington. The stamp FARRAR & WAIT without place name may mark a brief partnership similar to that of Farrar and Stearns, while the impression FARRAR & SOULE without place name documents a short-lived Canadian venture.

The Farrars were also active in the important potting community of Burlington, Vermont. Located on Lake Champlain as well as modern Route 7, a road which ran from Norwalk, Connecticut, to Montreal, Burlington was ideally suited to the stoneware trade, especially once the Champlain Canal had been opened, making it possible to ship suitable clay by water all the way from New Jersey.

There was a redware pottery here as early as 1806, but its owner, Norman L. Judd, who had trained under John Norton at Bennington, had left town by 1811. The existence of certain ovoid jugs impressed BURLINGTON/VT. raises the possibility of a stoneware kiln in the 1830s or '40s; but Lura Woodside Watkins claims in her *Early New England Potters and Their Wares* that the city's first stoneware manufactory was built on Pearl Street in 1854 by Ebenezer Lewis Farrar of Fairfax for the firm of Nichols & Alford.

That Farrar had some relationship with Nichols and Alford, who were probably businessmen, is supported by the existence of stoneware impressed E.L. FARRAR & CO./BURLINGTON, VT.; while the 1854 date is fixed by a molded pitcher bearing the impression NICHOLS & ALFORD/MANUFACTURERS/1854/BURLINGTON, VT.

Farrar had a pottery in Canada by 1857, but he also may have maintained some sort of relationship with the Burlington firm, as he was listed as a resident of the city upon his death in that same year. In any case, the Nichols firm was not a stable one. A price list published late in 1854 has Alford's name crossed out, and one used in 1855 describes the partners as Nichols & Boynton, a brief relationship memorialized by the rare stamp, NICHOLS & BOYNTON/ BURLINGTON, VT.

A period of relative stability was achieved when the Ballard brothers, Alfred K., Orrin L., and Hiram N., took over the works. They had owned a pottery at Gardiner, Maine, from 1854 to 1855; and their abrupt return to Vermont may reflect seizure of an opportunity to purchase the floundering Burlington manufactory. It appears that Hiram was in the city by 1855, his presence indicated by vessels stamped H. N. BALLARD/BUR-LINGTON, VT.

By late 1856 Alfred and Orrin were back in Burlington, and the firm name, as given in the New England Business Directory for that year, was O.L. & A.K. Ballard. Despite the fact that Orrin was associated with the Farrars in St. John, Quebec, off and on from 1857 through the end of the decade, the firm name remained unchanged until 1867, leaving behind a substantial quantity of ware impressed O.L. & A.K. BALLARD/BURLINGTON, VT., as well as many vessels impressed BALLARD & BROTHERS or BALLARD BROTHERS/BURLINGTON, VT.

From 1867 until 1874 Alfred K. Ballard was listed as proprietor, stamping his output A.K. BALLARD/BURLINGTON, VT. His successor in 1875 was F. Woodworth, who was in charge until at least 1878. Watkins maintains, though, that at some later date H. E. Sulls took over the factory and operated it until it shut down in 1895. Wares marked F. WOODWORTH/BURLINGTON, VT. are common, but nothing with the Sulls name is known.

If the beginning and ending dates are correct, the Burlington pottery operated for fifty years. Its output appears to have been substantial and in the first period, it may have attempted to compete with the United States Pottery at Bennington in the production of Rockingham. Watkins mentions that hound-handled pitchers, book flasks, vases, mugs, and other Bennington-type forms were produced here. This is supported by a Nichols price list that includes an impressive array of "fancy pressed ware"—pitcher and bowl sets, milk pans, beefsteak heaters, fountains (watercoolers), foot baths, and cake pans. However, after 1860 such wares were confined to the flowerpots, spittoons, pitchers, and teapots made by most Eastern stoneware factories.

The Fenton family of New Haven, Connecticut, was involved in yet another pioneer Vermont pottery. In 1804 Richard Webber Fenton,

a brother of Jonathan of Dorset, removed to St. Johnsbury in the northeastern part of the state and close to the New Hampshire border. It is thought he had a pottery there by 1808. Fenton was, of course, trained as a stoneware maker, but though it is assumed by some that he made salt-glazed wares, none bearing his name are known.

There is no doubt, however, that his son, Leander W. Fenton, whose mark, L. W. FENTON/ST. JOHNSBURY, VT. is common in the area, did manufacture stoneware. Since his father was born in 1771, Leander must have taken over the shop in the 1830s or '40s, but the exact date is unknown.

There are also vessels stamped FENTON & HANCOCK, ST. JOHNSBURY, VT., one of which is dated 1852, indicating a partnership at this time. Watkins assumed the associate to be Frederick Hancock, an English potter who was working at Bennington in the 1840s and who was, in 1858, one of the founders of the stoneware factory at Worcester, Massachusetts. There is, however, no evidence to support this, and it appears to contradict Frederick's history as he told it to Edwin Atlee Barber for his *Pottery and Porcelain of the United States*.

Whatever the case may be, the St. Johnsbury kiln burned to the ground in November 1859 and was never rebuilt. Among the vessels remaining are the usual blue-decorated crocks, jugs, and jars and at least one remarkable urn-shaped watercooler with applied decoration, always a rarity among American wares.

There may also have been one more, short-lived stoneware shop, this one in St. Albans, a sizable community on Route 7 near Lake Champlain and about twelve miles northwest of Fairfax. Watkins lists the firm of Boynton & Farrar as active there in 1860. Since a Farrar and a Boynton were working (though there is no evidence of a partnership) in Burlington in the 1850s, it is possible that they collaborated in such a venture.

# 5

# MASSACHUSETTS

THE STATE OF Massachusetts has a long and impressive history of stoneware manufacture. Though like the rest of New England the Commonwealth lacked suitable clays for stoneware, it did not lack for potters ambitious to produce it.

As early as 1742 the redware maker Isaac Parker of Charlestown (now a part of Boston) sought a loan from the colonial authorities to subsidize the making of salt-glazed wares since, as he pointed out in his petition, "there are large quantities of said Ware imported into this Province every year from New York, Philadelphia & Virginia."

His argument was persuasive enough that the loan was made, but Parker died three weeks later. His wife, Grace, and brother-in-law, Thomas Symmes, took up the work and employed a Philadelphia potter, James Duche.

Clay from Gay Head on the island of Martha's Vineyard was first tried, but it could not stand the high firing temperature, and both ware and kiln melted into a mound of slag. Convinced after three tries, the partners shipped in clay from New York and Pennsylvania. Enough pottery was produced that Symmes could advertise "blue and white stoneware of forty different sorts" in the *Boston Gazette* for April 16, 1745.

However, the business failed and Duche returned to Philadelphia in 1746. Grace Parker, in seeking relief from her onerous financial obligations, indicated the reason why. They had failed "on account of the Risque [sic] and Expense of transporting their Clay from afar, the Freight whereof only would cost them more than the ware when manufactured could be sold for." No examples of early Charlestown stoneware have been positively identified.

It was nearly fifty years before another attempt was made in Boston. In April 1793 the Boston Board of Selectmen granted the application of Jonathan Fenton of New Haven to "erect a stone pottery . . . at the North end." One of those passing judgment on the petition was William Little, a wealthy merchant born, like Frederick Carpenter, Fenton's associate in the venture, in Lebanon, Connecticut. Little apparently bankrolled the business, and its wares were sold through his store as well as from the kiln on Lynn Street.

An advertisement placed in the *Columbian Centinel* of August 14, 1793, is one of the earliest detailing the products of an American stoneware factory. Items available included jugs, butter and pickle pots, gallipots (small vessels used to mix and store medicines), mugs, and pitchers.

Like Grace Parker, Fenton and Carpenter had to import their raw materials. Thomas Pemberton in his 1794 *Description of Boston* noted that "(a)t the Stone Pottery lately set up in Lynn Street by Mr. Fenton from New Haven, all kinds of stone vessels are made . . . (t)he clay for this manufacture is brought from Perth Amboy in New Jersey."

The business lasted only three years. By Jan-

uary 1797 Fenton was in Walpole, New Hampshire, on his way to Vermont. Carpenter departed Boston late in that year for New Haven, where he worked in Jacob Fenton's stoneware factory until 1801.

Despite the brevity of their venture, Fenton and Carpenter left behind a surprisingly large number of recognizable vessels. These are customarily marked BOSTON in letters all of a single size. At least three examples also bear an impressed cartouche with the initials JF; and the decoration on these, an impressed and incised flower, an incised fish, etc., has made it possible to identify unmarked examples from the same kiln.

Interesting enough, despite their close association the partners worked in different styles. Fenton's was Germanic, with blue-decorated salt glaze, elongated necks, and vertical handles that flared widely from the body. Carpenter followed the English mode, preferring to dip his pieces in ocher, producing various shades of tan and brown while tucking his handles tightly against the body.

The failure of the Lynn Street works was not the end for Boston or for Frederick Carpenter. By the fall of 1801 he was back in Massachusetts, now residing in Charlestown where John Little, younger brother of his previous benefactor, had bought land for a pottery in July 1800. The shop was built by the Mystic River near the juncture of the present Medford and Lexington streets; and advertisements indicate that its wares were again sold through the Boston shop of William Little, who also held a mortgage on the premises.

Carpenter worked at his Mystic River shop until around 1811, producing numerous ovoid jugs and jars in rich tan and brown impressed

*Salt-glazed stoneware pot, 1793–96, attributed to Jonathan Fenton, Boston, Massachusetts. The decoration is filled with blue.*

*Stoneware jug impressed* BOSTON, *with a two-tone ocher or ferruginous glaze. Attributed to Frederick Carpenter, Charlestown, Massachusetts, 1804–11.*

either BOSTON with the "B" larger than the other capitals or with the addition of the date 1804. No one knows why the date was added, as the pottery was in operation prior to 1804. In any case, Carpenter's work is eagerly sought after by sophisticated collectors, and Lura Woodside Watkins, the unquestioned authority on New England ceramics, called it "as fine as anything ever turned in an American pottery."

In 1812 Frederick Carpenter made another move, going to work at a manufactory built early that year near the Charlestown prison by Barnabas Edmands. Edmands was a prosperous brass founder, and Carpenter ran the pottery for him until the potter died in 1827.

During this period Carpenter produced wares with a body more gray than tan, though often with the same ocher dipping found on his earlier examples. They were marked CHARLESTOWN.

The vessels were generally ovoid and often decorated with one or more small impressed designs which by their number also indicated the vessel's capacity in gallons. One collector has cataloged seventeen different stamps used to make these impressions. None are common, but among those sometimes seen are hearts, shields, eagles, circles, squares, tassels, and stars.

After Carpenter's death, Edmands hired another master potter and continued the firm until 1852. Marks for the period include BARNABAS EDMANDS/CHARLESTOWN and B.EDMANDS & CO./ CHARLESTOWN. In 1852 Barnabas passed control of the firm to his sons, Edward T. and Thomas R., who managed it until 1868. Their relatively common products are stamped EDMANDS & CO./ CHARLESTOWN. A third generation, John B. Edmands, carried on with various partners until 1905.

*Molded twelve-sided stoneware tobacco jar in an Albany-slip glaze, impressed EDMANDS on the base. Made by the Edmands Pottery, Charlestown, Massachusetts, 1868–1905.*

There was yet another eighteenth-century stoneware works in eastern Massachusetts. In 1772, William Seaver of Taunton, an important community in the southeastern part of the state not far from Providence, built a kiln on what is now Ingell Street. Seaver had previously worked at Dorchester, but there is no conclusive evidence that he made stoneware there. In fact, the first sign that he sold stoneware does not appear until 1791. Thereafter, however, there are numerous references in Seaver's accounts to the purchase of stoneware clay from New Jersey and the sale of salt-glazed pieces. A large, crude vessel attributed to his hand is impressed TAUN-TON/POT.

William Seaver died in 1815, by which time his sons John and William were connected with the business; however, the immediate future of the firm is unclear. Apparently, the pottery came into the control of Jonathan W. and William H. Ingell who owned brickyards in the vicinity. By 1837 they were turning out $10,000 worth of stoneware each year; much of it stamped WM.H. INGELL/TAUNTON/MASS. or J.W. INGELL/TAUN-TON/MASS.

In 1850 a portion of the pottery lot was sold to Alexander Standish, who since about 1846 had run a competing stoneware kiln on nearby Bow Street. His early ware is marked A.STANDISH/TAUNTON,MASS.; but in the early 1850s he took into partnership Franklin T. Wright. Examples impressed STANDISH & WRIGHT date before 1857 when Standish left the firm.

From then until about 1866, pieces from the Bow Street manufactory were marked F.T. WRIGHT & CO./STONEWARE/TAUNTON,MASS. However, in that year, Wright's son joined him under the logo F.T. WRIGHT & SON/ TAUNTON, MASS. The shop is thought to have continued into the 1870s. Its wares are common but generally rather ordinary in both form and decoration.

Another early kiln in the greater Boston area was that of Loammi Kendall in Chelsea. Kendall was born in nearby Charlestown and was, perhaps, encouraged by the success of the Edmands works; for in 1836 he bought land on the present Broadway and erected a factory. By 1837 he was winning praise for his wares at the Massachusetts Charitable Mechanics' Association Fair, and the business was continued into the 1870s. The output, which consisted of redware as well as stoneware, was not great; and examples marked LOAMMI KENDLE [*sic*]/CHELSEA or simply CHELSEA are not particularly common.

A competing shop at Medford in the northeastern section of greater Boston was less successful. Thomas and John Sables in association with Job Clapp were in business only from 1838 until 1844. Their wares, marked T.SABLES & CO./ MEDFORD or MEDFORD, were apparently intended primarily to house the products of a nearby distillery.

A much later Boston stoneware factory was located at Brighton, though its products, made by Joseph O. Bullard and Alexander F. Scott, were marked BULLARD & SCOTT/CAMBRIDGEPORT, MASS. The shop, located on Western Avenue, was established around 1870 and was still in business, under Bullard, in 1909. Little is known of its output.

In the Pottersville area of Somerset, a community on the river south of Taunton, the Chace family established a much more important manufactory. Somerset had been a potting town since the mid-eighteenth century, and Asa Chace was making redware there at least as early as 1768. Around 1847 his grandsons, Benjamin G., Clark, and Leonard, built a stoneware kiln on the family lot and incorporated as the Somerset Potters' Works, making the usual salt-glazed jugs, jars, pots, pitchers, churns, and so forth.

The shop remained in the family until 1882; but, as is often the case with a business controlled by several members of the same family, it is difficult to figure out who was in charge. Earlier vessels are often stamped B.G. & C. CHACE/SOMERSET for Benjamin and Clark, who were also listed as proprietors in the 1856 *New England Business Directory*. However, there are also pieces impressed L. & B.G. CHACE/SOMERSET.

More numerous are examples marked simply SOMERSET POTTERS WORKS, and these are believed to date from throughout the time the family operated the manufactory. From 1882 until 1891, when the Somerset works was merged with another firebrick shop owned by the same group of investors, little identifiable stoneware was made.

There were two other late-nineteenth-century stoneware works in eastern Massachusetts. Around 1880 an L. Willard set up shop in Ballardvale near Andover. The business was continued until the end of the century by him and his sons. The output, which was decorated either in freehand cobalt or with stencils, was marked L.WILLARD & SONS/BALLARDVALE or simply BALLARDVALE.

Amazingly enough, when Watkins visited the site in 1943 she found the kiln, clay preparation shop, potters' shop, and storage warehouse still standing.

The second of these kilns, the Dorchester Pottery Works on Victory Road in Dorchester, was not only standing but still in operation at the time Watkins wrote *Early New England Potters and Their Wares*. In fact, it remained in business until after World War II. The original owner was George H. Henderson, who had previously run

*Molded stoneware pitcher with dark manganese glaze in the form of a Nubian or Blackamoor head, attributed to the Medford, Massachusetts, pottery, 1838–44. So-called "face jugs" were made in the North as well as in the South.*

*Blue-decorated, salt-glazed stoneware jug with vase of flowers decoration, made and marked by the* SOMERSET POTTERS WORKS, *Somerset, Massachusetts, 1850–82.*

the Pewtress Pottery in New Haven, Connecticut. He was succeeded by other members of his family.

The secret of the firm's longevity was adaptability. Early hand production of salt-glazed stoneware crocks and jugs was abandoned in favor of mechanically produced wares glazed in colored slips and nontraditional forms such as jewelers' chemical dipping baskets and foot warmers. The stenciled mark DORCHESTER POTTERY WORKS/DORCHESTER MASS. is widely seen.

The first successful stoneware pottery in central Massachusetts was established in 1858 by Frank B. Norton and Frederick Hancock of Bennington, Vermont. They selected Worcester, a large industrial city served by major roads and railways, as the site. Since Norton was a member of the well-known Bennington potting family, he brought both skill and financial backing to the project, while Hancock had worked at potteries in New Jersey, New York, and Kentucky as well as in Vermont.

Norton and Hancock took over a small stoneware and terra-cotta works, which had been operated since 1856 by William Stone. Its rare ware is stamped, simply, WORCESTER.

Frank Norton was always the driving force at Worcester. The earliest ware was stamped F.B. NORTON & CO./WORCESTER, MASS.; after Frederick Hancock left the business in 1877, the impression used was FRANK B. NORTON/WORCESTER, MASS. until Norton's sons who had entered the business in 1868 were acknowledged with FRANK B. NORTON & SONS/WORCESTER, MASS.

They continued the firm after their father's death in 1886, using the impression F.B. NORTON SONS/ WORCESTER, MASS.

During its heyday, during the 1860s and early '70s, the shop turned out more stoneware than any other in Massachusetts, except the Edmands factory at Charlestown. In 1865 alone, the value of ware produced amounted to $10,000. The blue decoration employed reflected Bennington motifs and standards of quality and remains popular among collectors.

However, like other Eastern kilns, the one at Worcester was gradually strangled by changing customs and materials as well as Western competition. The making of emery wheels was introduced in 1873, and in 1894 the manufacture of traditional wares was abandoned.

Western Massachusetts stoneware production was centered in Franklin County. The earliest center was Whately, a small community just west of the Connecticut River. Stephen Orcutt, progenitor of an important Massachusetts stoneware family, was making redware here in 1797. Sometime before 1830, in partnership with Luke and Obediah Wait, he introduced salt-glazed wares, probably bringing clay up the river valley.

To judge by the relatively few examples marked ORCUTT & WAIT/WHATELY which remain, the business did not last long. However, it did stimulate Thomas Crafts, who had also been making redware in the vicinity since soon after 1800, to try his hand. Crafts not only succeeded locally, but other members of his family made stoneware in Portland, Maine, and Nashua, New Hampshire.

Crafts, whose products were stamped T. CRAFTS & CO./WHATELY, was active from 1833 until 1848. His brother Caleb returned from the family's Nashua kiln in 1845 and ran the Whately business under his own name, C. CRAFTS & CO./WHATELY, MASS., from 1848 until 1854. He

was succeeded during 1855 and 1856 by Edward A. Crafts in partnership with David D. and Isaac N. Wells under the uncommon mark, WELLS, CRAFTS & WELLS/ WHATELY, MASS. From 1857 until it was shut down in 1861, the factory was managed by Thomas's eldest son, Martin Crafts. His logo was M. CRAFTS/WHATELY. David Belding, a son-in-law of Thomas Crafts, may also have had a brief fling at ownership, for there are a few pots impressed D. BELDING/WHATELY.

In 1848, the year Thomas Crafts retired, the Orcutt family made another assay into the Franklin County stoneware field. Walter, a son of Stephen Orcutt, constructed a small kiln at South Ashfield about twenty miles northwest of Whately and then on a major peddlers' route. His partner was John Luther Guilford, whose family owned the land upon which the shop stood. An 1848 price list indicates that the firm made "fancy pitchers," mugs, and urn-shaped water fountains, as well as the usual stoneware items.

Stoneware marked ORCUTT, GUILFORD & CO./ ASHFIELD, MASS. was produced from 1848 until 1850, when Walter transferred his interest to Wellington Hastings and David Belding, the Whately craftsmen.

Though in business together only four years, this duo left behind a substantial number of pieces stamped HASTINGS & BELDING/ASHFIELD, MASS., including some remarkable watercoolers richly decorated in cobalt and embellished with applied or "sprigged" decoration in the classical manner. Raised figures found on such pieces include George Washington, Diana the Huntress, and several versions of the American eagle.

In 1854 Hastings & Belding went into receivership, and the bankrupt company was taken over by Staats Van Loon, an employee since 1851, and George W. Boyden. They struggled on for two years. Their products, marked VAN LOON & BOYDEN/ASHFIELD/MASS., are rare.

# 6

## CONNECTICUT

CONNECTICUT was home to New England's first successful stoneware works and to several other early manufactories, making it the linchpin of the region's pottery. Certainly, much of the credit for this thriving industry must go to the state's location. A rich source of stoneware clay at Huntington, New York, lay just across Long Island Sound, and the Bayonne, New Jersey, deposits were not far away.

The Nutmeg State's first potter was Adam Staats or States, a Dutchman who was in Manhattan by 1743 (probably working at the Crolius or Remmey potteries) and then had brief sojourns in South Amboy and in Pennsylvania, where he no doubt continued to perfect his trade. By 1750, however, States had reached Greenwich, Connecticut, just east of the New York State border, where he appears to have rented land on Indian Harbor from Ebenezer Mead, a well-to-do local landholder.

His kiln must have been operative by 1751;

for that year States entered into a contract with the trustees of the town of Huntington, Long Island, whereby the "Trustees above-said hath sold unto the Said Adam States above named a Considerable Quantity of white Clay by the Cord for one shilling per cord." The duration of the agreement was five years, and it is thought that at its conclusion States turned to New Jersey for his raw materials.

States was active at Greenwich until his death, which probably occurred prior to 1764, when Ebenezer Mead transferred the land on which the pottery stood to his son, Abraham, twenty-two years of age and States's apprentice.

Other than for a brief hiatus during the Revolutionary War, Abraham Mead operated the stoneware works at Indian Harbor until 1791. Among the more than sixty examples attributed to him are several made to mark the shop's termination, including two bearing the cobalt slip inscription, A.M. 1791.

54

*Blue-decorated, salt-glazed stoneware jar dated 1791 and attributed to Abraham Mead, Greenwich, Connecticut. The piece is believed to have been made for Hannah Lewis, wife of a local minister.*

Though little known among collectors, Mead's output is of great importance as it is the largest existent body of identifiable eighteenth-century American stoneware. Dated and initialed pieces and characteristic "watch spring" and patterned dot decoration make it possible to attribute to him a variety of wares, including jugs, jars, widemouth pots, tea or spirits flasks, pitchers, chamber pots, mugs, a mortar and pestle, and three batter jugs. The last are particularly important, as only one other eighteenth-century batter jug is known, an example from the Crolius factory in Manhattan, now at the New York Historical Society.

No one followed Mead at Greenwich; but other members of the States family played roles in coastal Connecticut stoneware potting. Adam States's brother, Peter, was a resident of Westerly, Rhode Island, as early as 1754, though there is no record of him or any other potter having made stoneware in that state.

However, Westerly is less than twenty-five miles southeast of Norwich, Connecticut, where Peter is known to have worked in the 1760s. It seems likely, in fact, that he established that community's first stoneware kiln.

Norwich, at the head of navigation on the Thames River, was ideally suited to serve as a commercial distribution point for inland eastern Connecticut and adjoining sections of Rhode Island. By the 1760s Christopher Leffingwell, a local entrepreneur, had established several industries, among which was a pottery, described by him in a deed of 1774 as "my Stoneware Kiln in the First Society of Norwich."

That Peter States was in charge of the business seems evident from the fact that in October 1769 Adam States's widow, Elizabeth, apprenticed her son, Adam, Jr., to learn the stoneware trade with his uncle at Norwich. Their agreement is typical of the arrangements under which young men entered into various skilled crafts during the eighteenth century: Elizabeth agreed that during the seven-year term her son would "faithfully serve & not absent himself from his Master's service without leave"; while Peter promised "to find Good Sufescent Clothing, Meat, and Drink, Washing & Lodging, during the said term, I learn the said Adam to read, rite, and civer [cipher], & find him one new sute Close when he shall arrive at the age of Twenty One, besides his wearing appreell."

Apparently, Peter was a better potter than he was a grammarian, because young Adam finished his apprenticeship and went on to produce pottery at Stonington, Connecticut. In the meantime the Leffingwell kiln was, by 1792, in the hands of a son-in-law, Charles Lathrop, who sold it four years later. It is thought that no stoneware was made at this site after 1796.

However, by 1786 Norwich had another stoneware factory, this one built on the banks of the Yantic River by Andrew Tracy and a partner named Huntington. Tracy maintained the business until 1801, when he quitclaimed it to Captain Joseph Hosmer of Salem, Massachusetts. Hosmer was not a potter, but he employed skilled operatives until 1803 when, upon his death, the pottery passed to William Cleveland who operated it until May 1814. None of these early proprietors appear to have left marked or otherwise identifiable ware.

However, the next owners, Peleg Armstrong and Erastus Wentworth, left behind a fair number of ovoid vessels, lightly touched in cobalt, and impressed ARMSTRONG & WENTWORTH/NORWICH. Erastus Wentworth was married to the daughter of Adam States, Jr., and was probably a skilled craftsman. Of his partner little is known. Their pottery operated from 1814 until 1834, first at the old site and later at a new location on the Yantic River at the Willimantic road bridge.

The closing of the Armstrong & Wentworth shop presented an opportunity for Sidney Risley, an East Hartford, Connecticut, potter; for

around 1836 he established a stoneware manufactory in buildings on Yantic Cove. Risley operated a successful business here until his death, April 26, 1875. The mark S.RISLEY/NORWICH is found frequently on wares acquired along the east Connecticut coast.

A son, George S. Risley, succeeded, but for only a brief time. On December 24, 1881, he was fatally injured in the explosion of a boiler, a blast so violent that the 1,500-pound tank was hurled through the pottery roof and into Yantic Cove over a hundred and twenty feet away! No ware bearing the name of George S. Risley seems to have survived.

The following year the shop was reopened under the management of Benjamin C. Chace of the Somerset, Massachusetts, pottery family, who dubbed it the Norwich Pottery Works. The mark, NORWICH POTTERY WORKS/NORWICH/CONN, was used by all successive managements. These included George B. Chamberlain, 1885–87, and Otto N. Suderberg, 1887–95.

Though basically a producer of utilitarian salt-glazed wares, the Norwich kiln turned out some unusual items. During Risley's time there were cast pitchers, some in a creditable Rockingham glaze, double bottles or gemels (most often associated with the New Haven potteries), and even miniature jugs to be worn as watch charms. At a later date the Norwich Pottery Works produced large watercoolers embellished with applied decoration in the form of eagles and floral sprays.

Soon after completing his apprenticeship in Norwich, Adam States, Jr., moved to Stonington on Fishers Island Sound and just west of the Rhode Island line. He married a local woman in 1778 and built a pottery in East Stonington on land provided by her father. Though Adam is believed to have worked at Stonington until his death in 1826, only a single piece stamped A. STATES is attributed to him.

However, there was another, better known manufactory in the town. It had been erected on land owned by Dr. Charles Phelps at Long Point or Stonington Borough and was sold by his son to William States in 1811. Since William was Peter States's son it is possible that this shop just a few miles from Westerly had been used by the old potter.

In 1812 Adam Jr.'s son, Adam III, bought a half interest in this pottery. The cousins worked together until 1821, when Adam III transferred his holdings to William, who continued the business until his death in 1823. The only mark so far found from this period is W.STATES.

Another son of Adam, Jr., Ichabod B. States, took over the factory in partnership with one Joshua Swan, Jr.; operating it until 1835 and leaving behind a few ovoid jugs and jars stamped SWAN & STATES/STONINGTON.

Another member of the States clan worked at New London some fifteen miles west of Stonington. There was a pottery here on Mill Cove as early as 1801. The original proprietor, Job Taber, got into financial difficulties, and his assignees in bankruptcy sold to Michael Omensetter in 1803. The property remained in his name until 1826 when the kiln passed into the hands of Daniel Goodale, Jr., a well-known Connecticut craftsman who was running a stoneware works in Hartford at the time.

However, Omensetter had died prior to the transfer, for the deed of 1826 describes the premises as "heretofore occupied by Michael Omensetter, dec'd. and said premises have lately been occupied by Mr. States." This "Mr. States" was William, grandson of Adam of Stonington (not to be confused with Peter States's son William who also worked at Stonington).

Though William States occupied Omensetter's land and may have used the kiln for a time following his death, he soon established another works. In November 1825 States, in partnership with Benjamin B. Knowles, purchased a plot of land at the corner of Mill and Main streets in New London. Within a year they had built a stoneware kiln that appears to have remained active until States was lost at sea in 1832. No examples associated with this venture have been identified.

In the meantime, Goodale, who probably never potted at New London (being fully occupied with a failing business in Hartford), sold a two-thirds interest in the shop in 1828. His new associate was Stephen T. Brewer whose wares, stamped S.T. BREWER/NEW LONDON, are rare. He and Goodale lost the property in 1830 for failure to meet mortgage payments; and the following year it was sold to Captain William Belcher, tavern owner, lottery agent, and potter.

Belcher continued the works until his death in 1836 at which point stoneware manufacture in New London seems to have come to an end. The few known examples from his hand are impressed W.BELCHER'S/FACTORY/N.LONDON or W.BELCHER/NEW LONDON C.

There were two other important coastal Connecticut stoneware centers. New Haven has a long but uncertain history. The Fenton family was active here as early as 1783, when the potters Nathan and Solomon Fenton advertised "Crucibles to be sold, wholesale or Retail . . . at their Potters-Works, near the Water-side."

While we cannot be sure these vessels were of stoneware, it is most likely; the craftsmen Jonathan Fenton and Frederick Carpenter are said to have learned the trade at the New Haven shop prior to their establishment of a stoneware factory in Boston.

Apparently, the Fenton manufactory either closed or passed into other hands in 1800 when Jacob Fenton, who was in charge, moved to Burlington, New York, and Jonathan and Richard Webber Fenton went to Vermont. By 1811 Dwight's *Statistical Account of the Towns of Connecticut* listed no potteries in New Haven.

However, if there was a hiatus, it ended in 1825 when Absalom Stedman terminated a Hartford partnership and moved to New Haven. It is likely that he occupied the old Fenton works, as he described his shop in an 1831 advertisement as located on East Water Street near the head of the municipal wharf. Stedman was a master potter, and among the examples bearing the impression STEDMAN/NEW HAVEN is an uncommon form, the decorated double or gemel bottle, known in several sizes. At some point Stedman was in business with one of the Seymour family potters from Hartford, an association reflected in pieces stamped STEDMAN & SEYMOUR/NEW-HAVEN.

The potter John Duntze took over the business around 1833 at which time his association with Noyes Darling was announced in a local newspaper. This relationship was a brief one, and Duntze ran the East Water Street works alone until 1852 when he disappears from local directories. Ware bearing the cipher J.DUNTZE/MANUFACTURER/N.HAVEN, CT. is fairly common.

There may have been a second pottery or another proprietor using the New Haven works during the 1840s. City directories from 1840 through 1845 list the "stoneware establishment in Water Street" of Edward E. Huggins, and there are examples marked E.E. HUGGINS/NEW HAVEN.

At a later date Samuel L. Pewtress, a member of a family of New Jersey potters and a former employee of the Worcester, Massachusetts, pottery, operated a stoneware manufactory at 71 Chatham Street in the Fairhaven area of New Haven from 1868 until at least 1887. His crocks and jugs are usually impressed S.L. PEWTRESS/N.HAVEN,CT., though a few examples marked PEWTRESS & CO./FAIRHAVEN, CONN. are known. These may date to the early 1880s when the shop was managed by George Henderson, who later owned the Dorchester, Massachusetts, stoneware company.

The most important stoneware center in southern Connecticut was located at Norwalk, a sizable community directly across Long Island Sound from the fine clay deposits at Huntington, New York. There were redware makers in

Norwalk before 1800, one of whom was Absalom Day who had been trained in Chatham, New Jersey, and had arrived in Norwalk around 1793.

In 1812 Asa E. Smith, a nephew of Absalom Day's wife, was apprenticed to Day and learned his trade at the earthenware works. However, Smith had grander ideas; and on October 31, 1825, he announced them in the *Norwalk Gazette*: "Stone Ware Factory/The subscriber informs the public that he has established a Manufactory of/ Stoneware/ in Norwalk at the foot of Mill Hill a few rods east of the Bridge where he will be able to supply Orders in that line to any extent." Though Smith appears to have operated as an individual proprietor from 1825 until 1837, only a single vessel bearing his mark, A.E. SMITH/NORWALK, is known.

In 1837 Noah Selleck, a merchant and operator of several steamboats on the Sound, became a partner, probably as a way of increasing the firm's capital. His name appears on no Norwalk ware.

Six years later, in 1843, Selleck was replaced by Asa's cousin, Noah S. Day. Though this partnership lasted only until 1849 and appears to have been fraught with personal and financial problems, it produced a vast quantity of stoneware marked SMITH & DAY/ NORWALK or SMITH & DAY/MANUFACTURERS/NORWALK,CON.

Asa Smith had several sons, and as they reached maturity they joined the firm; first Theodore, then Asa, and Howard Hobart, resulting in the marks A.E.SMITH & SON/NORWALK, CT. and A.E. SMITH & SONS/NORWALK, CT. During the latter period wares sold at a New York City wholesale outlet were also stamped A.E.SMITH & SONS/MANUFACTURERS/38 PECK SLIP,N.Y.

In the early 1860s, the father retired from the business and his offspring carried on under their own mark of A.E.SMITH'S SONS/MANUFACTURERS/NORWALK,CON. from about 1864 until 1874 when they incorporated as A.E. Smith's Sons

Stoneware preserve jar in a tan mineral glaze marked
STEDMAN/NEW HAVEN; made by Jonathan Stedman,
New Haven, Connecticut, 1825–33.

Salt-glazed stoneware pot with manganese brown decoration, impressed J.DUNTZE/MANUFACT'R/N.HAVEN,CT.
Made by John Duntze, 1833–52.

Pottery Company. In 1887 the firm became insolvent. A grandson, Wilford, took over for a few months; then, in 1888, the Norwalk Pottery Company was established by a group of local merchants. Pieces bearing the NORWALK POTTERY impression are plain, machine-made vessels, indicating that, though the company persisted until 1901, most of its products were made not at Norwalk but in mechanized Western factories, such as those of Ohio and Illinois.

Though a vast amount of ware was produced at Norwalk and much has survived, few of the pieces are particularly attractive. Examples tend to be heavy bodied; and cobalt decoration, where present, is usually scant and rather ordinary.

Hartford, the state capital on the Connecticut River, supplied most of the stoneware for the central portions of the state. Suitable clay could be brought up the river and finished wares distributed north and south along it.

Numerous potters worked in Hartford, and there is some confusion both as to dates of operation and as to relationships among family members, particularly the Seymour and Goodwin families that dominated the trade after 1830.

One of the earliest kilns was that of Peter Cross, who made salt-glazed wares at two different locations on Front Street between 1805 and 1815. His well-formed examples, marked P. CROSS/HARTFORD, are rare and valued by collectors. The second shop owned by Cross was taken over by two retired sea captains, George Benton and Levi Stewart, who employed the potter Daniel Goodale, Jr., to make wares stamped G. BENTON & L. STEWART/HARTFORD from about 1815 until 1822. Goodale bought the manufactory in March 1822 in association with Absalom Stedman. Stoneware marked GOODALE & STEDMAN/HARTFORD is fairly common and includes both pieces with incised decoration (made by several of the early Hartford kilns) and unusual long-necked bottles.

By 1825 Stedman had left to run a pottery in New Haven, while Goodale struggled on until 1830 when, overwhelmed by financial problems, he lost both this shop and his interest in a New London venture and disappeared from potting history.

The Goodale establishment was purchased in 1831 by Horace Goodwin and Mack C. Webster, who had bought Peter Cross's first pottery site about 1810. Goodwin was a son of Seth Goodwin, who had made redware in the Elmwood area of Hartford as early as 1795.

Goodwin and Webster ran both the Front

---

*Blue-decorated, salt-glazed stoneware jug impressed GOODWIN/ &/ WEBSTER/HARTFORD. Horace Goodwin and Mack C. Webster were active in Hartford, Connecticut, 1810–40.*

*Blue-decorated, salt-glazed stoneware crock made and marked by* SEYMOUR & BOSWORTH/HARTFORD. *The partners in this 1871–90 Connecticut firm were Orson Hart Seymour and Stanley B. Bosworth.*

Street shops for some ten years, and stoneware impressed GOODWIN & WEBSTER/HARTFORD remains common. The partnership came to an end around 1840. Webster and his son, Charles T., made ware marked M.C.WEBSTER & SON/HARTFORD until the death of the former in 1857.

Charles then took a new partner, Orson Hart Seymour, nephew of the well-known Troy, New York, craftsman, Israel Seymour. The mark WEBSTER & SEYMOUR/HARTFORD reflects a ten-year association that terminated in 1867 when Webster left the firm and Henry Phelps Seymour joined his brother. The pieces marked simply O.H.SEYMOUR/HARTFORD,CT. may date to this period. However Henry's death in 1871 required another reorganization. The new partner was Stanley B. Bosworth and the new logo SEYMOUR & BOSWORTH/HARTFORD,CT. The business continued until around 1890, though at some point Seymour ceased to be active, as reflected in wares stamped S.B.BOSWORTH/HARTFORD,CT.

Though the Front Street potteries operated under various managements for over eighty years, they had competition in the local stoneware trade. Thomas O. Goodwin modified his father's redware manufactory in Elmwood for the production of stoneware, which was carried on there from the 1820s until around 1870. Salt-glazed crocks and jugs impressed T.O. GOODWIN/HARTFORD are frequently seen.

# 7

## NEW YORK

FOR MANY COLLECTORS, New York is the stoneware state. Some of the nation's earliest potteries were located there. Pieces decorated in blue at Rochester, Utica, Fort Edward, and in Manhattan, are regarded as among the finest ever produced; and for sheer volume it is difficult to equal the output of the Empire State kilns. A complete documentation of the state's industry is not possible here and the reader should refer to my own *Potters and Potteries of New York State, 1650–1900.*

The earliest stoneware factories were located on Manhattan Island where they could take advantage of the plentiful supplies of suitable clay available either from Huntington, Long Island, to the east or the Amboys area of New Jersey to the southwest. The pioneer producers were members of the Crolius and Remmey families.

John William Crolius, from Coblentz, Germany, established a shop in the vicinity of present-day City Hall before 1728; and his descendants continued the business in the same

general area until 1849, possibly a longevity record for a major American stoneware factory.

Closely associated was the Remmey clan, whose kiln house was never very far removed from that of the Crolius family. John Remmey I was in business by 1735, and his lineal descendants, John Remmey II and John Remmey III, carried on until at least 1820. They too had German roots.

It is difficult to overestimate the importance to collectors of Crolius and Remmey examples. Both firms shipped their stoneware widely: pieces are found from Maine to the Carolinas, and bulbous vessels bearing typical incised and impressed decoration, richly bathed in blue, are found in all major museum collections as well as those of the most advanced collectors.

Marked examples include those of Clarkson Crolius (1800–38) and his son, Clarkson, Jr. (1835–49). The most common impression of the former was C.CROLIUS/MANUFACTURER/MANHATTAN WELLS/NEW YORK, while the latter usually stamped his output C.CROLIUS/NEW YORK. The most widely seen Remmey mark is that of John Remmey III (1791–1820), who impressed his vessels J.REMMEY/MANHATTAN WELLS/N.YORK.

Early competition in Manhattan was provided by a kiln on the East River at Corlear's Hook, which was run by Thomas H. Commereau and David Morgan, the latter almost certainly a member of the New Jersey potting family. Commereau established the business in 1797, operating it for only a year before Morgan took over. He remained in New York until 1802 when Commereau returned to continue the shop through 1819. Commereau's archaic looking vessels bear some variation of the impression COMMERAW'S/STONEWARE/N.YORK, while Morgan's rare and costly examples are stamped D.MORGAN/NEW YORK.

By the mid-nineteenth century Lower Manhattan was too congested to allow for the continuation of potteries that required much room for storage, were notorious pollutors and, most important, distinct fire hazards.

The first manufacturer to move north was Washington Smith, who began business on West 18th Street in 1833. Though his firm prospered, continuing until 1879 under guidance of a son, Washington I. Smith, little marked ware is found. Best known are twelve-sided bottles stamped PATENT/PRESSED/W.SMITH/N.Y. Some of these are dated 1849, making them among the first press-molded pop bottles.

There were only two other important Manhattan stoneware sites. The first was located in Greenwich Village on what is now Little West 12th Street. Several manufacturers were active here: J. and C. Varick (1846–49); Edward R. Roche (1849–50); Edward R. and John W. Roche (1850–58); Louis Lehman (1858–63), and, finally, William A. MacQuoid (1863–79).

All but the Varicks left marked wares, and the decorated examples from the MacQuoid era (usually impressed WM.A. MACQUOID & CO./NEW YORK/LITTLE WEST 12TH ST.) are among the most

charming examples of pictorial stoneware. Usually depicted in pale blue and the most whimsical manner are marching soldiers, drunkards, sailing ships, and various animals including cats and pigs.

Less well known but interesting in its own right is the pottery of Francis Laufersweiler, in business on West 27th Street from 1876 until 1889. Laufersweiler's pieces, usually preserve jars, were floral decorated and customarily stamped F. LAUFERSWEILER/EMPIRE CITY POTTERY/517 & 519 W. 27 ST./N.Y. They are uncommon.

The nineteenth-century communities that were to become part of greater New York City had difficulty competing in the stoneware field. There were only two manufactories of any consequence. In Brooklyn, near the navy yard, Thomas G. Boone, a Poughkeepsie potter, opened a works in 1839 which continued until his retirement in 1846. Examples are often stamped T.G. BOONE & SONS, POTTERY/NAVY STREET BROOKLYN. An employee, Dennis McLees, who also worked in New Jersey, appears to have continued the works for a few months more. A single vessel, impressed D.MCLEES BROOKLYN POTTERY/COR. SANDS & NAVY STS., has just come to light.

At a later date (1878–94) Cornelius Vaupel made stoneware as well as other ceramics in the Williamsburgh area of Brooklyn. His ware is uncommon, and marks indicate that the pottery was moved several times. The most frequently found impression is C. VAUPEL/NO 11 UNION AVE./WILLIAMSBURGH.

The most important stoneware factory on Long Island was established before 1805 at Huntington on the north shore. There were valuable clay beds here which provided material for kilns from Maine to Maryland; and by 1808 the firm of Samuel J. Wetmore & Co. in Huntington was selling stoneware jugs to a local store.

However, the earliest marked ware dates to the 1827–29 period when the firm of Henry

Lewis and Matthew H. Gardiner owned the same Huntington works. Examples stamped LEWIS & GARDINER/HUNTINGTON, L.I. are rare. Later proprietors include Henry Lewis (1829–54), whose impression was H. LEWIS/HUNT-INGTON, L.I., and the Poughkeepsie craftsman Frederick J. Caire (1854–63), producer of stoneware marked F.J. CAIRE/HUNTINGTON,L.I.

In 1863 the business came into the hands of the Brown brothers, George, Stephen, and Thomas. George, a potter who had worked at Poughkeepsie as well as Perth Amboy, New Jersey, and Somerset, Massachusetts, was always the dominant partner, with his brothers coming and going over the years. Nevertheless, the typical mark was always a variation of BROWN BROTHERS/HUNTINGTON/L.I. The pottery remained active until 1905.

The Huntington manufactory turned out the usual wares. A price list from the late 1850s or early 1860s lists pots, jugs, churns, beer bottles, jars, pitchers, and water kegs as well as a much more extensive inventory of redware, a staple that continued to be produced throughout the nineteenth century. Stoneware decoration is generally uninspired, though the use of stencils (a cow, an eagle, a bunch of grapes, and two variants of the rose) is unusual in New York State.

The redware shop at Greenport on the eastern end of Long Island also manufactured some stoneware. Its owner, Thomas Hempstead, produced it between 1857 and 1872; but the quantity must have been limited, for only a few pieces impressed T. HEMPSTEAD/GREENPORT, L.I. are known.

For generations the Hudson River provided access to the interior of New York State as well as eastern Connecticut, Massachusetts, and Vermont. It is hardly surprising, then, that the river valley spawned numerous kilns, the most important located at Poughkeepsie, Cornwall, Hudson, and Athens.

Closest to New York was the works at Cornwall on the west bank of the river some fifty miles north of Manhattan. The first reference to a pottery here is an 1811 notice for a runaway apprentice, but known stoneware potters appear in the census as early as 1800.

The first makers to mark their wares were members of the Bell family. Moses C. Bell, whose seldom seen wares are stamped M.C.BELL, was active by 1830; and another member of the family, Nathan C. Bell, who had run a small shop in Kingston to the north, ran the Cornwall business from 1834 until around 1840. His stoneware bore the stamp NATHAN C. BELL/CORNWALL, N.Y. A partnership between the two is indicated by pieces impressed M. & N.C. BELL/CORNWALL.

By 1850, though, the business was in the hands of two New Jersey craftsmen, Isaac V. Machett and his son, Isaac, Jr. By 1859 the father's participation, reflected in examples marked I.V. MACHETT & SON, was at an end. Isaac, Jr., continued until 1867 when he moved to Pennsylvania, where he worked as a potter for the rest of his life. His New York wares bore the cipher I.V. MACHETT.

Poughkeepsie, an important east bank town about eighty miles north of New York City, was a much longer lasting site. It too can be traced to the late eighteenth century. A 1799 map of the community shows a building marked "pottery." However, the earliest piece of stoneware attributed to the community is dated 1813; and the first potter to produce marked wares was William Nichols, in business around 1823. His mark, W. NICHOLS/PO'KEEPSIE, is hard to find.

Nichols was succeeded by William Reynolds (1824–30) whose stoneware bore the oddly phonetic stamp PO'KE'PSKE/W.REYNOLDS. Then, throughout the 1830s and early 1840s a substantial group of potters and investors entered into a variety of brief and unstable endeavors, most of which have left marked ware. These included

Charles W. Thompson, first with the Massachusetts craftsman Eleazer Orcutt (1830–31); then alone (1831–33); and finally (1833–35) with Francis Bogardus (who continued the business on his own until 1836). Perhaps the most interesting aspect of Thompson's period was the manufacture with Orcutt of finely cast stoneware pitchers of a quality comparable to those then being made in New Jersey.

Other short-lived firms included Jacob G. Ball & Co. (1836–41); Thomas G. Boone, later a potter in Brooklyn (1833–37); Edward Selby with various partners (1839–44); and Mabbett & Anthone (1837–39).

The arrival of the French potter John B. Caire in 1839 brought some stability. By 1842 he had acquired one of the town's two pottery sites, and in 1845 installed his son, Jacob, in the other. The mark JOHN B.CAIRE & CO./MAIN ST./PO'KEEPSIE,N.Y. may be found on a variety of stoneware, including well-formed hound-handled pitchers similar to those made at Bennington and in several New Jersey factories.

One of the Poughkeepsie plants, that on Union Street, was closed in 1853; and the other, the Main Street works, was sold out of the family in 1854. The buyers were Louis Lehman (later to work in Manhattan) and Philip Riedinger.

However, in 1857 Adam Caire, John's youngest son, bought Lehman's interest and established a partnership that lasted until 1878. The mark RIEDINGER & CAIRE/POUGHKEEPSIE, N.Y. is frequently seen. Following Riedinger's death, Adam became sole proprietor and continued the works until his own death in 1896. His stamp was ADAM CAIRE/POUGHKEEPSIE, N.Y.

Around 1845 Edward Selby left Poughkeepsie for Hudson, a busy whaling and river port about fifty miles upriver. His shop there lasted only until 1850; but a surprising number of pots bear the stamp E. SELBY & CO./HUDSON, N.Y. The business was revived briefly, 1868–69, by Amos S. Hover and Charles Fingar. Among their un-

common marks was HUDSON POTTERY CO./
HUDSON, N.Y.

Directly across the river from Hudson was
Athens, New York, where the Clark family established one of the state's most successful potteries. Its founder Nathan Clark was from
Cornwall, where he had probably learned the
trade.

In 1805 he built a manufactory at Athens that
was continued by his descendants until 1900.
Clark's first partner was Thomas Howe (1805–
13). He then operated independently until 1829
when he took as associate Ethan S. Fox, a relative by marriage. By 1838 Nathan was ready
to retire, so he left the business in Fox's hands
until 1843 when a son, Nathan Clark, Jr., took
command. The latter guided the destiny of the
pottery until his death in 1891. Though there is
marked ware associated with all the prior periods, none is so common as that impressed
N.CLARK, JR./ATHENS, N.Y.

One of the most interesting aspects of the
Athens firm was its colonizing effect on upper
New York State. Nathan Clark sent employees
to open potteries in Lyons, Rochester, and
Mount Morris; and others worked in such major
potting communities as West Troy, Fort Edward, and Utica. Probably no other single individual had as great an effect on development
of the state's stoneware industry.

The other important stoneware factory in the
Hudson Valley was located at Ellenville in Ulster
County, a hamlet thirty miles west of the river.
It was founded in 1829 by Horace Weston and
continued after 1849 by his son Daniel, whose
products bore the cipher D. WESTON/ELLEN-
VILLE, N.Y.

Daniel Weston retired in 1875, but the shop
was maintained by other potters: James and
John J. Ryan (1875–78) and John J. Ryan with
Samuel Brady from 1878 until 1897. A substantial quantity of marked ware, including many
of the popular "chicken pecking corn" crocks,
survives.

The Albany-Troy area 150 miles north of
Manhattan marks the head of navigation on the
Hudson; prior to the building of canals or rail-
roads, it was here that clay from New Jersey
was unloaded. Understandably, much of that
clay went into local stoneware kilns.

Troy, on the east side of the river, had the
earliest known kiln, operated about 1799–1803
by Branch Green, who later worked in Old
Bridge, New Jersey, and at Philadelphia. However, it was the partnership of two Quakers,
Josiah Chapman and John Gifford (1803–15),
that produced the first marked ware, a few pots
stamped J.CHAPMAN/TROY FACTORY.

Next on the scene was Israel Seymour of the
Hartford, Connecticut, family of craftsmen. He
was in Troy by 1809 and had taken over the
Chapman works before 1816. Though he had
various partners and competitors during the
1820s, by 1837 Seymour had gained control of
the Troy market. His factory, under his own
guidance until 1852 and that of his son, Walter J.,
through 1885, produced much of the stoneware
found in the Capital district.

Early examples (usually impressed I.SEY-
MOUR/TROY FACTORY) may bear incised decoration; while those from the 1830–50 period are
generally stamped I. SEYMOUR & CO./TROY and
are embellished with rather ordinary floral designs. Son Walter's wares are similarly decorated
and are marked W.J. SEYMOUR TROY POTTERY 44
FERRY STREET.

Most important among early rivals were
George Lent (1813–24), whose wonderfully
ovoid jugs bore the inscription G.LENT/TROY;
Calvin Boynton and Russell Elsworth (1825–29)
and Boynton alone until 1835; William Lundy
with various partners (1824–28); Sanford S.
Perry with several associates (1826–33); and Eleazer Orcutt, the Massachusetts and Poughkeepsie potter with different partners from 1823
through 1830.

These relationships spawned enough marked
stoneware to make any collector happy; and as

is the case with Poughkeepsie, it would be possible to build a substantial collection around just the pre-1840 output of this single city.

In 1825 George Lent moved from Troy to Lansingburgh, then a separate community, where he made stoneware until around 1843. Eleazer Orcutt then took over the kiln, operating it until 1848. In the meantime, another potter had appeared on the scene. Pliny Thayer, who built a separate works in 1841, operated with great success until 1855. His mark, PLINY THAYER/LANSINGBURGH, N.Y., appears not only on blue-decorated crocks and jugs but also on some well-molded brown-glazed spittoons.

Thayer's successor at Lansingburgh was the young Troy potter James B. Reiley. He lasted only until 1858 but left behind a number of charming pieces, including miniatures, all decorated with sophisticated floral and avian designs. The mark J.REILEY & CO./LANSINGBURGH is uncommon.

Albany's first known stoneware maker was William Capron (1800–01); but the first to mark his ware and the collector's favorite is Paul Cushman, who worked from 1807 until his death in 1833. Cushman's pieces are crude, his incised decoration often grotesque; but in combination with large impressed marks such as PAUL CUSHMAN'S:STONEWARE:FACTORY:1809: HALF:A:MILE:WEST OF ALBANY:GAOL, they are irresistible!

Cushman's initial competition came from the Boynton family. Jonah (1816–18) and Calvin (1818–25) produced equally crude and folksy wares. Their marks J. BOYNTON and C. BOYNTON are rare.

During the 1820s and 1830s Albany, like Troy and Poughkeepsie, was in the midst of what one might call the "stoneware wars." A dozen or so potters in shifting alliances tried to make a go of the business. Few lasted long, though most left at least some identifiable ware to mark their passing. Among the better known are James Trice and A. Atherton (1820–26); Moses Tyler,

first with Charles Dillon from 1825 until 1834 and then alone until 1847; and Augustus Smith, who worked with the peripatetic Eleazer Orcutt (1841–43) and John Brickner (1844–47). Tyler's mark, a variation of M.TYLER, ALBANY/MANU-FACTURER, is particularly common.

The major figure was Jacob Henry. He began producing portable furnaces (they looked like a pottery bucket but were cheaper to operate and more warming than open fireplaces) in 1826 and was still active in 1865. Along the way he made stoneware with a variety of partners, including Charles Dillon and Nathan Porter, both of whom were to be pioneer potters in nearby West Troy.

Albany's last stoneware pottery was established, appropriately enough, by Eleazer Orcutt. In 1853 he and his sons, Charles F. and Edwin B., opened a shop which remained in the family until 1866. It was then transferred to Stephen Pepson, who had been employed by Pliny Thayer in Lansingburgh. Pepson's wife, Ellen, was still selling salt-glazed wares in 1893; and her mark, E.PEPSON/ALBANY,N.Y., is one of the few associated with a female pottery owner.

West Troy, now Watervliet, just a few miles north of Albany but located on the Erie and Champlain canals, gradually usurped Albany's trade during the 1830s and 1840s. The first potter was Sanford S. Perry, active in Troy from 1826 to 1833, when he erected a kiln on Champlain Street. Stoneware impressed S.S.PERRY/WEST TROY was made until 1836 when, beset by financial problems, Perry fled to Virginia where he is known to have been working as late as 1850.

There was no dearth of successors. Foremost was William E.Warner, who had worked at both Perth and South Amboy, New Jersey, in the early 1830s. Warner's career in West Troy was a spotty one. During the 1840s and early 1850s he bought substantial parcels of land, produced not only salt-glazed wares but also cast, hound-handled pitchers described in a local newspaper as "Extra Glazed Fancy Ware" and lived in a large house fronted by four clay pillars in the form of jugs. Yet, he was bedeviled by fire and financial setbacks. In the mid-1850s his attempt to open a pottery in Canada resulted in bankruptcy; and though he continued to be listed as a potter in West Troy until 1871, it is doubtful that he owned his own shop.

More successful was Nathan Porter who worked first with Charles Dillon (1839–41), then alone (1841–45), and finally with George Fraser (1846–63). All these men were former Albany craftsmen; and their wares—marked variously DILLON & PORTER/WEST TROY; NATHAN PORTER/WEST TROY or PORTER & FRASER/WEST TROY, N.Y.—provide a fertile field for collectors.

Porter & Fraser were followed in West Troy by George W. Seymour (1863–67), son of the well-known Troy potter; Andrew J. and John L. Russell (1867–79); Daniel Shepley with various partners (1879–97); Lewis Smith and Lysander Luther (1897–98), and finally again by John L. Russell through 1899. The last tore down the old factory and erected a row of brick houses.

The most important stoneware works north of Albany were located at Greenwich, Galway, and Fort Edward. The first, in Washington County over thirty miles northeast of Troy, had a potter as early as 1810, but his first stoneware, impressed L.ROWELL/GREENWICH, dates to the 1830s. Lemuel Rowell was succeeded in 1849 by his son-in-law, Otto V. Lewis, who moved the shop to nearby Galesville about 1852.

Lewis was a gifted craftsman who made decorated stoneware and the finest Rockingham produced in New York State, but he also had financial problems. In 1857 he transferred the business to his brother, William A. Lewis; in 1860 Frederick A. Gale, a local businessman, took over, using the services of itinerant potters until 1865. A variety of marks reflect these changes in ownership.

There was an even smaller pottery at Galway in Saratoga County some thirty-five miles northwest of Albany. The first owner was Abraham Hodgson (1840–50); his son, Nathanial Hudson, carried on until 1866. The marks A.HODGSON/GALWAY and NATHANIAL HUDSON/GALWAY VILLAGE,N.Y. are found on plain, lightly decorated pots which often show a pink tinge from the local soil mixed with more expensive stoneware clay.

Following his failure at Galesville, Otto V. Lewis went to Fort Edward on the upper Hudson sixty miles north of Albany. There he founded the first of a series of large stoneware factories that dominated the trade in northern New York until the end of the nineteenth century.

Lewis soon vanished from the scene, but his financial backer, George A. Satterlee, in partnership with Michael Mory, ran the New York Stoneware Company from 1859 until 1885. After Mory's death in that year, Satterlee went on until retirement in 1891. The impression SATTERLEE & MORY/FORT EDWARD, N.Y. is common.

The community's second pottery, operated by J. A. and C. W. Underwood from 1865 to 1867, came into the hands of Haxstun, Ottman & Company in 1867 and was continued by the brothers William R. and Gilbert Ottman after 1872. They remained in business until 1892.

An erstwhile partner, Andrew K. Haxstun, opened his own works in 1875. His associate, George S. Guy, took over in 1882, operating the shop for another decade.

A mere recitation of these changes of ownership fails to adequately reflect the magnitude of the Fort Edward operations. In 1883 alone these three firms employed seventy potters, had a total capital of $83,000, and an annual product of $115,000. Their ware was sold from Maine to Ohio, and a marketing organization called the Fort Edward Stoneware Association was established to reduce the murderous competition.

Nevertheless, times change; and after 1892

*Blue-decorated, salt-glazed stoneware jug marked* FORT EDWARD STONEWARE CO./FORT EDWARD,N.Y *with unusual "ghost" decoration. Made by A. K. Haxstun & Co., Fort Edward, 1875–82.*

now relatively inexpensive earth, and kilns were built throughout the region.

Among the earliest were those at Utica, Rome, and Syracuse. Utica's first manufactory was established in 1825 by Justin Campbell who was succeeded in 1828 by Amos Gay. In the meantime two other stoneware manufactories had been built, both in 1827. The proprietors were the firm of George Brayton, Aaron Kellogg, and Sylvester Doolittle, and David Roberts, who worked alone or with various partners.

The population of the surrounding countryside was expanding but it still couldn't absorb this much stoneware. The first to go was Gay, who went bankrupt in 1830; the business passed into the hands of Samuel Addington and from him to Noah White in 1838. Another casualty of 1830 was Roberts whose financial backers, the mercantile firm of Field & Clark, abandoned him late that year. Brayton, Kellogg, and Doolittle underwent several changes in management and by 1833 was in the hands of George Brayton's son, Jonathan. He had retired from the field by 1837.

The last to attempt the business in Utica were Henry and George Nash who used the old Brayton, Kellogg, and Doolittle works (left empty when Brayton had removed his business to the Roberts Pottery around 1831) from 1832 until 1839. After that there was only Noah White.

During the approximately fifteen years of intermittent activity at these three kilns a vast amount of marked stoneware was turned out including quite a few pieces with incised decoration and even one with applied or "sprigged" decoration.

Once he had eliminated his competition, Noah White built a business that lasted under the guidance of sons and grandsons until 1907 and must be considered one of the East's most successful potteries. The sequence of ownership was as follows: Noah White (1838–49); Noah White and sons Nicholas A. and William (1849–

there was but a single pottery in Fort Edward. It was operated by the Hilfinger Brothers (Alexander, Frederick, Rupert, and Theodore) whose father, John, had worked at West Troy, Worcester, Massachusetts, and Bennington. The Hilfingers carried on until 1942, but their products after 1900 were primarily flowerpots.

With the opening in the 1820s of the Erie Canal stretching from Albany to Buffalo, it became possible to ship New Jersey stoneware clay to central New York. Potters arrived with the

*Blue-decorated, salt-glazed stoneware crock stamped* WHITES UTICA. *Manufactured at the White Pottery, Utica, New York, 1865–86.*

Syracuse, another important community about sixty miles west of Utica, had a stoneware factory by 1840. Its owner, William H. Farrar (another member of that ubiquitous Vermont family), worked intermittently at several locations until 1868, turning out not only blue-decorated, salt-glazed stoneware but also much brown-glazed molded ware; spittoons, poodles, spaniels, and even lions, many of them impressed on the base W.H.FARRAR.

Farrar's competitors at Syracuse included Joseph Shepard (1857–64), C. E. Pharis & Co. (1864–67), and Charles E. Hubbell and Dennison Chesebro. The latter were active from 1867 until 1887 and among their innovations was a stoneware preserve jar patented in 1875.

There was an even earlier stoneware pottery at Jordan, on the canal twenty miles west of Syracuse. It was established in 1827 by the Connecticut craftsman Sidney N. Norton and continued from around 1852 by James McBurney and his sons, William, Harvey, and Justen memorialized in the stamp, J.MCBURNEY/ & SONS/JORDAN. The business came to an end before 1860, and some members of the family are said to have opened a pottery in Ohio.

The potter John Darrow and his sons were active at Baldwinsville some fifteen miles northeast of Jordan from 1845 until 1876, though they did not make stoneware until 1852. Examples from this site are fairly common, and among the marks is BALDWINSVILLE STONE-WARE.

The other significant stoneware manufactories in the area were at North Bay on the shore of Oneida Lake northeast of Syracuse and in the tiny community of Westmoreland some ten miles south of Rome. A kiln was established in North Bay around 1848 by Peel Webster and

65); Nicholas A. White and his sons, William N. and later Charles N. (1865–86), and finally Charles N. White (1886–1907) under whose guidance the firm specialized in molded decorative stoneware in the German manner, becoming the nation's leading manufacturer in this field. Long spurned by collectors, these cast mugs, pitchers, crocks, and vases are now considered prime collectibles.

Rome, another canal town less than twenty miles northwest of Utica, had two early stoneware kilns. By 1824 the brothers Norman and Arden Seymour were making stoneware there. Though they remained in business until around 1848, few pieces bearing the mark N. & A. SEYMOUR/ROME can be found. However, a remarkable watercooler with incised floral decoration is in the collection of Utica's Munson-Williams-Proctor Institute.

Norman L. Judd, a Bennington trained craftsman who had been turning redware in Rome since 1811, also made some stoneware in the late 1840s. At present the only known examples are jugs stamped JUDD.

continued by E. H. Farrar until 1851. It was then acquired by John C. Waelde who was active until 1875. Waelde's mark, J.C.WAELDE/NORTH★ BAY, is found on the usual crocks and jugs, a substantial number of which are embellished with cobalt stenciled animals, cows, deer, eagles, and roosters.

Pottery from Westmoreland is considerably less distinguished. The owner there was Dwight W. Graves, who made stoneware on a part-time basis (he was also a farmer) from 1855 until 1875. His crude vessels are marked D.W. GRAVES/ WESTMORELAND in very large letters and are usually of a rosy hue reflecting the generous admixture of local clay.

South-central New York also had its share of stoneware works, most of them located on the various canals that proliferated in the area during the 1830s and 1840s. Early sites were at Cortland and Homer, neighboring communities forty miles south of Syracuse.

Homer's first manufactory was active before 1830 under the management of a Utica potter, Thomas H. Williams. He was probably in partnership with a local merchant, Thomas D. Chollar, who controlled the business from 1832 to 1836 with Lucius Bennett and then, until 1844, in association with Joseph Darby.

Sylvester Blair had a kiln in Cortland from 1829 until 1835, when he sold out to Mason & Russell. They, in turn, transferred the business four years later to Chollar & Darby of Homer. Following Darby's retirement in 1849, Chollar sold the shop to Madison Woodruff, a potter who had been employed at both Homer and Cortland since at least 1831. Woodruff continued the manufacture of stoneware until 1885. His

frequently seen ware is usually impressed M.WOODRUFF/CORTLAND,N.Y.

Binghamton, fifty miles south of Cortland and close to the Pennsylvania border, was the most important southern center after 1850. Around 1848 William Roberts, son-in-law of Noah White of Utica, opened a branch of the family pottery there which he continued until his death in 1888. The stamp W.ROBERTS/BING-HAMTON, N.Y. is most frequently encountered, though the continuing involvement of members of the White family is reflected in pieces marked N.A. WHITE & CO./BINGHAMTON and WHITES' BINGHAMTON.

One of the most interesting pieces of Amer-

*Blue-decorated, salt-glazed stoneware jug impressed W.ROBERTS/BINGHAMTON,N.Y. Made at the pottery of William Roberts, 1848–88. The only piece of American stoneware to celebrate a hanging!*

ican decorated stoneware comes from this shop. It is a jug bearing the figure of a hanged man and the inscription in slip, "Friday/March 3/Rulloff," which alludes to the hanging in 1871 of Edward H. Rulloff, a homicidal maniac who had killed at least five people, including his wife and daughter.

Other stoneware factories in the southern portion of the state included ones at Ithaca, Havana, Elmira, Penn Yan, Dundee, and Olean. Ithaca's first stoneware maker was James B. Magee (1853–55), followed by James M. Mott (1855–60), and with Griswold Apley until 1862 and Dennis Mooney (1862–64).

A period of stability arrived in 1864 when James Macumber took over the facilities which he operated with Isaac Van Arsdale (later a potter in Canada) until 1867; with Matthew Tannahil through 1886 and, finally, until 1890 with Lynford M. Mood. All but the last partnership have left marked ware; and the old pottery still stands on Lake Street in Ithaca.

Havana, now called Montour Falls, is located some twenty-five miles southwest of Ithaca. Its stoneware works was built by Stephen T. Brewer (probably the same man who had worked in New London, Connecticut, during the late 1820s) around 1852. He continued the business until 1860 when it was taken over by an employee, Henry M. Whitman.

Following a fire in 1862, the shop was rebuilt by a local businessman, Albert O. Whittemore, who remained active until a second fire brought things to a conclusion in 1893. A substantial number of highly decorated pieces, including ones adorned with "star faces," animals, houses, and castles, bear the mark A.O. WHITTE-MORE/HAVANA, N.Y.

Wares produced at Elmira, sixty miles west of Binghamton, were more ordinary. The city's only stoneware manufactory was built in 1865 by Albert O. Whittemore of Havana, but two years later it was taken over by a wealthy local merchant, James B. Farrington, who managed it with various partners until 1882 when he took his son, E. Ward, into the business. The latter operated independently from 1887 until 1893. All Elmira stoneware bears the Farrington name, with the impression J. FARRINGTON & CO./ELMIRA, N.Y. most often seen.

Penn Yan, at the head of Keuka Lake, is fifty miles northwest of Elmira. A redware pottery was established here before 1830 by John Campbell, and by 1850 his son, George, was making

*Blue-decorated, salt-glazed stoneware crock marked* PENN YAN *and attributed to James Mantell, Penn Yan, New York, 1856–76.*

stoneware, though examples stamped CAMP-BELL/PENN YAN are rare.

In 1854 George Campbell sold the business to James Mantell, who had previously worked at a pottery in Lyons, New York. Mantell had a partner until 1856, Shem Thomas, later to have his own pottery in Harrisburg, Pennsylvania. From 1856 until 1876 Mantell ran the pottery alone, producing a substantial quantity of well-decorated stoneware impressed J. MANTELL/PENN YAN.

At the tiny town of Dundee, less than twenty miles southeast of Penn Yan, there was a pottery run by the Holmes family. It was built between 1845 and 1850 by James Holmes. Working with various associates and, later, with his son, Bryan, Holmes remained active into the 1860s. Marked Dundee stoneware, which is uncommon, includes at least one example bearing incised decoration.

The stoneware shop at Olean over a hundred miles west of Elmira was the westernmost of the southern kilns. It was built in 1852 by Isaac Wands, who always described himself in advertisements as "a practical potter." His Eagle Pottery Works was an immediate success, continuing under the guidance of its founder until 1869. His successors—Edwin A. Montell (1869–74), Clarence A. Crane (1874–75), Elisha M. Johnson and Samuel A. Knapp (1875–77), and James M. Brooks (1877–83)—appear to have been less so. While ware marked I.H. WANDS/OLEAN, N.Y. is common, that of the other owners is seldom seen.

The stoneware history of central New York is largely written in terms of two families, the Clarks and the Harts. Both were pioneers in the trade, and both recognized the need to develop branch factories under the control of a single company which might between them carve up and control large market areas.

First in the field was Nathan Clark, the Athens potter. In 1822 he established a pottery at Lyons, a town on the newly opened Erie Canal about forty miles east of Rochester. The local manager was George G. Williams, who had been trained at Athens; and the usual mark was N.CLARK & CO./LYONS.

When, in 1835, Williams was assigned to open another pottery, this one at Mount Morris, he was replaced by Thompson Harrington who had previously worked in Hartford, Connecticut. By 1840 the business was one of the largest in upstate New York, producing $16,000 worth of ware annually.

Nevertheless, in 1852 the Clark family sold its interest in the shop to Thompson Harrington, who continued it for another twenty years. His mark, T. HARRINGTON/LYONS, appears not only on stoneware decorated in blue with animals, flowers, and human figures, but also on cast pitchers and mantelpiece figures in the Staffordshire manner.

Blue-decorated, salt-glazed crock impressed T.HARRINGTON/LYONS and attributed to Thompson Harrington, Lyons, New York, 1852–72. This decoration is often referred to as "man in the star."

The last owner at Lyons was the German potter Jacob Fisher, who leased the works from Harrington in 1872 and bought them six years later. He too was successful. By 1896 his was the largest pottery in the state, and he maintained the business until 1902. Ware impressed J. FISHER/LYONS, N.Y. is found throughout the Northeast.

The Clark establishment at Mount Morris forty miles south of Rochester had a much briefer history. Williams was sent there as manager in 1835, but by 1846 Nathan Clark had turned the business over to him; and there is no evidence that stoneware was made after that time. The factory was always small, and the stamp N. CLARK & CO./MT. MORRIS is seldom seen.

The third Clark colony, at Rochester, proved much more profitable. Others had recognized the potential of this thriving mill town at the Genesee Falls. As early as 1822 the Porter family, Micah and his sons William and Samuel, was making stoneware there. The rare mark, M. PORTER/ROCHESTER, memorializes a business that continued until sometime after 1830, when the Porters moved to western Pennsylvania and carried on their craft in the Oil City-Pleasantville area.

In 1839 Clark made his move. Acting through another Athens employee, John Burger, he acquired the old Porter works. Though initially associated with Thompson Harrington and G. G. Williams, Burger bought the business in 1854. The impression CLARK & CO./ROCHESTER was replaced with JOHN BURGER/ROCHESTER, a mark used until 1867 when sons John Burger, Jr., and George Burger took over the business. The firm was Burger & Lang (reflecting admission of brother-in-law George Lang) from 1869 through 1877; Burger & Co. during the period 1877–79; and in the sole control of John Burger, Jr., from 1880 until it shut down a decade later. A vast amount of marked ware remains.

For some ten years beginning in 1849 the Burgers had serious competition in Rochester from the German craftsman Frederick Stetzenmeyer, who for part of this period was in partnership with the grocer Gottlieb Goetzmann. Though out of business by 1860, they left behind some extremely well-decorated pieces stamped F. STETZENMEYER & CO./ROCHESTER, N.Y. In fact, these along with pieces made by John Burger, Sr., during the 1840s, 1850s, and 1860s constitute a body of decorated ware equal to anything produced elsewhere in the United States. The birds, animals, and flowers, often done in a pointillist manner, are both charming and sophisticated.

While less ambitious, the Hart potteries were equally successful. The brothers Samuel and James Hart erected their first manufactory in 1832 at Fulton, thirty miles northwest of Syracuse. In 1840 James left for Sherburne, New York, where he established a second kiln. Samuel continued alone until 1876, and his impression, S. HART/FULTON, N.Y., is among the most common of the several family marks.

In 1876 a son, Charles Addison Hart, joined his father; two years later Samuel retired and was succeeded by a second son, Elwyn Erskine. Together, these offspring guided the fortunes of the Fulton works until they were destroyed by fire in 1892. The mark HART BROS./FULTON, N.Y. is often seen.

The business established at Sherburne, fifty-five miles southeast of Syracuse, was continued through 1885. The founder, James Hart, and his son, Charles, were in charge from 1841 through 1850. In the latter year Charles went north to Ogdensburg to open yet a third branch of the family empire, leaving his father alone until 1858.

However, upon James Hart's retirement in that year, Charles returned to assume control at Sherburne. He had sole responsibility until 1866 when a son, Nahum, entered the business which

*Blue-decorated, salt-glazed stoneware crock made and marked by J. (John)* BURGER,JR./ROCHESTER, N.Y., *1880–90.*

they operated together until Charles's death in 1885. The stamp, C.HART & SON/ SHERBURNE, marks this period.

The third pottery at Ogdensburg on the St. Lawrence River in far northern New York had a somewhat checkered history, with various family members attempting to make a go of it. From 1850 until 1853 the proprietors were Charles and Samuel Hart (an absentee landlord) and Albert Lobdell, a potter who had married into the family. Lobdell sold out in the latter year; and in 1858 Charles returned to Sherburne to be replaced by his younger brother, William, who remained in charge until his death in 1869.

The mark W.HART/OGDENSBURGH reflects the high point in the history of this factory; a time during which some remarkable blue decoration was done. Fish, faces, and even a hand pointing to the heavens embellished graceful semiovoid vessels.

Upon William's death the pottery was taken over by his half brother Joseph J. Hart who operated it until a fire in 1874 destroyed everything. Though the works were rebuilt in 1877 by other members of the Hart family, lack of business led to a final shutdown in 1879.

Buffalo was the westernmost center of New York stoneware manufacture. The potential of this great port city on the Lake Erie shore had been recognized as early as 1835 when Godfrey Heiser, who had worked in Albany about 1826–32, established a factory on East Seneca Street to "sell to . . . friends and customers as good an article . . . and as cheap as any fair dealer" (*Buffalo Patriot and Commercial Advertiser*, May 13, 1835).

Heiser was active with various partners until 1848, when he became a brewer. The mark G. HEISER/BUFFALO is most common of the several from this era. For the next nine years Heiser's sons, John and Henry, and a close associate, Philip Mugler, operated the pottery. All left marked ware.

However, in 1857 the business was purchased by Charles W. Braun, another German potter, who operated it until his retirement in 1896. His mark, C.W. BRAUN/BUFFALO, is found on much stoneware, including some extremely well-decorated bird and flower crocks.

Braun's only local competition was Christian Bruel, who worked intermittently from the mid-1860s into the 1890s. His output could never have been significant, as only a single marked piece, CHR. G. BRUEL/COR-PECKHAM & WATSON ST./BUFFALO, N.Y., is known.

# 8

# NEW JERSEY

THE IMPORTANCE OF New Jersey in the history of American stoneware should never be underestimated. Some of the earliest potteries were located here; and, perhaps equally significant, it was in the South Amboy area on Raritan Bay that deposits of stoneware clay were discovered that served to fuel the Northeastern industry from the middle of the eighteenth into the twentieth century.

There were also close relationships with potters and potteries in New York, Pennsylvania, and New England; for greater detail on these one should see M. Lelyn Branin's authoritative *The Early Makers of Handcrafted Earthenware and Stoneware in Central and Southern New Jersey*.

The most important eighteenth-century site was at Cheesequake, a few miles east of South Amboy along the bay. Charles Morgan of Westchester County, New York, purchased a large plot of land here in 1710, including a vast bank of stoneware clay only a mile from South Amboy. However, there is no present evidence that Charles was a potter; and it seems likely

that his son, James, to whom a portion of the estate was left in 1750, is the one who both discovered this valuable earth and established the area's first kiln, probably during the 1760s.

There is no doubt that James Morgan owned a stoneware manufactory by the time of the American Revolution; for in 1782 he filed a compensation claim for war damages that included "1 kiln of Stone Ware not burnt" destroyed in a British raid. Moreover, the exploration of the pottery site in the 1940s led to the discovery of numerous shards, including one bearing the cobalt slip inscription, "Danniel Holmes/ . . . September 23,1775/ . . . mboy James Morgan/& . . . ."

James (titled Captain Morgan for his Revolutionary War exploits) died in 1784, leaving responsibility to his son, also named James and also a former officer in the Colonial army. James, Jr., sold the pottery site in 1801, and there is no indication that ware was made there after that date.

In fact, James Morgan, Jr., was probably associated by then in a stoneware manufactory established around 1799 in Troy, New York, by the potter Branch Green. The name Morgan appears as a partner there in an 1801 advertisement; and by 1805 James, Green, and Jacob Van Wickle had built another shop at Old Bridge some ten miles west of Cheesequake. By 1809 Green had removed to a Philadelphia pottery, and it is not known how long Morgan retained an interest in the Old Bridge firm; dated shards found at the site indicate ware was made until at least 1824.

In the meantime, Thomas Warne, who had married a daughter of James Morgan, Sr., took advantage of the closing of the Morgan kiln at Cheesequake. Warne, who had probably trained with the Morgans, bought a piece of land just a few hundred feet from their kiln site, and by 1800 he was turning out stoneware impressed WARNE/S.AMBOY N.JERSY.

In 1805 Warne's daughter married Joshua Letts, a local man and a potter. His partnership with Morgan is reflected in various examples marked either with the simple monogram, T.W. J.L., or the elaborately patriotic, LIBERTY FOR EV/WARNE & LETTS/S.AMBOY.N.JERSY (often with a date such as 1806 or 1807 added).

Joshua Letts continued the business for about four years after Thomas Warne's death in 1813, leaving behind a few vessels stamped MADE BY J.LETTS/LIBERTY FOR EV. By 1815 the pottery had been sold to James Morgan, returning again to the pioneer potting family of Cheesequake.

Warne and Letts stoneware is (with that of the early Manhattan and Boston kilns) the crème de la crème for sophisticated collectors. The wide variety of impressed decoration (crescents, scallops, holly leaves, sawtooth panels, and dentil molding) is a primer of neoclassic design; and

*Blue-decorated, salt-glazed stoneware pot attributed to James Morgan, Jr., Cheesequake, New Jersey, 1784–1801. Some of the earliest surviving American stoneware may be traced to New Jersey.*

the large, boldly placed marks make for instant identification.

When James Morgan died in 1822 he left the Cheesequake works to his granddaughter, Catherine Bowne, who mortgaged them in 1831 and lost them through foreclosure to her uncle, Charles Morgan, in 1835. It is likely that the manufactory was in operation under various managers at least until 1831.

Potters known to have been living in the community during the 1820s include three members of the Remmey family from Manhattan (Joseph, John, Jr., and William); Benjamin Lent from Lansingburgh, New York; and Benjamin B. Knowles, who was later connected with a stoneware factory at New London, Connecticut. Moreover, when James Morgan died in 1822 one of the assets included in his estate was a bill for clay sold to yet another Connecticut firm, Armstrong and Wentworth of Norwich!

In the 1840s another pottery was established in the area, this one at the head of Cheesequake Creek about a mile north of the village. The proprietor, Noah Furman, maintained salesrooms in Manhattan; and known examples of his work are marked N.FURMAN NO.11,PECK SLIP, N.Y. or N.FURMAN, NO. 39, PECK SLIP, N.Y. The Furman shop is believed to have burned in 1856.

Due to the abundance of suitable clay and excellent shipping facilities, the Raritan Bay and River area attracted other potters as well. The Price family established a stoneware works around 1800 in the so-called ''Roundabouts'' (alluding to a great bend in the Raritan River at this point) area of Sayreville a little over five miles north of Old Bridge.

Though operated for over forty years by various members of the family, the firm never appears to have been very successful. The first known stoneware makers here were the brothers Ebenezer Price, Jr., and Xerxes Price. The former died in 1820, leaving control of the firm to his sibling whose wares, impressed MADE.BY. XERXES/PRICE/AT.S.AMBOY, are rare.

By this time the business was encountering financial difficulties. A judgment obtained by James Morgan against Ebenezer (probably for clay) was included among the former's assets at the time of his death in 1822, and Xerxes's farm was sold to satisfy another judgment in 1830. Following the seizure of more property two years later Xerxes committed suicide. His son, George W. Price, ran the business until 1843 when the sheriff once more appeared on the scene. During this latter period Xerxes's brother-in-law, Henry French, had an interest in the manufactory, and there is at least one piece marked HENRY.FRENCH.

Another member of the Price family, Ebenezer's son, Abial, who had been trained at Sayreville, established his own works at present-day Matawan some five miles east of Cheesequake about 1844. His seldom seen wares were impressed A.PRICE/MIDDLETOWN POINT, N.J.

Following Price's death in 1852, the factory was taken over by Josiah Van Schoick, who had at one time been associated with Abial, and Ezra Dunn. The partnership appears to have been successful, though marked ware, impressed VAN SCHOICK & DUNN/MAKERS/MIDDLETOWN POINT, N.J., is not often seen. In 1862 the business was moved to a new location in Matawan, and in 1868, a third partner, William A. Dunlap, joined the firm.

Dunn, Dunlap & Company added earthenware and tile making facilities but continued making stoneware into the last decade of the nineteenth century. Though Van Schoick and Dunn died in the 1890s and Dunlap in the early 1900s, the firm they founded still exists, though all manufacturing operations ceased in the 1950s.

From 1842 until 1849 Thomas Cottrell ran a second kiln at Middletown Point, this one turning out both stoneware and redware. It was closed following the proprietor's suicide and little is known of its products.

There was also another pottery at Old Bridge. In 1823 Asher and David Bissett bought a tract of land on River Road, where they constructed a wharf and stoneware kiln. In 1846 Asher sold his share of the business to his brother; David was then joined by a relative, Evert Bissett, who had previously worked at South River. Though the kiln apparently remained active until 1865 when the property was leased for other purposes, no ware associated with it can be positively identified.

The other Bissett kiln, at South River (formerly Washington) about four miles northwest of Old Bridge, was built around 1826 by William and Evert Bissett. William died two years later, and in 1831 his interest was sold to the potters Jacob Eaton and Samuel Stout who had been renting space for a stoneware factory nearby since at least 1826 (as evidenced by a single piece impressed SAM STOUT/1826). Since Evert Bissett sold his 50 percent of the Bissett kiln to them in 1835, Eaton & Stout owned the South River factory outright after that date. Their wares, impressed EATON & STOUT/WASHINGTON, are uncommon. Evert Bissett's role is memorialized by a single vessel marked E.BISSETT/1832.

After a series of financial reverses, Samuel Stout lost his share in the pottery around 1842. Jacob Eaton continued to operate it until 1856, leaving behind a few vessels stamped J.EATON. The new owner was James Holmes to whom Branin ascribes a few pieces bearing the letter "H." He sold out in 1864, and thereafter the factory remained active under various ownerships until 1868.

By the late 1820s the community of South Amboy had become the most important center in the area. It was located at the mouth of the Raritan River in the heart of the clay belt and less than twenty miles by water from Manhattan. In 1831 the brothers David and Henry Cotheal, well-to-do merchants with New York City interests, bought a stoneware factory here, which according to some sources was built in 1826 by the English potter William Hancock.

The existence of a stoneware jar stamped W.H. HANCOCK lends some credence to this.

Since the Cotheal brothers were not potters, they appear to have brought in professionals to run the shop. The first may have been Horace Humiston who had made stoneware at Troy, New York. He left there in 1830 and appears in the South Amboy Township census for the same year. There is ware marked H. HUMISTON/SOUTH AMBOY as well as HUMISTON&/STOCKWELL/S.AMBOY,N.J., which indicates a partnership with Henry Stockwell who had worked at Utica, New York, in 1828, in Troy in 1829, and is listed in South Amboy during 1830 and 1831.

Humiston died at South Amboy in 1833, and his illness may have been the reason why William E. Warner, who had been running his own pottery across the river in Perth Amboy since 1831 moved to South Amboy. Though there are examples stamped HUMISTON & WARNER/SOUTH AMBOY, there are none bearing Warner's name alone; and by 1837 he was in West Troy, New York, where he took over a pottery formerly operated by Sanford S. Perry.

Warner's departure coincided with that of the Cotheals who sold the land in 1836; by 1846 it was in the hands of Caleb A. Townsend, whose manager was George W. Price, the Sayreville potter. Another experienced craftsman entered the lists in 1847 when Townsend sold out to John P. States of Stonington, Connecticut, scion of that state's well-known family of potters. However, within a year the business was back in Townsend's hands; and his manager was probably Dennis McLees who had been working in Brooklyn, New York, during the 1840s. There is at least one piece impressed, D.MCLEES POTTER/S.AMBOY,N.J.

Late in 1848 Townsend sold the factory to Abraham Cadmus of New York who, by 1850, had converted it into a major producer of yellow and Rockingham wares. It is likely that at this point McLees returned to Brooklyn where he had his own stoneware pottery in 1850.

Perth Amboy, north across the Raritan from South Amboy, had at least one pottery. William E. Warner was active here for short time, his stay memorialized by a jug in the collection of the Brooklyn Museum, which is incised "This is the first jug made in the Columbian Pottery Sept 1st 1831 William E. Warner manufacturer." It was signed as maker by Henry Stockwell. But within a year or two Warner and Stockwell were working at South Amboy.

However, Gordon's *A Gazetteer of the State of New Jersey* for 1834 refers to "an extensive pottery of excellent stoneware" in the community; and it is likely that the business was continued by John B. Pewtress whose family later owned a factory at New Haven, Connecticut. Though as yet little is known about the Pewtress firm, the abundance of 1835–50 form vessels impressed JOHN B. PEWTRESS/PERTH AMBOY indicates an operation of some duration.

Though primarily a Rockingham and yellowware manufactory, W. H. P. Benton's Eagle Pottery at Perth Amboy, active 1858–65, turned out a substantial number of brown-glazed, molded stoneware pitchers as well as rare coffee-pots. Except for a presentation pitcher with the embossed logo W.H.P. BENTON/1860, this ware does not appear to have been marked.

Though it came to be the most important community in the area, New Brunswick, on the Raritan west of the Amboys, has a brief ceramics history. A redware pottery built in 1810 was redesigned in 1835 by Ralph Stout to accommodate stoneware production. By 1855 the firm was Stout and William Atkinson; and in 1862 it was sold to Alfred J. Butler, whose wares, stamped A.J.BUTLER/MANUFACTURER/NEW BRUNSWICK,N.J., are fairly common. In 1868 Butler transferred the works to a shop on Burnet Street which had been run since 1850 by George W. Price of Sayreville; and in 1875 he sold the factory to Charles W. McMullen and Thomas F. Connolly, whose mark was MULLEN & CONNOLLY/MANUFACTURERS/NEW BRUNSWICK, N.J.

They returned the business to him in 1880; and he promptly transferred it to Connolly, whose imprint, T.F. CONNOLLY/MANUFACTURER/NEW BRUNSWICK, N.J., identifys ware made until May 1881. Connolly's partner then became Charles T. Palmer, until 1888 when the firm was sold to Adam Green. Examples stamped CONNOLLY & PALMER/NEW BRUNSWICK, N.J. are occasionally found. Green's stoneware, marked ADAM GREEN/NEW BRUNSWICK,N.J., was the last made at New Brunswick. The factory closed in 1901.

There appears to have been a second early manufactory, this one operated 1830–32 by James T. Horner and William W. Shirley. Located on Water Street in New Brunswick, the firm exhibited molded "flint stoneware" at Philadelphia's Franklin Institute exhibition in 1831, making it one of the earlier American producers of such wares.

A much more important manufacturer of molded wares was located at Woodbridge, two miles north of Perth Amboy. Around 1835 the proprietors of the Salamander Works (which may have been active on Cannon Street in Manhattan since 1830) established a shop on the Woodbridge-Metuchen road. The firm advertised "flint and fire-proof" wares and in 1835 received a diploma from the American Institute of the City of New York for "a fine speciman of flint stoneware." Other awards followed in 1838 and 1839.

In 1842, the principal owner of the firm, Michel Lefoulon, transferred it to his son, Louis M., and to Jules Decasse with the latter gaining full control by 1848. Jules passed the business on to another member of the family in 1850, and by the end of the decade the firm was no longer making molded wares.

*Molded stoneware pitcher with embossed eagle decoration and tan mineral glaze, attributed to Woodbridge or Jersey City, New Jersey, 1830–45.* ▶

The Salamander works made cast stoneware and yellowware with a Rockingham glaze, and known examples are sometimes impressed SAL-AMANDER WORKS/WOODBRIDGE,N.J.

At Manasquan on the Atlantic coast some twenty miles southeast of Cheesequake, Nicholas Van Wickle established a stoneware shop around 1824. His father, Jacob, had been James Morgan's associate at South River in the early 1800s, and Nicholas followed in his footsteps.

Like his sire, Nicholas Van Wickle was not a potter. He appears to have employed one Asher Applegate to fashion ware, as there is a jug incised "Asher Applegate/Maker/Manasquan/Monmouth County/New Jersey." The Van Wickle manufactory advertised "a general assortment of Stone Ware such as Pots, Jugs, Jars, Pitchers, &c." in the January 25, 1838, edition of the *Monmouth Inquirer and General Advertiser*; and the company may have been active as late as 1850.

North of the Amboys there were several important stoneware factories. Keen Pruden, who had apprenticed with his uncle, Joseph, at Morristown, took over a redware pottery at Elizabeth in 1819; and around 1832 he began to make stoneware. His early pieces are impressed ELIZ-TOWN/POTERY.

When Keen retired in 1835 he turned the business over to a son, John Mills Pruden, who ran it until 1877. His first wares were marked J.M. PRUDEN/ELIZ-TOWN, N.J.; but, after establishing a Manhattan distributorship, he stamped them J.M. PRUDEN/185 DUANE-ST,N.Y. A brief partnership, 1865–71, with Augustus Olcott, a New York merchant, is memorialized in pottery impressed PRUDEN & OLCOTT/185 DUANE-ST,N.Y. Around 1877 the business was sold to L. B. Beerbower & Company, who continued it through the 1880s.

At Newark, a few miles to the north, there was a later stoneware manufactory, this one built on Bloomfield Avenue in 1871 by Conrad Haidle and John C. Sonn. Their ware, impressed

C.HAIDLE & CO./UNION POTTERY/NEWARK, N.J., mirrors a partnership that lasted only until 1875 when J. Zipf replaced Sonn; and the imprint became HAIDLE & ZIPF/UNION POTTERY/NEWARK, N.J. Zipf became sole proprietor in 1877, remaining in business until 1906. His mark was UNION POTTERY/NEWARK, N.J./J. ZIPF PROP'R.

Jersey City, five miles east of Newark and directly across the bay from Manhattan, was the site of the earliest successful American manufactory of cast or mold-made stoneware. In 1828 David Henderson, with his brother John, bought the shop formerly occupied by the Jersey Porcelain Works and began to make elaborate flint-glazed pitchers, spittoons, and soap dishes based on English designs.

The wares, whose various marks included D & J/ HENDERSON/ JERSEY/CITY and HENDERSON'S/FLINT STONEWARE/MANUFACTORY/JERSEY CITY, met with immediate success. In 1830 alone there was a silver medal from the Franklin Institute and first Premium from New York's American Institute.

In 1833 the business was incorporated as the American Pottery Manufacturing Company; and, until David Henderson's death in 1845, the works turned out a variety of sophisticated stoneware, much of which was impressed AMER-ICAN/POTTERY CO./JERSEY CITY, N.J. Marked examples are much in demand and bring high prices, $750 to $1,500, when they appear on the market.

There were also scattered manufactories to the north and west of the metropolitan district, though not a great deal is known about them. Peter Peregrine Sandford worked at Hackensack (then known as Barbadoes Neck) from the 1780s until sometime after 1800 when he removed to Westchester County, New York. His extremely rare work, impressed in large letters, P.P. SAND-FORD/BARBADOES NECK, includes examples with incised, blue-filled fish.

It is possible that Peregrine's shop was taken over by Isaac V. Machett and his son, who were active in Hackensack from about 1819 until they moved north to Cornwall, New York, around 1850. Since all Machett ware seems to be marked I.V.MACHETT or I.V. MACHETT & SON with no locality, it is hard to determine at which of these locations it was produced.

At Bergenfield, a few miles northeast of Hackensack, the redware potter George Wolf-kiel also made some stoneware 1855–67 at his shop on New Bridge Road.

Benjamin Lent, who had worked at Cheese-quake, appears to have operated a shop in the community of Caldwell, some ten miles north-west of Newark, 1825–31. A few pots stamped B.LENT/CALDWELL are known.

About the same distance west of Caldwell is Morristown, where the brothers Josiah and Louis E. Meeker made both stoneware and red-ware from 1844 until 1894. Salt-glazed examples bear the uncommon imprint J. & L.E. MEEKER.

By far the most important pottery in central New Jersey was located at Flemington in Hunterdon County. Abraham Fulper and his son William began to make stoneware around 1860 in a kiln on Mine Street, which had been built about 1814 by the redware potter Samuel Hill.

Fulper had five sons, all of whom were connected with the business at one time or another; and following Abraham's death in 1881, ware was marked G.M. FULPER & BROS./FLEMINGTON, N.J. or FULPER BROS./FLEMINGTON, N.J. In 1898 a mortgage foreclosure led to the establishment of the Fulper Pottery Company, which made art and utilitarian ceramics until 1980.

The Fulper manufactory is best known for an extraordinary group of blue-decorated pieces made during the 1880s which featured folksy renditions of circus scenes, bathing beauties, and

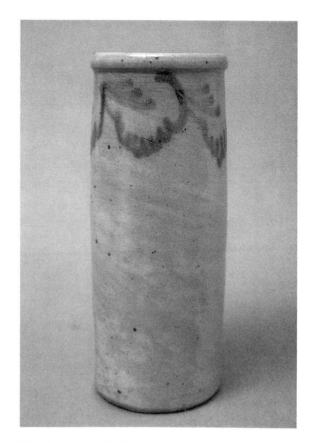

*Blue-decorated, salt-glazed stoneware vase, central New Jersey, 1830–50. An unusual form in this medium.*

*Blue-decorated, salt-glazed cream pot marked I.V.MACHETT and attributed to Isaac V. Machett, active in Hackensack, New Jersey, 1819–50.*

local characters. The artist remains unknown, but the art is among the best in this medium.

A much smaller and less successful stoneware maker was Oliver H. Smith, who with one or more brothers established a small works at Flemington in 1889. He lasted only until 1894, and his ware, impressed SMITH BROS. & CO./FLEMINGTON, N.J., is uncommon.

In western New Jersey, the Trenton-Camden area on the Delaware River was home to some of the state's earlier stoneware factories. The merchant William Richards advertised in 1774 that he had "erected a manufactory at Lamberton about a half-mile below Trenton, for making the useful Dutch Stone Ware." The property was occupied by Washington's troops in 1777, and nothing more is known of the venture. However, there may be some connection with one Bernard Hanlon who advertised his "Stoneware potting Manufactory at Trenton" in the *New Jersey Gazette* for November 3, 1778. Hanlon, who had various other business interests, maintained his pottery at least until 1780.

Another early stoneware business was located at Ringoes in Amwell Township some ten miles northeast of New Hope, Pennsylvania. In 1746 the potter John Peter Kemple purchased land at Ringoes on which he and his son, Phillip, built a pottery. The site has been located, and excavation has revealed a substantial quantity of shards, both redware and stoneware. However, since neither the estate inventory of John Peter or of Phillip indicated the presence of salt-glazed wares or the materials necessary to produce them, it is likely that stoneware was not made until sometime after Phillip's death in 1778. At this point the shop passed into the hands of Phillip's son, Onteil, and he appears to have made

stoneware (which is specifically listed in his estate) until his death in 1798. The pottery seems to have been discontinued at this point.

No marked pieces have been associated with the Ringoes works. Shards indicate ovoid jugs, jars, pots, and flasks with vertical handles decorated with crude abstract designs of loops and coils.

Burlington on the Delaware River midway between Trenton and Camden was the site of a kiln owned by Charles C. Lawrence, who advertised "STONE WARE OF AN EXCELLENT QUALITY, consisting of POTS, JUGS, JARS, PITCHERS, &c, &c." in an August 1810 edition of the local *Aurora of the Country.*

Lawrence's shop remained active until 1813, when the property was seized by creditors and its owner removed to Philadelphia and Chester County, Pennsylvania. He eventually ended up

*Blue-decorated stoneware watercooler with incised and applied decoration and rare matching lid, attributed to William and Charles Wingender, Haddonfield, New Jersey, 1883–1900.*

making portable furnaces in Manhattan, 1827–30. There is at least one jar bearing the stamp LAWRENCE/BURLINGTON/N.J.

Haddonfield, now part of Camden, was a separate community in 1869 when Richard Snowden built a stoneware kiln on the grounds of an earlier redware pottery. Following Snowden's death in 1883, the factory was taken over by several members of the Wingender family of German immigrant potters. William and Charles Wingender made elaborate blue-decorated steins, mugs, and related items until about 1923. Their work is so similar to contemporary German work that unless it is marked C.W. & BRO. or W.W., it is hard to distinguish. A third brother, Jacob, eventually moved to Alabama where he made stoneware for some years.

Southern New Jersey had but two stoneware factories, both in Cumberland County. In 1866 George W. Kellogg and his sons opened a works at Vineland which closed three years following Kellogg's death. Ware stamped G.KELLOGG & SONS/ VINELAND, N.J., is rare.

In Bridgeton, on the Cohansey River, the redware pottery of William J. Smith, established in 1866, was converted to stoneware production around 1880 and remained in business until 1908. I know of no marked examples.

# 9

# PENNSYLVANIA

PENNSYLVANIA was home to a stoneware industry so vast that as yet no scholar has been courageous enough to undertake its total evaluation. There have been regional studies of Philadelphia and of the Greensboro-New Geneva kilns, and, most important, Jeannette Lasansky's *Made of Mud*, which deals with the manufactories of central Pennsylvania. These and similar examinations of local potteries reveal a business that encompassed dozens of shops, hundreds of craftsmen, and an output of marked ware rivaling that of New York.

The earliest kilns were located in Philadelphia, where Anthony Duche, Sr., English-born but equally familiar with the German Westerwald wares, established a works on Chestnut Street in the early eighteenth century. Duche was in Philadelphia by 1705 but is not thought to have gone into business on his own much before 1720. His "Pott-House" is referred to in a 1724 advertisement; and in 1730 he and his four potter sons applied to the Pennsylvania Assembly for a local monopoly on stoneware production pointing out that "for several Years past they have, with great Industry, applied themselves to the Art of making Stone-ware, heretofore unknown in these Parts."

Despite denial of this application and his sons' gradual abandonment of the business (one of them, James, was the potter who assisted Grace Parker in her attempts, 1742–46, to introduce stoneware manufacture to Boston), Anthony Duche, Sr., continued the firm until his death in 1762.

Excavation in the area where the Duche kiln was located has revealed a vast quantity of stoneware shards, including about a dozen bearing his mark, the initials AD within a cartouche, establishing him as the earliest known maker of marked American stoneware. The majority of the fragments identified are those of blue-decorated salt-glazed chamber pots and large mugs or tankards half-dipped in a brown ferruginous slip in the English manner.

The next Philadelphia manufacturer of some consequence was Branch Green, a New Jersey and New York craftsman, who established a kiln near Second Street around 1809. The uncommon mark B. GREEN/PHILAD is associated with his tenure at a works purchased about 1827 by Henry H. Remmey (son of the Manhattan stoneware manufacturer) and a partner named Burnett.

Henry's rarely seen stamp is HENRY REMMEY/MANUFACTORY/PHILADELPHIA. Under his guidance and, after 1859, that of his son, Richard Clinton Remmey (whose impressed logo, RCR/PHILA, is well known to collectors), this manufactory flourished into the twentieth century, though the making of utilitarian stonewares was largely abandoned by the 1880s. Remmey pottery is characterized by fine form and deep blue floral decoration.

The Remmeys were not without competition in Philadelphia. Thomas C. Haig, who arrived in Philadelphia about 1812 as a redware potter, established a manufactory that was making stoneware by mid-century. Though Haig died in 1833, the pottery was continued by a son, also named Thomas, late into the nineteenth century. Marked examples include a blue-decorated bank in the form of a log cabin marked T.HAIG, 1852.

Other manufacturers within the city included William Henry (1823–59), whose wares were stamped HENRY/PHILA., and John Brelsford (1846–58), whose pottery bore the impression JOHN BRELSFORD/MAKER/PHILADELPHIA.

Chester County, just west of Philadelphia, is renowned for its redware manufacturers, several of whom also produced stoneware. One of the largest kilns was at Mt. Jordan, where John P. M. Grier was active from 1850 until 1866, followed by his son Ralph J. Grier until 1902 and his son E. Stanley Grier through 1910. The firm's wares were sold throughout eastern Pennsylvania and into Maryland and Delaware. An early employee was Joseph Remmey of the Phil-

*Blue-decorated, salt-glazed stoneware miniature house attributed to Thomas C. Haig, Jr., Philadelphia, Pennsylvania, 1850–60. This piece is slab built and hand modeled, a rare thing in Northeastern stoneware.*

adelphia potting family, who left behind a blue-decorated, salt-glazed bank incised "Joseph B. Remmey, made at J.P.M. Grier Pottery, Chester County, Pa. July 20, 1850."

Other stoneware producers included Edwin Brosius of Kennett Square near the Delaware border (1880–85); Levi Coates of Cochranville in the western part of the county, who turned some salt-glazed wares in the 1880s; and Darlington Cope of New London Township who made stoneware from 1870 until 1888.

The major pottery at Reading, an important industrial center north of Chester County, was run by the Shenfelder family. Their mid-to-late-nineteenth-century stoneware was most often stamped D.P. SHENFELDER/ READING, PA.

There appear to have been few stoneware factories in northeastern Pennsylvania, both because the area was rugged and sparsely settled and because it was on the natural distribution routes of major New York State firms. However, there were kilns at Honesdale and Pittston.

In 1848 Horace Weston, who was operating a successful pottery at Ellenville, New York, established a branch at Honesdale, the southern terminus of the Delaware and Hudson Canal. Ware was initially marked H.WESTON/HONESDALE, PA., even though the founder died in the very year that the shop was built.

However, a son, William Weston, continued the enterprise until 1854, stamping his output W.W.WESTON/HONESDALE, PA.; and he was succeeded by a second son, Horace Weston, Jr., who operated the factory into the 1870s.

Pittston, less than ten miles southwest of Scranton, had an important mid-nineteenth-century manufactory. The mark EVAN B. JONES/PITTSTOWN,PA. reflects a business active on North Main Street from 1870 into the late nineteenth century and one which produced well-made pots widely distributed throughout New York and Pennsylvania. Following a fire in 1888, the property was sold to longtime employee James Ryan, a Massachusetts and New York potter who continued active into the 1890s.

South-central Pennsylvania, particularly the area along the Susquehanna and Juniata rivers, was an important center of production during the mid-nineteenth century. Harrisburg, the state capital, had two kilns. The first, established in 1852 by the Wilson brothers, Daniel and Thomas H., was near the railway depot on Filbert Street. The Wilsons sold to Shem Thomas and John Young in 1856; and their own ware, marked T.H.WILSON & CO./HARRISBURG,PA., is uncommon.

The new owners had New York State connections. Thomas had worked at Lyons and Penn Yan and Young was later employed at the Burger works in Rochester. They owned the Harrisburg kiln only until 1858 when Young returned to New York, and Thomas went to work at the Cowden Pottery, which opened in 1860. Their stoneware, seldom seen today, is impressed JOHN YOUNG & CO./HARRISBURG, PA.

The next tenant at the Filbert Street works was William Moyer, active only through 1860 when the manufactory appears to have shut down. He left behind a few pieces marked WM. MOYER/HARRISBURG,PA., including a monumental urn-shaped watercooler. The floral decoration on this piece is identical to that found on 1849–59 Rochester, New York, pieces, suggesting that a New York decorator found brief employment in Pennsylvania.

The termination of activity on Filbert coincided with the establishment of one of Pennsylvania's most important stoneware factories. In July 1860, John W. Cowden bought land for a kiln along the Pennsylvania Canal between Cumberland and Herr streets. His Harrisburg Stoneware Pottery remained active there until 1915 under the management of various children.

The founder, whose products were impressed W.COWDEN/HARRISBURG,PA., was in charge until his death in 1872; from 1863 until 1887, much ware was stamped COWDEN & WILCOX/HARRISBURG,PA., reflecting a partnership with Isaac J. Wilcox. From 1887 until 1895, a son, Frederick H. Cowden, ran the business under the logo F.H. COWDEN/HARRISBURG. His son, also John W. Cowden, entered the firm in 1895, and ware was marked COWDEN & SON/HARRISBURG, PA. until 1905 when Frederick retired. Stoneware from the period 1905–15 bore the stamp COWDEN & CO./HARRISBURG.

Cowden and Wilcox produced a vast amount of stoneware that was sold from New York

*Blue-decorated, salt-glazed stoneware jug with variation of "man in the moon" design; made and marked by COWDEN & WILCOX/HARRISBURG,PA., 1863–87.*  ▶

south to Virginia and west to Ohio. Marked examples are plentiful, and blue-decorated pieces, including birds, human faces, figures, ships, and animals, are eagerly sought by collectors.

Waynesboro, on the Maryland border, southwest of Harrisburg, was the site of a kiln established by John Bell in 1833. Though better known for its decorative redware, this factory produced a substantial quantity of salt-glazed pottery appreciated for its fine blue-gray surface and charming floral decoration. The senior member of the family was active until 1880, and most examples found are impressed JOHN BELL/WAYNESBORO,PA.; his sons, John W. Bell (active 1880–1895) and Upton Bell (active 1885–99) also placed their names upon salt-glazed vessels.

Other, smaller stoneware manufactories in the area included that run by Henry B. and George B. Pfaltzgraff at Emigsville outside York, 1876–1906, and the Newville pottery some twenty-five miles west of Harrisburg. The York establishment evolved into an important twentieth-century business concentrating on fine tablewares. The earlier stoneware was often marked H.B. PFALTZGRAFF/YORK,PA.

The rather isolated works at Newville were built in 1852 by Michael Zigler and run by his son Henry, whose wares were stamped H.H.ZIGLER/NEWVILLE,PA. A wide variety of products, including foot warmers, beer bottles, milk pans, and pitchers, were made until 1865 when Henry Zigler removed to Illinois.

Michael Zigler then sold the plant to the brothers John S. and Edwin R. Hayes, who continued the business until about 1877. An unusual characteristic of their management was that they never placed their own names on the ware, preferring to use the mark SAM'L I. IRVINE/NEWVILLE,PA for their agent and brother-in-law, Samuel Irvine.

There were also two potteries on the Juniata River northwest of Harrisburg. George Miller

established a redware shop at Newport in 1838; following his death in 1864 his sons, Michael and Theophilus, began to manufacture salt-glazed wares impressed M.& T. MILLER/NEWPORT, PA. Though ordinary in form, many of these crocks and jugs were decorated with large floral patterns or even human heads and figures.

The business remained active until around 1895. An apprentice, Henry Markel, had bought in around 1877; and Michael Miller died in 1890, leaving the firm to Markel and his brother.

The manufactory at Lewistown, a larger community about thirty miles upriver, was located on Valley Street and was also the successor to an earlier redware pottery. In 1868 John H. Dipple began to make stoneware here. However, his career was cut short by one of those accidents that plagued the lives of potters. In

_Blue-decorated, salt-glazed stoneware cream pot impressed LEWISTOWN/POTTERY and attributed to John H. Dipple, Lewistown, Pennsylvania, 1868–72._

1872 he was struck by a train when crossing the local tracks to reach his clay pit.

His wife, Anna Margretta, maintained and expanded the business, first with the assistance of a potter son-in-law, Austin L. Hyssong, and later her sons, John, Jr., and Andrew G. Following Anna Dipple's death in 1901 the sons marched on into the twentieth century. Amazingly, Andrew Dipple did not stop turning stoneware until 1929! John Dipple simply marked his products LEWISTOWN/POTTERY; Anna used the logo A.M.DIPPLE/LEWISTOWN,PA., and the sons, J.H.DIPPLE/LEWISTOWN/PA and A.G.C. DIPPLE/LEWISTOWN,PA.

Northumberland County, up the Susquehanna, had factories at Sunbury on the river and Snydertown a few miles to the east. Snydertown's was the earlier, having been established in 1868 by William R. F. Weimer and his brother, George Y. Weimer. There is no firm evidence that the business continued after 1872; and ware, stamped W.R.F. WEIMER & BRO., or, conversely, G.Y. WEIMER & BRO., is exceedingly rare.

Though the pottery at Sunbury may have been operated by its owner, Thomas D. Metcalf, from around 1870 until 1889, pieces impressed T.D. METCALF/SUNBURY PA. are even harder to find; and practically nothing is known about the business.

There were also kilns at Mooresburg about fifteen miles to the northeast and at Bloomsburg on the east branch of the Susquehanna some twenty miles northeast of Sunbury. The Mooresburg firm was headed by Daniel Ack, who bought a pottery site in 1857 which he did not sell until 1909. A warehouse, once part of the original factory, still stands. Products were stamped D.ACK/MOORESBURG,PA. until 1886 when sons John F. and Clyde C. entered the business under the logo J.F.ACK & BRO./ MOORESBURG,PA. From 1888 until 1904 John alone was in charge, marking his crocks, jugs, and ornate garden urns J.F.ACK/MOORESBURG,PA.

The Bloomsburg works was one of Pennsylvania's longest lasting, remaining active until 1929. The shop was established in 1858 by John Rehm. Augustus Rabb became his partner in 1866 under the logo RABB & REHM/ BLOOMSBURG,PA., which continued to be used after 1874 when Augustus was replaced in the partnership by his brother, John.

In 1891 the manufactory passed into the hands of Austin L. Hyssong who had previously worked at the Lewistown pottery. His mark was A. L. HYSSONG/BLOOMSBURG. Austin had four sons in the business, and in 1914 one of them, Charles, took over the shop operating it until 1929. His output does not appear to have been marked.

There was another smaller stoneware works at Berwick, about ten miles east on the Susquehanna. Its owners, Jessie Edwards and a man named Wessler, were active from 1882 until around 1890; and only a single piece marked WESSLER & EDWARDS/BERWICK, PA. is known.

Williamsport in Lycoming County on the west branch of the Susquehanna had an important stoneware manufactory whose products are found frequently both in Pennsylvania and New York. Though a pottery had existed there since 1859 there is no evidence that stoneware was made prior to 1875 when William Sipe, Joseph Nichols, and Abram S. Young built a works on Market Street.

Getting started must have been difficult, for the impression SIPE,NICHOLS & CO./WILLIAMS- PORT, PA. records a partnership that lasted only until 1877. For the next two years the mark was MOORE,NICHOLS & CO./WILLIAMSPORT, PA., as Logan C. Moore replaced Sipe, who nonetheless remained an employee until 1879, when he bought the company outright.

Under Sipe's guidance the business flourished until 1893. By the mid-1880s earnings exceeded $25,000 per year, a very substantial sum for a pottery; and the output was three thousand gallons per month. Ware was marked SIPE & SON or SIPE & SONS/WILLIAMSPORT, PA. (reflecting the participation of Luther R. and Oscar W.) throughout the life of the firm, despite the fact that the founder died in 1891.

On up the west branch, there were manufactories at Lock Haven and in the Sugar Valley area south of there. Around 1867 a German craftsman, Bernard Hoffard, took over a pottery established at Lock Haven in 1855 by a countryman, William Shroat. Hoffard remained active with various partners until 1884. Stoneware impressed LOCK HAVEN, PA. is attributed to him or to Shroat.

Loganton, a small community in the lush Sugar Valley area, had at least one stoneware maker, John Gerstung. He worked from about 1870 until 1880; and his products were marked, appropriately enough, SUGAR VALLEY, PA.

In the mountainous west-central region of the state there were several stoneware centers concentrated for the most part about local clay sources. Centre County had two such kilns. The first was built at Mount Eagle in 1862 by John B. Leathers. His well-formed and attractively decorated wares are impressed J.B. LEATHERS/MT. EAGLE, PA. Around 1878 John appears to have

joined his older brother, Ira, in establishing a second kiln at Howard about five miles to the northeast. Ware stamped LEATHERS & BRO./HOWARD, PA. is traceable to this venture. Though it is not known when the Mount Eagle concern ceased production, both shops appear to have been discontinued by 1889.

There were much longer lasting manufactories at Huntingdon, some forty miles to the southwest. John Glazier established a redware shop here around 1810, and when his son, Henry J., joined the firm in 1831 they began to make stoneware. Those pieces bear the stamp H. GLAZIER/HUNTINGDON, PA. John Glazier retired in 1847, and his son went into politics seven years later. Then, as now, politics was the more lucrative field; operations were terminated at the pottery.

However, years later, in 1871, William H. Thomas, a son of the Harrisburg potter Shem Thomas, built a new factory in Huntingdon, this one on the present Standing Stone Avenue. Initially, his brothers Edward and Ephraim were active in the business; but they were gone by 1873, and five years later William lost the shop to creditors. Known examples from this kiln are usually marked THOMAS & BRO./HUNTINGDON, PA. or W.H. THOMAS/HUNTINGDON, PA.

The last of the Huntingdon potters was Austin L. Hissong of Lewistown, who reactivated the Thomas shop in 1881, continuing through 1885. His mark, A.L. HISSONG/HUNTINGDON, is not common.

Other communities in Huntingdon County claimed their own kilns. There were two at Cassville only ten miles south of Huntingdon Borough. The earliest was that established in

*Blue-decorated, salt-glazed spittoon bearing the stamp J.B. LEATHERS/MT. EAGLE, PA. John B. Leathers worked at Mount Eagle in Centre County, Pennsylvania, from 1862 until about 1886.*

1842 by Jacob Greenland with his three sons, one of whom, Norval W., became sole owner in 1881. He continued the business until 1913. Despite this lengthy tenure, the Greenland family left behind only a single marked example, a miniature jug incised N.W.GREENLAND.

Elisha B. Hissong, who started the other local manufactory in 1851, was much more traditional. He marked his products CASSVILL/E.B.HISSONG. With the assistance of his four sons, Elisha maintained the shop until his death in 1893; and Charles B. and Russell Hissong continued it until 1912.

Shirleysburg, about eight miles due east of Cassville, sat right on top of a large vein of stoneware clay, so it is not surprising that in 1864 Philip Kabis purchased an existing redware kiln in the town and began to make stoneware. Kabis had an unusual specialty, the making of salt-glazed water pumps and pipes; but since he did not mark his ware his products cannot be identified with any certainty. He too got into financial problems and shut down in 1888, despite having informed the public as early as 1876 that he sold a variety of stoneware "which I will practically give away"!

In 1873 Rebecca Myton and her son, Kennedy, established a pottery at Petersburg some five miles north of Huntingdon Borough. Since they were not potters, they employed itinerant craftsmen who remained active at the site until 1896. No marked ware is known.

Though the most important pottery complex in western Pennsylvania was located in the Greensboro–New Geneva area, there were several other centers. One of the earliest was located at Pleasantville in Venango County.

Around 1830 Micah Porter and his sons, William and Samuel, who had been making stoneware at Rochester, New York, removed to the Pleasantville–Oil City area in northwestern Pennsylvania. Members of the family are listed in the 1840 census there, and rare examples from the kiln are impressed PORTER/PLEASANTVILLE. It

is not known how long this shop operated, but it is possible that the family retired to enjoy its wealth: One of Pennsylvania's first oil wells was discovered on the lands of William Porter!

Erie, an important port on the lake and midway between the Ohio and New York borders, had two later manufactories, both located conveniently on the Erie Extension Canal. In 1851 Reuben J. and Charles Sibley bought land between West Second and Third streets upon which they erected a stoneware pottery. The Sibleys came well recommended, as members of the family had been associated with the well-known Bennington, Vermont, stoneware factory since the 1830s. However, they did not appear to thrive in Erie. In December 1852 the business was sold to George Webb and Daniel Brennan; and two months later Brennan was replaced by Oscar C. Thayer.

The firm of Webb and Thayer ran the business from 1853 until 1859 when Webb took a new partner, David McAllaster, who, in turn, transferred his interest to Sidney Kellogg in the following year. Among the few pieces of identifiable Erie stoneware are vessels stamped WEBB & KELLOGG/ERIE,PA.

Kellogg left the firm following a serious fire in 1864. Webb and his newest partner, Jay S. Childs, continued the business only until 1867 when the property was sold for the benefit of creditors.

By this time Erie had a second stoneware manufactory, built on West Ninth Street in 1860 by Samuel Cummins and Oscar Thayer, who had just left his partnership in the West Second Street works. The Erie City Stone-Ware Manufactory, as it was known, was successful enough to last until 1888. Throughout this period the property was always owned by Thayer, though there were several different partnerships.

The first was Thayer & Cummins, active until the latter's departure in 1863. Thayer then ran the business with William Price until 1865 when he was replaced by Calvin Bachelder. A rare 1867 price list indicates that Price & Bachelder made the usual salt-glazed jars, jugs, churns, pots, and pitchers.

In 1868 Oscar Thayer resumed his role in the firm, which operated as Thayer & Price until 1881. Following Price's departure in that year, the company name became O. C. Thayer & Co. until 1886, when the admission of James N. Thayer resulted in a new title, O. C. Thayer & Son, used until termination of activity in 1888.

Oddly enough, despite nearly thirty years of activity, there is no marked ware that can be associated with the West Ninth Street pottery.

Little is known of the several potteries once located in Beaver County northwest of Pittsburgh. The name J. WEAVER impressed in a semicircle is associated with a stoneware kiln operated 1850–80 by John Weaver and his son, George; and the New Brighton-made pottery of James Hamilton, who later worked at Greensboro, was impressed J.HAMILTON/BEAVER.

Other Beaver County stoneware manufacturers included members of the separatist Economy Society, active at Beaver Falls 1834–81; Sherwood Brothers (1877–90), and D. G. Schofield & Co. (1877–1893), both located in nearby New Brighton; the Fallston Pottery (1875–1900) and the Enterprise Pottery (1880–1900), in Fallston about two miles to the south; and the McKenzie family whose kiln was located at Vanport on the Ohio River just a few miles southwest of New Brighton. This firm was known as McKenzie Brothers from 1840 until 1870 and from then until 1900 as Fowler & McKenzie. Early examples were impressed J. MCKENZIE/BEAVER, PA.

Pittsburgh's early craftsmen included James Barr who made both stoneware and redware from 1815 until 1847; Hugh Donaldson, active 1839–45; Adam Burchfield (1860–70); S. M. Kier & Company (1867–1900); and Henry Pettie & Company in business from 1850 until 1870.

One of the city's most important works was located in the area known during the nineteenth century as East Birmingham. The owners, 1857–72, were Foell & Alt, and their wares, which were decorated with both stenciling and freehand work in cobalt, were marked FOELL & ALT/MANUFACTURERS/EAST BIRMINGHAM,PA.

There were two manufactories southeast of Pittsburgh, that of Michael Straw at Greensburg in Westmorland County, in business 1835–45 and the Swank Pottery in Johnstown, active during the 1860–80s period. The Swanks had a competitor during the mid-nineteenth century, as evidenced by stoneware marked, A.J. HAWS/JOHNSTOWN, PA.

However, the greatest concentration of Pennsylvania stoneware potteries during the second half of the nineteenth century was in the southwest corner of the state along the Monongahela River. These firms were important not only for their output, which in 1860 amounted to over 42 percent of all stoneware made in the state, but also for the distinctive appearance of their wares.

Decorative stenciling, often combined with freehand painting, was the norm rather than the exception; and the stenciled eagles, flowers, and classical scrollwork are the most sophisticated employment of the medium to be found on American stoneware.

It was also the Greensboro–New Geneva area that spawned "Tanware," the use of stenciled or freehand decoration in manganese or Albany slip on an unglazed buff surface.

The reason for all these potteries and all this creative activity may be found in a rich bed of stoneware clay located along the river about fifty miles south of Pittsburgh. Between 1850 and 1915 this vein supported at least fifteen different manufacturing centers.

The earliest was at Greensboro about five miles north of the West Virginia border where Daniel Boughner, who had taken over the Vance family redware pottery in 1819, began to make stoneware in the late 1840s. His impressed mark, BOUGHNER/GREENSBORO,PA., is not common. By

1859 his sons Alexander and William had entered the business under the logo D. BOUGHNER & SONS / GREENSBORO, PA. Following Daniel's death in 1861 they continued the business until 1868; their rare stenciled mark is A. V. BOUGHNER/ GREENSBORO, PA.

Formidable competition arrived on the scene in 1850 when James and William L. Hamilton of New Brighton shifted their operation to Greens-boro. James continued their business until 1880 when he sold to Thomas F. Reppert and William T. Williams. Early wares are stenciled JAS. HAMILTON/&CO./GREENSBORO/PA. Reppert, after initially marking his output WILLIAMS & REPPERT/ GREENSBORO, PA., capitalized on his predecessor's reputation by using the stamp T. F. REPPERT/ SUCCESSOR TO/JAS. HAMILTON & CO./ GREENSBORO, PA. He remained in business until 1893.

*Blue-decorated, salt-glazed jar stenciled* FOELL & ALT/ MANUFACTURERS/EAST BIRMINGHAM, PA. *This firm was active in East Birmingham, now a part of Pittsburgh, from 1857 until 1872. The combination of freehand and stencil decoration seen here is particularly attractive.*

*Blue-decorated, salt-glazed stoneware pitcher made and marked by* J. SWANK & CO./JOHNSTOWN, PA., *1865–1900. Both form and decoration are typical of pieces made in western Pennsylvania.*

William L. Hamilton left his brother's business in 1857, establishing a pottery transferred in 1866 to his son, Frank, and son-in-law, John Jones. The founder's wares were impressed HAMILTON GREENSBORO, while the new partnership used variations of the name HAMILTON & JONES/STAR POTTERY/GREENSBORO,PA. Second in size only to James Hamilton's pottery, Hamilton & Jones was active until 1898.

Just across the river from Greensboro was New Geneva, Pennsylvania, another busy stoneware center. Around 1855, George Debolt, a former employee of Boughner, went into business with the New Jersey craftsman Henry Atchison. Debolt was gone before 1860, and there are only a very few pieces marked DEBOLT & ATCHISON (in freehand cobalt). However, examples impressed H.K. ATCHINSON & CO./NEW GENEVA,PA, may reflect the same partnership.

Atchison remained active until 1861, when he entered the Union Army. He lost an arm at the battle of Petersburg, Virginia, and though he returned to New Geneva, he never took up his craft again.

The other claimant for the position of first stoneware maker in the community is Samuel R. Dilliner who is said to have begun work in 1854, continuing until 1866. The existence of a jar stenciled DILLINER & ENEIX/NEW GENEVA/PA. suggests that Dilliner, who apparently was not a potter, was allied with James D. Eneix. At a later date (1874–98) Eneix had his own pottery about a mile south of New Geneva, marking his output J.D.ENEIX/NEW GENEVA.

Dilliner's business passed into the hands of Adolph Eberhart and J. G. Williams (A.EBERHART & CO. was the mark), one of the numerous partnerships that attempted to make a goof stoneware production at New Geneva during the second half of the nineteenth century. Others included Alexander Conrad, in business from 1870 until 1882 with wares marked variously A. CONRAD or A.CONRAD & CO./NEW GENEVA/ PA.and NEW GENEVA/POTTERY; John P.

Eberhart (1880–87) whose stencil was JOHN P. EBERHART & CO./NEW GENEVA,PA., reflecting an early partnership with Thomas Eberhart; and Leander Dilliner, whose shop, active from 1874 to 1880, was sold to the Eberharts.

Perhaps the most successful of all was Robert T. Williams, who was trained by Hamilton and Jones, ran his own pottery in West Virginia from 1875 until 1878, and in 1882 took over Conrad's New Geneva Pottery Works. Williams, whose products bore the stenciled legend R.T.WILLIAMS/NEW GENEVA/PA., was a maker of "Tanware," which was typically produced in the form of pitchers and flowerpots.

Despite his financial triumphs, Robert Williams appears to have come to a bad end. In 1895, with the factory still operating profitably, he vanished on a selling trip downriver into West Virginia. Some said that he fell out of a boat and drowned, but others believed that he had just "gone west" as so many men (and a few women!) did when things got difficult at home or in the shop.

Whatever the case, the business was sold to another Williams, Charles L., who ran it for a few years before turning things over to Arthur Robbins. He maintained the kiln until 1914, at which point stoneware production in New Geneva ceased. Interestingly enough, Charles Williams stenciled his wares C.L.WILLIAMS & CO./ SUCCESSORS/TO/R.T.WILLIAMS/MANUFACTURERS/ OF STONEWARE/NEW GENEVA,PA.

There were other stoneware factories in the area. North along the river were Isaac Hewitt at Rice's Landing, 1870–80, with ware stenciled EXCELSIOR WORKS/ISAAC HEWITT,JR./RICE'S LANDING, PA.; the firm of Donnaho & Beal, active around 1870 in Fredricktown; and Stephen Ward, whose pottery in nearby West Brownsville operated at about the same time. There was also the partnership of Hall and Greenland working in Uniontown northeast of New Geneva during the 1870s, as well as other smaller shops in the Greensboro–New Geneva area.

# 10

# MARYLAND, DELAWARE, AND WEST VIRGINIA

BOTH MARYLAND AND WEST VIRGINIA had important stoneware manufactories. The former produced wares similar to those made in New York and eastern Pennsylvania during the same period of time, while the latter is best known for stencil-decorated examples resembling pottery produced in the Greensboro–New Geneva area of western Pennsylvania. Delaware, small and surrounded by states with large stoneware industries, turned out only a small amount of documented ware.

## MARYLAND

The Maryland stoneware industry can be traced with some certainty to the late eighteenth century. By the early 1800s Baltimore had several manufactories, large enough not only to supply the vicinity but to ship goods north to New England and south along the Virginia and Carolina coasts.

One of the state's ambitious proprietors was Jacob Myers, who announced in the *Alexandria Gazette* of May 4, 1820, that "(m)y Stone ware establishment is conducted by Henry Remmey & Son, late of N. York." Myers certainly recognized quality, for Henry Remmey's family had been making salt-glazed wares in Manhattan since the 1730s, and his son, Henry, Jr., bought a Philadelphia pottery in 1827 which remained in the family until well into the twentieth century. Henry, Sr., appears to have taken over the Baltimore works around 1822, as the city directory for that year lists him as "Henry Remmey, Stoneware Factory, N.W. corner of Bond and Pitt." It is likely that this venture came to an end with the purchase of the Philadelphia factory. The mark, which is extremely rare, is H. REMMEY/BALTIMORE. Among the pieces upon which it is found is a pitcher with incised, blue-filled, floral decoration in the New York manner.

Two other important names in early Baltimore stoneware are Amos and Morgan. William

H. Amos and Thomas Morgan worked together there from 1812 until 1822, leaving behind various marked pieces. Included is a jar with free-standing handles and incised floral pattern which has "Morgan & Amoss/Makers/Pitt Street/ Baltimore/1821" scratched on the base.

Morgan, however, is thought to have worked in Baltimore as early as 1810, and, following his partner's departure, he continued alone from 1823 until 1837. The impression MORGAN MAKER is associated with this later period. Morgan was very likely a member of the far-flung New Jersey–New York–Virginia clan of Morgan potters.

By 1830 William H. Amos was associated with the Miller pottery in Alexandria, Virginia, where he turned a piece incised B.C.MILLER/ MAKER/Sept. 1st 1830/W.H.AMOS. Another member of the family, Thomas Amos, who had made stoneware in Baltimore 1810–17 (one of his apprentices in 1813 was Enoch Burnett, later Henry Remmey, Jr.'s partner in Philadelphia), also moved to Virginia. He was running a Richmond kiln by 1820.

There were other pioneer manufacturers. David Parr established the Maryland Potteries at Baltimore in 1815, and they were continued by his wife Margaret and son James L. until around 1855 when this business, too, was moved to Richmond. Peter Perine's factory, opened in 1793 and making stoneware by 1827, was still in business after 1900 as Mauldine Perine & Sons. Although, like many similar potteries, it diversified in later years, the Perine shop always relied on its output of utilitarian stoneware (for which it won an award at the 1876 Centennial exhibition).

One of Perine's former associates, William Linton, proved an active competitor from 1845 until around 1867. He had taken over an older shop, that of James E. Jones & Company (1834–45). Like his predecessor, Linton made ordinary salt-glazed crocks, jars, and jugs.

Even after 1850 Baltimore continued to have a flourishing stoneware industry. Peter Hermann, whose business was located on Eager Street and who marked his wares PETER HERMANN, was active 1850–72, while H. S. Taylor's Jackson Square Pottery advertised crocks and watercoolers, 1872–83. Another local rival was Benjamin Greble, a maker of both redware and stoneware during the 1860s.

A few other Maryland craftsmen made stoneware, such as Henry Weise, working 1865–75 in Hagerstown on the Great Wagon Road from Pennsylvania to Tennessee, but the business was largely concentrated in Baltimore. And there is no doubt that it is the Baltimore marks that most collectors seek.

## DELAWARE

The Delaware stoneware industry seems to have been dominated by the shop of William Hare, who worked in Wilmington, the capital city, from 1857 until 1887. Though Hare usually described himself as a manufacturer of "earthenware," he has left behind an amazing number of small, undecorated, straight-sided preserve jars and jugs, most of which are covered with a tan or brown slip glaze and impressed WM.HARE/WILMINGTON,DEL.

## WEST VIRGINIA

Though West Virginia had an earthenware maker by 1784, stoneware production did not become important before the mid-nineteenth century. Morgantown, close to the Pennsylvania border and the Greensboro–New Geneva manufactories, was the most important center.

The first producer of salt-glazed wares at Morgantown was John Wood Thompson, a Maryland-born potter who had purchased a local redware kiln in 1827. It was not, however, until the 1840s that Thompson began to make

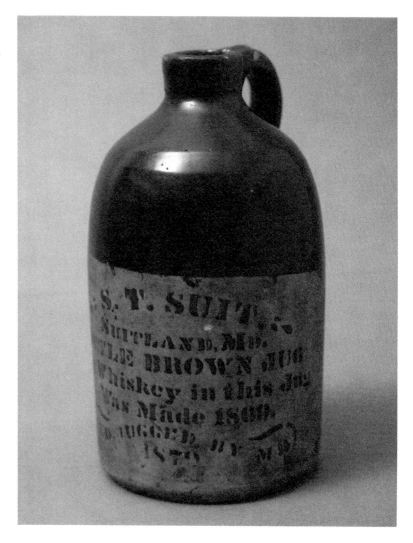

*So-called "brownware" pitcher; stoneware partially glazed and stenciled in Albany slip. Attributed to Maryland, 1875–80. The inscription reads S.T.SUIT/SUITLAND,MD./ LITTLE BROWN JUG/The Whiskey in this Jug/Was Made 1869/AND JUGGED BY ME/ 1879. Suitland is now part of the greater District of Columbia area.*

stoneware. Upon his retirement in 1853 the firm passed to three sons, the most active of whom was David Greenland Thompson, who managed the works until his death in 1890.

Though it closely resembles the output of nearby southern Pennsylvania shops, Thompson stoneware may be distinguished by the impressed mark, D.G.THOMPSON or MORGANTOWN, and the skillful combination of freehand floral decoration with the usual stencil designs. Also, certain earlier examples bear impressed decoration; rosettes, coggling, and even a scene of houses, trees, fences, and farm vehicles, rarely seen in West Virginia ceramics.

A second Thompson son, James J., competed briefly with the family kiln. From 1875 until 1878 he was in partnership with Robert T. Williams, a New Geneva craftsman. Their ware was impressed THOMPSON,WILLIAMS/CO./MORGANTOWN/WV. Another early stoneware pottery, about which little is known, was established in the 1840s at nearby Collins Ferry on the Monogahela River. The owner was William Critchfield whose only known example is a jar inscribed in cobalt slip, "Home Manufacture/Independence/High Tariff/William Critchfield/August,1844."

In Marion County, less than twenty miles southwest of Morgantown, was Palatine, once an important center for the manufacture and dis-

tribution of salt-glazed wares. The firm of Richey & Hamilton, 1870–90, is best known. As was so often the case in this area of West Virginia, Hamilton was probably a member of the Greensboro, Pennsylvania, clan, and the mark, RICHEY & HAMILTON/PALATINE, W. VA., was stenciled in blue. Other known stamps are T.H. HARDEN/PALATINE, W.VA. and PALATINE/ POT TERY/CO. Both date to the last quarter of the nineteenth century, and the latter may feature stenciled representations of prancing horses, a unique decorative element in this area. Yet another local firm was Knott, Sunderland & Co., whose stenciled cipher, KNOTT & CO./PALATINE/ W.VA., appears on crocks and jugs dating to 1870–1900.

Nearby Shinnston in Harrison County also had a sizable community of potters. Here, too, makers' names and decoration were done in stencil work. WILKINSON/&/FLEMING/SHINNS-TON, W.VA. (1885–95) is the mark most frequently encountered. However, an earlier manufacturer appears to have been Alexander Conrad who, after being involved in the stone-ware business at New Geneva from 1872, established himself at Shinnston in 1882. He continued there for nearly a decade.

There were several other important stoneware making sites scattered through the state of West Virginia. Parkersburg in Wood County on the Ohio River and the state's western border had a substantial kiln owned by the Pennsylvania craftsman A. P. Donaghho. During the period 1874–1900 this factory turned out a very large volume of salt-glazed utilitarian stoneware decorated with stenciled geometric devices and marked, in the same manner, A.P.DONAGHHO/ PARKERSBURG, W. VA. The not uncommon stencil, EXCELSIOR/POTTERY/PARKERSBURG, indicates the existence of another firm, owned by Donaghho or others 1880–1900.

Wheeling, an important city in the "neck" of West Virginia and some seventy miles northeast of Parkersburg on the Ohio, had at least one stoneware manufactory. The name J.MILLER/ WHEELING, W.VA. (1869–80) is associated with this locality as is the mark H.F.BEHREN/CO./ WHEELING.W.VA., believed to date from the 1880s.

At the opposite end of the state, in Linside, a tiny Appalachian Mountain community on the Virginia line some forty miles west of Roanoke, was the shop of Rice and Doyle. Their products, decorated with a combination of stencil and freehand floral patterns, were customarily imprinted RICE & DOYLE/POTTERY/LINSIDE, W.VA. Like so much West Virginia ware, these pieces may often be distinguished from Pennsylvania examples only by identifiable makers' marks.

# 11

# VIRGINIA AND THE DISTRICT OF COLUMBIA

## VIRGINIA

THE STATE OF VIRGINIA is a rich source for the stoneware collector. Both the English and Germanic traditions are evident in a variety of salt-glazed wares dating from the eighteenth to the early twentieth century.

Moreover, Yorktown, Virginia, was the site of one of our nation's earliest stoneware kilns. In 1732 Governor William Gooch reported to London's Lord Commissioner of the Board of Trade that "(t)he same poor Potter's work is still continued at Yorktown without any great improvement or advantage to the owner or any injury to the trade of Great Britain."

The pottery to which he referred, near the York River, has been excavated. Contrary to what Gooch led his superiors to believe, its products were far from "poor." During the period 1720–45 a vast quantity of fine redware and stoneware was made here by unknown craftsmen.

The owner of the factory appears to have been William Rogers, a merchant, and among its products were brown salt-glazed bottles, bowls, storage jars, pipkins, chamber pots, and mugs. The last, customarily twice dipped in a ferruginous glaze characteristic of London half brown/half tanware, are of such quality that they would have been largely indistinguishable from contemporary English examples.

While Governor Gooch allayed the commercial jealousy of English pottery owners, he could not fool other colonists. When Isaac Parker of Charlestown sought financial assistance from the Massachusetts Bay Colony to establish a stoneware works in 1742 he pointedly referred to the "large quantities of said Ware imported into this Province every year from New York, Philadelphia and Virginia." There can be little doubt that the Virginia ware came from Yorktown, for shipping records indicate that ceramics were frequently sent north to New England.

Rogers died in 1739, but the pottery appears to have remained active until at least 1745 and, possibly, 1750. Stoneware shards associated with it have been found at several locations in Virginia, but no intact pieces have as yet been identified.

Richmond was the site of another early kiln. In 1811 Benjamin DuVal, a local apothecary, advertised in *The Enquirer* for August 9 that he had opened the Richmond Stoneware Manufactory in buildings near Main Street where he had run a tile factory since at least 1808. By 1814 he was making jugs, pots, pitchers, bottles, churns, chamber pots, milk pans, inkstands, and flasks (referred to locally as "ticklers"); and a year later he offered to deliver "Ware in any part of the City, free of the expense of cartage, and at the New York prices."

Despite a kiln failure in 1815 and competition from Manhattan and Baltimore stoneware, DuVal persisted until 1817, when he turned the works over to his son, James. It seems likely that the business came to an end before 1820, as it does not appear in the industrial census for that year. The only known example is an ovoid pot similar to examples made in New York with freestanding handles and the impressed, blue-filled mark, B.DUVAL & CO./RICHMOND.

DuVal had ample competition in the immediate vicinity. A New York potter named John P. Schermerhorn, who had probably worked for him, opened a rival works in Richmond before 1820, and by the latter year he was employing three men and producing "stoneware of all kinds." There was also Thomas Amos, who had worked in Baltimore 1810–17, Samuel Frayser, and a Samuel Wilson who may be the same potter who was active about 1813 in Albany, New York. Clearly, no one had a monopoly on the Richmond trade in 1820. However, little is known of the duration of these various shops.

Much later stoneware makers in Richmond included David Parr and Sons, members of the Baltimore family, who were active in the 1860s and 1870s. They called their business the Richmond Pottery and offered the public "Best quality stoneware, such as jugs, pitchers, jars, milk pans, spittoons, bread risers, butter pans, churns and water jars."

Petersburg, some fifteen miles south of Richmond, also had an early kiln. Thomas Lowndes established a stoneware factory there in 1806, operating it until his death in 1812. It is likely that his shop was taken over by William Harwood, who was running the Petersburg Stoneware Manufactory in 1818. There was also a similar business operated by Richard Randolph 1813–15 on the James River twelve miles east of Richmond. This would not have been far from Trees Point in Charles City County where Moro Phillips bought land for a pottery in 1850. Though Phillips opened a second shop in Philadelphia in 1853, it is thought that he continued the Trees Point works for some years, probably under the supervision of Sanford S. Perry, a Troy, New York, craftsman who had come to Virginia around 1836.

Germanic potters brought a much different heritage to western Virginia when in the mid-nineteenth century they settled along the Great Wagon Road through the Shenandoah Valley in towns such as Winchester and Strasburg. First in the field was Peter Bell, a Maryland craftsman, who reached Winchester in 1824 but made nothing other than redware until 1832. Though he was active until 1845, marked examples are rare.

His sons, Samuel and Solomon, founded their own pottery in Strasburg in 1833; they continued to make slip-decorated earthenwares, and also produced some remarkable stoneware. Among the examples known are a double-handled watercooler impressed SOLOMON BELL/ STRASBURG, VA., lavishly decorated in cobalt in the German manner and embellished with applied, impressed, and incised decoration; and a jar marked S. BELL (for Samuel Bell), decorated

*Blue-decorated, salt-glazed jar stamped S.BELL and attributed to Samuel Bell, Strasburg, Virginia, 1850–70. Charming decoration is a characteristic of Bell family wares.*

with four horses, the outlines of which were impressed, then blue filled. Their shop remained active until 1882, turning out a multitude of stoneware vessels.

There were several other late-nineteenth-century manufactories in Strasburg, all of which produced marked, often blue-decorated, stoneware. They include Samuel H. Sonner (1870–83), followed by his son, John H. Sonner (1883–92); Amos and Jeremiah Keister (1880–85); James M. Hickerson (1884–98); L. D. Funkhouser (1899–1905); and William H. Lehew (1880–90).

Marks most often seen are W.H. LEHEW & CO/STRASBURG,VA.; S.H.SONNER/STRASBURG,VA. and L.D.FUNKHOUSER & CO./STRASBURG/VA. Less common are J.M.HICKERSON/STRASBURG,VA. and

J.H.SONNER/STRASBURG,VA. Much of the ware is stencil decorated and bears a distinct resemblance to that made in western Pennsylvania and West Virginia.

Though the Strasburg-Winchester potteries are best known to collectors, there were many other kilns scattered down along the Great Wagon Road all the way to the Tennessee border. John D. Heatwole, active at Dry River in Rockingham County, 1850–80, made not only the usual line of stoneware but tombstones as well. One of these, gray with cobalt lettering and an eight-pointed star, bears the inscription, "IN MEMORY OF MARY S. HEATWOLE, WHO WAS BORN SEPT. 10, 1848 & DIED MARCH THE 24, 1851, AGED 2 YEARS 6 MONTHS & 14 DAYS/ J.D.HEATWOLE/1853."

The Coffman family, Andrew and his offspring, John, William, Robert, and Edward, whose shop was located at nearby Mt. Herman (1840–65), also made tombstones. An example signed by John Coffman may be seen in the Lutheran burying ground at New Market some thirty-five miles southwest of Strasburg. Other unusual marked Coffman examples include a covered sugar bowl impressed A.COFFMAN/ ROCKINGHAM CO.,VA. and a stoneware druggist's mortar on which is inscribed "for Dr. L.L.Painter made by B.R.L. Coffman."

Andrew Coffman appears to have previously worked at a much earlier pottery established by Johannes Zigler in 1830 at Timberville west of New Market. Though much of the earlier production there was redware, a stoneware pitcher dated 1832 is attributed to this kiln.

The important center of Harrisonburg had several manufactories, including one run by Mathius Ireland (1860–70) and partners, succeeded by his son into the 1880s. Ware was frequently impressed MT.CRAWFORD,VA., reflecting location of the shop in this community a few miles down the Pike from Harrisonburg.

Rockbridge County, southwest of Harrisonburg, had several stoneware makers, among them the mysterious John S. Morgan who had been born in New York State in 1768 and who in Virginia during the 1830s and 1840s produced stoneware with incised blue-filled swag-and-tassel decorations remarkably similar to that made in Manhattan by David Morgan (1795–1809). He is quite possibly the John Morgan who appears in the Manhattan directories from 1802 until 1812.

To make the whole thing more intriguing, Morgan's partner in the shop at Rockbridge Baths some ten miles north of Lexington appears to have been John Campbell, a redware maker. There were several John Campbells active in Manhattan during the late eighteenth century making earthenware and they would have known the Morgans.

In any case, the Morgan-Campbell Pottery came into the hands of a Virginia-born craftsman, Isaac D. Lam, around 1854, and he operated it until his death in 1882. Lam's products were often marked ROCKBRIDGE.

Further south was the manufactory of George N. Fulton near Fincastle in Botecourt County. Fulton was from an Ohio family, had worked at the Parr factory in Richmond, served in the Civil War, and had a shop near Jordan Mines in Allegheny County from 1867 until 1875. In the latter year he moved from this isolated location to Fincastle a few miles north of Roanoke, where his business prospered until his death in 1894. His floral-decorated pieces were sometimes signed G.N. Fulton or G.N.F. in blue or brown slip.

Fulton often sold his wares in Blacksburg, where they were in direct competition with redware made by Thomas Waddle (1850–80). Marion Rawson in *Candleday Art* (1938) quoted Daniel Arrit, who as a youth had worked for Fulton, on this rivalry:

You know, marm, this was good stoneware, not that no 'count red earthen ware. You could bile [boil] in our stoneware. I've drive the wagon many a time to Blacksburg, and there old Waddel that sold the redware would see me coming and shout, "what you bringing that no 'count stuff to this town for?" And I'd shout back, "yours is the no 'count stuff, ain't burnt to a body. Mine's burnt to a stone body. Give me a piece of your old no 'count ware, I want to pitch it down the road a little piece." So I pitched one of my crocks down the road twenty feet and it never broke none. His'n? He daren't give me any. He went out of business afore long.

Few descriptions of the economic struggle between stoneware and redware makers are more eloquent than this one.

Stoneware shops were scattered throughout southwestern Virginia with the majority located in Washington County at the Tennessee border. J. M. Barlow began making pottery near Abingdon around 1880 and later worked at Alum Wells and Ocola into the 1890s. Known marks include J.M.BARLOW/ALUM WELLS and J.M.BARLOW/OCOLA,VA. His Alum shop may have been continued until 1893 by Edward William Mort whose uncommon impression was E.W.MORT/ALUM WELLS, VIRGINIA. Other Abingdon Township potters included Charles F. Decker and his son, Charles, Jr., Pennsylvania potters active from 1870 until 1880 when they moved to Tennessee, and the firm of Hamilton & Stuart. In 1870 the Deckers, in partnership with a man named Mallicole, turned out 144,000 gallons of stoneware; a huge amount, particularly when contrasted with the bare 3,600 gallons produced by Hamilton & Stuart in the same year.

Another Abingdon craftsman was John B. McGee or MaGee (1870–80) whose ware was impressed J.B.MCGEE. McGee was from Maryland and had worked in New York State. He is probably the Ithaca, New York, potter whose stamp was J.B.MAGEE/ITHACA.

## THE DISTRICT OF COLUMBIA

Several nineteenth-century stoneware manufacturers were active in the District of Columbia and in Alexandria, Virginia, which until 1846 was a part of the district. The earliest was John Swann (1811–41), while most prominent were members of the Smith and Milburn families.

Hugh Smith (1825–41) is memorialized by rare examples marked H.C.SMITH/ALEXA./D.C.; while Benedict C. Milburn (1841–67), who bought the Swann business, was followed by sons J. A. and J. C. Milburn (1867–77). The father's impression was B.C.MILBURN/ALEX.

A later Alexandria firm was that of E. J. Miller (1856–67) whose impression was E.J.MILLER/ALEX. B. J. Miller, a son, managed the company into the 1880s. His period under the guidance of his father is marked by wares stamped E.J.MILLER & SON/ALEXANDRIA, VA.

The District of Columbia also had later manufactories. William H. Ernst made salt-glazed wares from 1840 until 1880, marking his products WM.H.ERNST/WASHINGTON/D.C.; while Enoch Burnett ran his shop at West Eighth and I streets from 1853 until 1869. Pieces impressed R.BUTT/W.CITY,D.C. suggest another presently undocumented maker. Most examples from the District of Columbia–Alexandria area resemble in form and decoration wares made in Pennsylvania, Maryland, or New York.

*Blue-decorated, salt-glazed stoneware jar with lug handles made by Hugh C. Smith (1825–41) and impressed* H.C.SMITH/ALEXA./D.C. *At this time Alexandria was part of Washington, D.C.*

# 12

# NORTH CAROLINA AND SOUTH CAROLINA

NORTH AND SOUTH CAROLINA were important stoneware manufacturing states in which both English and Germanic traditions had full play. Salt-glazed stoneware was the first product; but alkaline glazing, developed first in South Carolina, soon spread into its sister state, and craftsmen from here carried the tradition throughout the South and as far west as Texas.

## NORTH CAROLINA

The North Carolina stoneware industry rivals in age that of the earliest Northeastern centers. The three most important localities were Randolph and Moore counties where Seagrove was the traditional hub; Forsyth County, dominated by Moravian potters at Salem; and the Catawba River Valley area. During much of the nineteenth century these areas produced enough pottery that it was not only sold locally but also exported north to Virginia and west into Ten-

nessee. There was also a smaller concentration of potters in Buncombe County just north of Asheville.

The earliest stoneware maker may have been the Moravian Rudolph Christ (master at Salem, 1789–1821). Community records establish that he burned a kiln (probably salt glazed) on November 3, 1795; and by 1803 a separate listing of stoneware cream pots, "narrow neck jugs," mugs, and "night pots" (chamber pots) appeared in annual inventories. Despite this early start, the Moravians do not appear to have continued this line of business after Christ's retirement in 1821.

Another pioneer was the firm of Robins & Co. at Fayetteville in Cumberland County. Gurdon Robins, a transplanted Hartford, Connecticut, businessman, announced in the *Fayetteville Gazette* for March 16, 1820, that he had established a "MANUFACTORY OF STONE-WARE" in that community. The products listed—jugs, pots, pitchers, mugs, churns, kegs, chambers, and both common and fountain inks—were similar to those being made in the Northeast.

This is hardly surprising, for the master potter employed by Robins was another former Hartford resident, Edward Webster, who had learned his trade at the shop of his uncle McCloud Webster (active Hartford, 1810–40). Webster's wares were a mottled dark brown produced by salt glaze applied over an iron wash and in form showed the high-shouldered, delicate ovoid profile characteristic of the best early American stoneware. Excavation of the pottery site has revealed shards with incised decoration including elements of an eagle-and-shield design similar to known examples from Hartford and New Haven, Connecticut. A rare marked jug is impressed Gurdon Robins/& Co./Fayettville.

Though Robins's manufactory started off with high hopes and at the time of the 1820 industrial census was listed as having an annual production of $5,000, things did not go well. By 1823 Robins had failed and returned to Hartford. The mortgaged pottery passed to Charles McAllister, a local attorney.

However, the business did not come to an end. It appears that Webster ran it, first for McAllister and, by 1827 at the latest, in his own name. He remained active until 1838 when he removed to South Carolina. Four pieces stamped either EDWARD WEBSTER/Fayettville or simply EDWARD WEBSTER are known.

The first potters to work in Randolph County some fifty miles northwest of Fayetteville were Englishmen from the Staffordshire area. The patriarch is Peter Craven who was in Randolph County by 1760 after living first in New Jersey and Virginia. There is no evidence that he or his sons, John and Thomas, produced anything but redware. However, the third generation were stoneware makers, and it is possible that this too is due to the Webster family.

By 1830 Chester Webster, Edward's older brother, was in Fayetteville and shortly thereafter he moved to Coleridge in southwestern Randolph County. There he was employed as a potter first by Solomon Craven and then his son, Bartlet Yancy or B. Y. Craven. Chester, too, was trained in the Connecticut tradition, and, though no marked ware of his is known, he seems to have worked in Randolph County into the late 1870s; and his vocabulary of Connecticut form and decoration greatly influenced ceramic traditions in the area.

Particularly important is a group of twenty-one pieces of salt-glazed stoneware, some bearing dates from 1842 to 1879 and embellished with incised decorations of birds, fish, and flowers, which are attributed to Edward, Chester, and possibly Timothy Webster, the latter a younger brother who was in Randolph County about 1840. Known as the "Bird and Fish" group, these pieces show a level of sophistication in incised decoration seldom achieved elsewhere in the South.

Other members of the Craven family maintained the stoneware tradition in Randolph County until 1917. Among the better-known members of this prolific clan were Enoch S. Craven (1850–60), whose mark was E.S. CRAVEN, and Henry Craven (1845–55), whose son, Emery John (1870–80), impressed his wares E.J.V. CRAVEN. Most prolific was Jacob Dorris Craven (1855–90), who worked both in Randolph and in the Browers Mill area of adjoining Moore County. By 1860 he was producing 60,000 gallons of ware annually. Among his several marks are J.D. CRAVEN and J.D. Craven/Browers Mill, N.C.

Nor were the Cravens the only potting family in the vicinity. From the late eighteenth until the early twentieth century over two hundred potters worked in the Randolph, Moore, Chatham, and Montgomery County area. Prominent among these were members of the Cole family. William Cole was making redware in Randolph County before 1790, and his trade was continued by son Stephen and grandsons,

*Salt-glazed stoneware preserve jar, made and marked by Jacob Doris Craven, Randolph County, North Carolina, 1855–85. Craven was one of the state's most important potters.*

*Alkaline-glazed stoneware churn with cobalt blue band, North Carolina, 1870–90. Southern churns are characterized by one or more freestanding handles high on the body and an opposite lug handle.* ▶

Mark and Matthew, who began to produce salt-glazed wares early in the 1800s. The next generation settled in the Whynot area where Evan Cole (1860–95) was the first to mark his wares, stamping them COLE & CO. Many other members of the family were involved in the field well into the twentieth century.

Other Randolph County manufacturers were John F. Brower (1870–1900) whose shop produced blue-decorated salt-glazed wares stamped J.F.BROWER; William Henry Chrisco (1880–1920) whose pottery shop was, in 1969, purchased by the Smithsonian Institution and moved to Washington, D.C.; James M. Hayes of New Salem (1855–1900) whose stamp was J.M.HAYES; and Daniel Cagle whose pottery

was located (1880–1920) at Whynot. His mark was D.CAGLE.

Perhaps the most influential craftsmen in Chatham County, east of Randolph, were members of the Fox family. Jacob Fox came to the area from Bucks County, Pennsylvania, in 1779. While the father made redware, a son, Nicholas Fox (1797–1858) began to produce blue-decorated, salt-glazed stoneware in the 1830s.

Several pieces impressed N.FOX are known. The kiln at Siler City near the Randolph County line was continued by his son, Himer Jacob Fox (1850–85), whose pieces, stamped H.FOX, often bore an inscribed masonic emblem. So well done was the family work that the term "fox jug" came to be used for any particularly fine piece.

Other Chatham County artisans included Baxter N. Welch whose shop at Harper's Crossroads was in business from 1890 until 1905. Welch was both shrewd and optimistic. He leased a clay pit for $1 per year and for a term of ninety-nine years!

Moore County was home to a large number of potters, many of whom set up shop along the northern boundary close to Seagrove in Randolph County; the area became known in the late nineteenth century as "Pottersville." Early practitioners of the art were members of the Owen or Owens family. One branch was headed by Joseph Owen (1850–80); the other by James J. Owens (1855–90), whose mark J.J.OWENS Patent Jar appears on preserve jars. Members of both clans have continued to work in the ceramics field up to the present time. The Coles and Cravens were active here, too. Ruffin Cole established a small works at Carthage in the northeastern corner of the county in 1889, continuing it into the twentieth century, and his brother, Alfred, had a shop nearby 1900–10. J. D. Craven had a shop at Browers Mill, which was continued after 1890 by his son, Daniel.

The third major area of stoneware manufacture in North Carolina was located along the valley of the Catawba River in Lincoln and Catawba counties. The potters here were for the most part of German extraction rather than English, and the ware they produced was usually alkaline rather than salt glazed.

No firm link to the Edgefield, South Carolina, innovators in the field of alkaline glazes has yet been established; but it appears that some potters in both states had earlier migrated from

*Pig-form stoneware bank with a tan mineral glaze, attributed to North Carolina, 1870–1900.*

other locations in North Carolina where they may have been neighbors if not business associates, and from the mid-nineteenth century on craftsmen moved freely back and forth between the areas.

One of the most important Catawba sites was the rural community of Vale in the northwest corner of Lincoln County. Two important potteries were located here; those of Daniel Seagle and David Hartzog (Hartsoe). Seagle was working at the redware trade as early as 1828, and sometime around 1840 he began to make alkaline-glazed stoneware, often embellishing the finish with a drip glaze produced by melting glass fragments placed on the rim or handle of a piece.

Daniel Seagle died in 1867, and his shop was carried on by a son, James Franklin Seagle, until the late 1880s. Father and son produced very similar wares, often marked upon the shoulder, D.S. or, later, J.F.S.

A neighbor was David Hartzog, who also employed the melted glass technique on his alkaline-glazed vessels produced 1840–80. David had two potter sons, Daniel, who continued the family shop until at least 1896; and Sylvanus Leander (1875–1910) who worked nearby at two different sites; the first a few miles northwest of Vale, the second on the Lincoln-Maiden Road some ten miles east of Vale. The father's cipher was DAVID HARTZOG/HIS MAKE; while the sons used the stamps D.H. and S.L.H.

By 1850 five separate potteries were in operation around Vale, and as well as the more customary wares they were turning out small kegs or rundlets, ring jugs, and various trick jugs similar to those made in redware by Pennsylvania potters. Other forms closely resembled those made at Edgefield.

At Blackburn near Newton in adjoining Catawba County was the kiln of John Wesley Hilton (1870–1917). Like other western North Carolina artisans he employed both glass drip and cinder glazes on vessels stamped J.W.H. The business was continued until 1927 by his three sons. A second Catawba County shop was located (1900–15) near Probst Crossroads and owned by Thomas Phillips.

One of the first alkaline-glaze stoneware makers in western North Carolina was Edward W. Stone, who was active near Candler some ten miles southwest of Asheville as early as 1841. He was selling his wares in Edgefield that year, so he would have been well acquainted with the glazes used there. His mark, E.STONE, is rare. The business was continued until about 1865, with son, James Henry (mark, J.H.STONE) involved after 1860.

A few outlying North Carolina manufactories are also known. These include the salt-glaze works of W. W. Ballard (1872–94) located at Dockery (now Mt. View) in Wilkes County west of Winston-Salem, and an establishment at Jamestown in Guilford County a few miles southwest of Greensboro which was owned by a Quaker, Benjamin Beard. He made salt-glazed stoneware 1820–40 which was impressed BENJAMIN BEARD/GUILFORD COUNTY, N.C. In adjoining Alamance County was N. H. Nixon's

pottery (1860–80). His stoneware was stamped N.H.NIXON. Finally, there is the Broome Pottery in Alton, Union County, not far from the South Carolina border, The founder, Nimrod W. Broome (1850–90), was succeeded by his son "Jug Jim," who ran the works into the 1920s. Both Albany-slip and salt-glazed stoneware, including grave markers, were made here.

## SOUTH CAROLINA

Catherine Wilson Horne, the editor of *Crossroads of Clay: The Southern Alkaline-Glazed Stoneware Tradition,* calls South Carolina a "crossroads where European forms and technology, Asian glaze formulas and the distinctive forms and decorations produced by the African-Americans commingled." And, indeed, this seems to be the case.

The first potters were from the British Isles, familiar with both the techniques of stoneware manufacture and traditional redware slip decoration, which they adapted to embellish stoneware vessels glazed not with salt but with wood ashes or lime mixed with clay and water, a medium previously employed in China, Japan, and Korea but never in Europe. And many of the pottery employees were slaves or freemen whose memory of African forms may have influenced development of the face jug, the Southern vessel most familiar to collectors.

The focus of this activity was the Edgefield District in western South Carolina, along the Georgia border and in close proximity to Augusta. The first known manufacturer of any importance was Dr. Abner Landrum whose works at Pottersville (Edgefield) appears on an 1817 map of the area and who is thought by some to have originated local use of the alkaline glaze.

Speculation (and it will probably always remain just that) is that an Englishman, William Cookworthy, had access to letters by a French missionary that described the alkaline-glazing process as practiced in China; that Cookworthy transferred certain letters patent including this information to an English company, one of whose directors was Richard Champion; and that Champion came to South Carolina in 1784 where he may have imparted the secret of the glaze to local craftsmen. The fact remains that by 1821 (the date of an alkaline-glazed South Carolina vessel) the finish was being used in the Edgefield District. That it continued to be employed late into the nineteenth century reflects the fact that salt was scarce and expensive in the area. Though tedious to prepare, alkaline glazes could be made from materials that were cheap and readily available. Once commercial Albany-slip-type glazing materials, which were both modestly priced and easy to mix, appeared in the area, in the 1880s, most craftsmen abandoned alkaline finishes.

Though Abner Landrum sold his Pottersville Stoneware Manufactory in 1828, the business was continued by Reuben Drake with various partners through 1836; then by Nathaniel Ramey and associates until 1840. Later owners included Jasper Gibbs with various partners until the early 1850s and, finally, Francis W. Pickens who owned the shop until it was shut down about 1860. Known marked ware, all alkaline glazed, associated with this pottery includes a syrup jug signed in slip Drake,Rhodes/ Improved Stoneware and several pieces impressed N.RAMEY & CO.

Another early manufactory was that of Landrum's older brother, John, at Horse Creek just north of Vaucluse in Aiken County, some fifteen miles southeast of Edgefield. He was in business as early as 1817, and the trade was maintained by his son Benjamin F. and son-in-law Lewis Miles (who had had his own kiln at nearby Stoney Bluff since at least 1834) from 1847 until the 1860s; and by their sons, Benjamin F. Landrum, Jr., and John Miles into the late nineteenth century. It is clear that during at least some of this period the principals maintained

*Alkaline-glazed stoneware pot incised "Lm May 7, 1861 Dave" and made by Dave, a slave potter employed by Lewis Miles in the Edgefield District of South Carolina.*

separate shops. In 1850 they were valued at $1,800 and $4,000 respectively.

Lewis Miles is perhaps best known for the work of his slave, Dave, a turner active 1834–63, who threw large storage jars (to forty-gallon capacity), which were frequently incised with his master's mark, LM, dates, and charming doggerel such as "1858/This noble jar will hold 20/Fill it with silver and you will have plenty" or "Great and noble jar/Hold sheep, goat or bear." Marked Dave pieces now are among the highest priced of all Southern stoneware.

The youngest Landrum sibling, Amos, also had his own pottery, on Shaw's Creek a few miles east of the John Landrum site. Established about 1830, this shop passed to his son-in-law Collin Rhodes, and was continued by various owners until 1860.

Rhodes, however, is better known for his interest in another Shaw's Creek enterprise, the

Phoenix Factory, which he established with Robert Mathis in 1840, and which was the first South Carolina pottery to produce any quantity of decorated stoneware.

It is likely that the man primarily responsible for this innovation was Thomas Chandler, a Virginia-born potter who was probably trained in the Northeast (in 1832 he enlisted in the U.S. Army while in Albany, New York). Chandler's wares are much more in the North Atlantic States tradition than anything else being made in the Edgefield District at the time. The forms are more sophisticated, walls thinner, and the decoration of loops, swags, and tassels mirrors the Federal style evident in New York, Baltimore, and District of Columbia work. Moreover, his bold stamps, PHOENIX/FACTORY/ED.SC and FLINT WARE (a term for salt-glazed stoneware employed in the Northeast), stand out in a society where potters often were reluctant to add more than bare initials to their products.

Though it lasted only until 1846, the Phoenix Factory turned out some of the finest slip-decorated wares ever made in the South. Included among these are a remarkable water-cooler with a black wedding scene and a syrup jug embellished with the figure of a woman in a hoopskirt. Both are done in brown-and-white slip against a pale green ground and are attributed to Thomas Chandler. The wedding piece, in particular, is reminiscent of incised, blue-decorated wares from the Hudson Valley area of New York State.

Collin Rhodes acquired full ownership of the Phoenix Factory in 1846 and ran it under his own name through 1853. Ware was frequently inscribed in slip, C.Rhodes Maker or C.Rhodes/Factory, and a modest tradition of loop and floral slip decoration was continued.

Chandler, however, had moved on. From 1845 until 1849 he managed a pottery in McCormick County north of Edgefield; it was owned by his father-in-law John Trapp, who had purchased it from John Durham in 1843. Some finely decorated vessels, impressed TRAPP &/CHANDLER, date to this period. By 1850, however, Thomas Chandler had his own factory. In May of that year he announced in the *Edgefield Advertiser* that "believing that a good article of this useful and necessary Ware is much needed, (he) has come to the conclusion to make and keep on hand a splendid article, which he will not only recommend but will warrant to be good."

It is likely that this kiln, at Kirksey's Crossroads, was the same one or near the one he shared with Trapp. In any case, Chandler seems not to have been successful. Though the 1850 census listed him as having eleven employees and a business valued at $2,500, he left the state soon after, dying in North Carolina during the year 1854. A substantial number of Chandler's vessels have survived, most impressed CHANDLER, CHANDLER WARRANTED, or CHANDLER MAKER.

By the mid-1850s the creative period of the Edgefield District had passed. The innovators were gone, many of them to spread the doctrine of alkaline glaze throughout Georgia, North Carolina, Alabama, Mississippi, Florida, and Texas. However, ordinary ware continued to be made for local consumption. John W. Seigler, who had bought Collin Rhodes's Shaw's Creek shop in 1853, continued it with his son G. P. Seigler until late in the century. Two marks are known: J.W.S. & CO./Pine House, S.C. and G.P. SEIGLER/TRENTON,S.C. Another German potter, W. F. Hahn, established his business at Trenton in the 1880s, leaving behind some jars stamped W.F.HAHN/TRENTON/S.C.

Jesse P. Bodie, another manufacturer during this period, owned a kiln on Martintown Road near Kirksey's Crossroads which had been built

---

◀ *Alkaline-glazed stoneware jar with brown mineral slip decoration attributed to Amos Landrum, Shaw's Creek, South Carolina, 1830–40.*

around 1840 and was sold to him in 1870 by J. H. Burnett. Bodie remained active until 1884. His pots often bear the impression J.P.BODIE/ MAKER. There was also a stoneware factory at Miles Mill, south of Trenton, South Carolina; it was owned by John Miles in 1870, continued as the South Carolina Pottery Company (manufacturers of Majolica, Rockingham, and yellowware as well as stoneware) during the late 1880s and was still in business under the aegis of one Duke Harley in 1900.

Nor was the Edgefield District South Carolina's only source of stoneware. After leaving Pottersville, Abner Landrum owned a factory in Columbia 1832–59 which was continued by his son Linneaus Mead Landrum and son-in-law John Stork and their descendants into the twentieth century. Known marks include L.M.LANDRUM/COLUMBIA/S.C. Another émigré, Thomas Owensby, moved north to Cherokee

County near Spartanburg, where he worked until 1850. His son, Thomas Owensby, Jr., is said to have turned the jug inscribed "August the 30/ 1864/ Made and sold at/ a low price for Confederant/ Money by me Thomas Owenby." Other descendants ran this shop until the 1940s.

Another active center was "Jug Factory" near Gowensville on the Greenville/Spartanburg County line. First on the scene was William Henson, active 1840–80. His three sons guided the trade into the twentieth century. At the nearby community of Norah in Greenville County was the late-nineteenth-century establishment of Whelchel & Smith. One of their jugs is incised "Whelchel & Smith/Mfg. Co. Norah, S.C./ July 19, 1893." South of this area, in Laurens County near Clinton, was the rural shop of Joe Johnson, a North Carolina craftsman who turned ware during the 1880s.

Appropriately enough, considering what

they contributed to the early history of South Carolina stoneware, there were also some kilns owned by blacks. Josh Miles, whose shop was in the Horse Creek area of Aiken County, was employing a half-dozen workers in 1880, and Rich Williams was working on the Tyger River near Gowensville in the first decade of this century; his vessels were stamped WILLIAMS. In form and decoration his ware resembles that of his white competitors.

*Alkaline-glazed stoneware face jug with kaolin eyes and teeth attributed to the pottery of Thomas J. Davies, Edgefield District, South Carolina, 1860–65.*

# 13

# OTHER SOUTHERN KILNS

DURING THE mid-nineteenth century the stoneware traditions nurtured in Virginia and the Carolinas spread rapidly into adjoining states. Potters trained in the alkaline-glaze tradition were joined by others, particularly from Pennsylvania and Ohio, who were accustomed to salt glazes; while all were influenced after 1880 by the availability of commercial Albany-slip and Bristol-type finishes.

## GEORGIA

Lying on the direct route south and west for craftsmen migrating out of the Carolinas, Georgia played an important part in developing the Southern stoneware tradition. No less than eight different geographic areas in the state had large enough concentrations of potters to be termed "jug towns"; and alkaline glazes (often with a high concentration of lime producing an olive-green hue) were used by many shops well into the twentieth century.

Washington County, southwest of Augusta, was one of the earliest centers. Abraham Massey, trained in the Edgefield, South Carolina, district, was here by 1820 producing his distinctive "coffee boilers." Another Edgefield potter, Cyrus Cogburn, was in Washington County before 1840 but gone to Alabama by 1850, a common pattern of migration.

A more influential figure was James Long, a Maryland-born craftsman, who reached Crawford County near Macon in 1826 after working briefly with Massey. Long founded a ceramic dynasty that can be traced into the 1930s. Equally important, he made a monumental two-handled alkaline-glazed jar that bears a variety of applied decoration, including reliefs of Presidents Jefferson and Jackson, and is one of the few decorated pieces to come out of Georgia.

Long had four potter sons, one of whom, Jesse, created in 1871 a second rarity, a jug incised with a complete panorama of the fox hunt: hunters, hounds, dogs, and fox. Jesse's mark was JBL, and marked ware from other members of the family is also known: Jasper N. Long (1900–38), JNL; Henry Newton Long (1880–1902), HNL; and Virgil Oscar Long (1895–1900), *V.O. Long* in script.

Other Crawford County potters included members of the Becham family. John Becham, Sr., active 1830–50, had five sons who followed his trade over a forty-year period from 1850 until 1890. Two were Benjamin J. Becham, whose stamp was BB; and Washington Becham, whose impression, WB, appeared on the shoulder of his alkaline-glazed vessels. Washington's son, C. Jackson Becham (mark, CJB), continued the shop until the end of the century.

About thirty miles to the northwest along the line separating Upson and Pike counties was another "jug town," this one founded about 1841 by Thomas B. Bishop. His sons, Jasper A. and Henry H., appear to have abandoned their father's alkaline glaze. Jasper, whose known stamps are J.A.BISHOP/DELAY,GA. and J.A.BISHOP/KENZIE,GA., began working in the traditional manner in 1860; but by 1890 he was using an Albany-slip finish. Henry, who had his own shop at Digby in adjoining Spaulding County, 1860–80, is said to have made salt-glazed stoneware. A grandson, William Bishop, employed the same glaze (1880–1900) on vessels impressed W.D.BISHOP/MEANSVILLE,GA.

Another early jug town manufacturer was Bowling Brown, active in the Pike–Upson County area from the 1840s until he moved to Atlanta in 1864. Working with him were his sons, John S. Brown and Bowling P. Brown.

A third son, Thomas O. "Boss" Brown, had moved to Howell's Mills in northwest Atlanta around 1850; and by 1871 his father and two brothers had joined him at a pottery that the family continued to run until after 1900. Family marks include those of grandson Ulysses Adolphus Brown (U.A.BROWN), who operated the Howell's Mills business 1880–1900; William S. Brown (a brother of Bowling Brown), W.S. BROWN/HOWL'SMILLS,GA.; Bowling P. Brown (B.P.BROWN/ATLANTA,GA.); and Edward C. Brown (E.C.BROWN).

Some of these men appear to have worked at a second Atlanta vicinity site, in the Buckhead District of Fulton County, where Bowling Brown was residing by 1880. Ulysses's son, Horace V. "Jug" Brown, kept this shop active until the mid-1930s. Both kilns made primarily salt- and Albany-slip-glazed stoneware.

Nor were the Browns the only ones supplying Atlanta with stoneware. An earthenware shop established there in 1846 by J. R. Craven was converted to alkaline-glazed stoneware manufacture and continued until at least 1859 by Isaac Newton Craven. His hard-to-find wares are impressed I.N.CRAVEN. William Washington Rolander, whose mark was W.W.ROLANDER/ATLANTA,GA., made Albany-slip-glazed vessels 1875–1920; and his son, Ivon, maintained the shop until 1948. Around 1890 one C. S. Kline was also making stoneware in the city.

There was another manufactory of alkaline- and Albany-slip-glazed wares in Paulding County less than twenty miles northwest of Atlanta. The proprietor was John H. Sligh and the foundation date 1870. Upon Sligh's death in 1897 his wife, Sara Ann, assumed the management; and when she died in 1901 a son, Jacob, took over, maintaining the works until 1925.

By far the greatest concentration of Georgia potters was in White County and portions of adjoining Union and Habersham counties, in the mountainous northeast corner of the state. The Mossy Creek District just south of Cleveland, Georgia, was the heart of this activity.

One of the best-known family names here is Craven: John V. Craven was active before 1850. He was succeeded by Isaac Henry Craven (1860–1880), whose alkaline-glazed wares were stamped IHC. A third member of the clan, Isaac Newton Craven, left for Atlanta around 1850. Other early potters include Frank Anderson (1850–65), Bunk Holcomb (1850–80), and Clemmens Quillian Chandler (1840–50).

Perhaps first to exploit the clays of White County was a Virginia native, Nathan Pitchford, who was making stoneware there by 1822. He had four sons who, after Nathan's death in 1846, inherited the pottery. A third generation, in the form of grandson John Henry Pitchford, brought the business to the century's end. All used an alkaline glaze.

Members of the Dorsey family proved equally resilient. David L. Dorsey, from North Carolina, settled in Mossy Creek around 1840 but didn't run a pottery until 1860. However, his four sons all became potters, and spawned a number of local operations, some of which persisted into the 1920s and 1930s. Oddly enough, though, the most successful was a relative, William "Daddy Bill" Dorsey, who was not even a potter. He did, however, employ quite a few (1875–1920) at his manufactory near Cleveland; and his ware, stamped W.F.DORSEY, is not hard to find.

A much later pottery, though one that has received a great deal of collector attention, is that established at Cleveland in 1893 by John Milton Meaders. All six of his sons became potters, and a third generation, adapting to demand for "art" wares, face jugs, and similiar items, has carried the business down to the present day. Best known of these later artisans is Lanier Meaders.

Union County, northwest of White, had a manufactory of some consequence. It was owned from about 1870 until his death in 1903 by Wesley Jones. Part of this time he was in partnership with J. H. Thomas, and following Jones's death his son, Dock Jones, ran the shop until 1915. Alkaline- and Albany-slip-glazed stoneware were the products.

Another important area of activity, listed on local maps from 1847 until 1889, is "Jug Factory" on the Oconee River in present Jackson County. Charles H. Ferguson, who had worked in the Landrum Pottery in South Carolina, owned a pottery here 1826–46. His sons, William F. and James S., continued it through the 1860s; and grandsons, Van G. and George D. Ferguson, guided the business into the present century.

Other craftsmen active in the Jug Factory area of Jackson and Barrow counties included James M. Delay (1865–75) and his brothers Russell V. (1870–80) and John Milton (1860–97); and Nathaniel H. Hewell (1857–87) and his four sons. A descendant, Harold Hewell, continues to operate their factory at nearby Gillsville.

Elbert County, to the east and on the South Carolina border, had a late stoneware shop whose wares, produced by the Cade family, were stamped, simply, CADE. There were many other local kilns whose histories remain to be explored.

## ALABAMA

Though individual potters worked throughout the state, there were three main focal points of the Alabama craft: Baldwin County near Mobile, Randolph County in the east, and the northwestern counties of Lamar and Marion.

By far the earliest was Baldwin, where French and later English potters were active during the eighteenth century. Initial products were brick, tile, and earthenware; but early in the nineteenth century craftsmen from the Northeastern states brought salt-glazed techniques to the area. A jug form of 1820–40 with abstract cobalt floral decoration in the New York–Pennsylvania manner and the mark BAMA CITY is attributed to Fairhope, on the eastern shore of Mobile Bay some ten miles south of Mobile. Its maker is unknown, but later Baldwin County craftsmen reflect a wide ethnic range.

By 1850 the firm of L. & L. Lafever (1845–60) was producing three thousand gallons of stoneware yearly; and another potter of French descent, named LaCoste, was working at Daphne, five miles north of Fairhope, in the 1860s. His daughter married Abraham Miller, a German-American from Lancaster County, Pennsylvania, who after working at Daphne 1866–72 established his own kiln in Pickens County northwest of Tuscaloosa. By 1883 he was at Sprott in Perry County, where his son, grandson, and great-grandson continued to make stoneware from local clay until 1980.

Another German craftsman was Jacob Wingender, whose family ran an important manufactory in Haddonfield, New Jersey. Jacob

moved to Marlow about ten miles southeast of Fairhope in the 1890s and was still in business in 1910. His Albany-slip-glazed stoneware was impressed J. WINGENDER/MARLOW, AL.

The Scotsman John McAdams settled at Montrose on the coast between Daphne and Fairhope in the 1870s. He and his children remained in business until around 1890. The only identifiable piece from this kiln is a face jug, far more sophisticated than most, which is Albany-slip glazed and incised McAdams/Montrose/Pottery.

Other potters included Joseph Gabel of Montrose (1875–85), whose daughter, Belle, was an accomplished turner; Edward Boudy, a potter who had worked in New York and Ohio and was employed during the 1850s in Baldwin County; and Homer Howard, another Ohio craftsman active during the mid-nineteenth century.

Later marked ware from Mobile County bears the impressions of Owen Farley (OWEN FARLEY/MOBILE), active 1875–80; James Beasley (JAMES BEASELEY/MONTROSE) who worked at Montrose during the 1880s, and MOBILE POTTERY/M.F. KIRKSBRIDE, PROP., for M. F. Kirksbride, whose manufactory turned out a substantial quantity of Albany-slip-glazed ware during the last quarter of the nineteenth century.

Another important area was Randolph County on the Georgia border. Potters from North and South Carolina, familiar with alkaline glazes, paused here on their way west during the 1840s and 1850s; some remained to establish kilns at Rock Mills and nearby Bacon Level.

One of the earliest of these pioneers was Elijah McPherson, a South Carolina craftsman, who was in Randolph County by 1840 and still running his own kiln a decade later. William and Napoleon B. McPherson, probably his sons, had their own shops in Rock Mills by 1860. William's operation was quite extensive, producing no less than 36,000 gallons of ware annually. Also from South Carolina was Matthew

*Salt-glazed stoneware jar attributed to Alabama, 1850–1900. These large vessels served a variety of storage purposes.*

Duncan, who remained in the county from 1840 until 1846 before going west to Texas. His son, Samuel W., continued to work near Rock Mills until sometime in the 1850s; but by the time of the 1860 census he had established a thriving business just to the south in Chambers County. He continued there until at least 1880.

Sharp competition was provided by the Boggs family, the Pittmans, and the Usserys. Andrew Jackson Boggs began making alkaline-glazed stoneware in the Rock Mills vicinity around 1830, and his descendants, particularly James Andrews Boggs (1890–1930), continued the business into this century. A salt-glazed vessel incised J.A. Boggs/June 19, 1895 is known. The Pittman family was allied during the 1870s with the Boggs clan in a partnership that produced salt-glazed wares impressed PITTMAN & BOGGS; but by 1880 the firm had become Pittman and Brothers. It continued until 1920. The mark was PITTMAN & BROS./ROCK MILLS, ALA. The first Ussery was Milton J., who appears in the 1850 census. By 1860 Jackson Ussery was making 13,000 gallons of stoneware each year; and a descendant, A. A. Ussery, was still busy at Rock Mills in 1880.

Among the better-known workers at nearby Bacon Level was E. T. Mapp, 1870–1910, whose well-formed wares were given an alkaline finish and often stamped E.T. MAPP. His competitors also included members of the Ussery family. Calvin J. Ussery ran a pottery as well as a sawmill at Bacon Level at the turn of this century. Yet another Ussery, W.J., went west to Walker County, northwest of Birmingham, where the 1850 census recorded him as a potter producing a modest thousand gallons a year in alkaline-glazed stoneware.

DeKalb County, to the north along the Georgia line, also had its share of potters. The Alabama Pottery Company (1890–1910), makers of Bristol- and Albany-slip-glazed wares stenciled ALABAMA POTTERY CO./FT. PAYNE, ALA., was heir to a tradition going back to Elizer McPherson, who made alkaline-glazed wares embellished with glass melt decoration at Fort Payne from 1875 until 1900.

The other major location was Lamar and Marion counties in northwestern Alabama at the Mississippi border. Here the emphasis was on salt glazing, probably due to the influence of Peter Cribbs, an Ohio potter from the Canton area. After a period in Mississippi, Peter settled near Bedford in Lamar County in 1841. Following his death around 1875 his widow continued the business until 1900, employing two former Cribbs slaves, Major and Captain. One of Cribbs's offspring, a son named Fleming, had his own kiln at Sulligent in Lamar County during the last quarter of the nineteenth century.

His competition came from J. D. Green, active 1890–1900, and the firm of Lloyd & Guthery at Pine Springs which made both stoneware and earthenware from 1870 until 1887.

Adjacent Marion County also produced a great deal of stoneware. The Lloyds were active here, too. Isham James Lloyd, from Tennessee, settled at Bull Mountain Creek between 1840 and 1850; and his son, Steven C., continued the shop until his death in 1868. Among the items for which this family is known are blue-decorated, salt-glazed tombstones. Another important potting clan was that founded by Billy Rye, also from Tennessee, who moved to Detroit, Alabama, in the late 1850s or early 1860s. He and his sons, William and Washington, founded a dynasty that persisted until the time of the Second World War. Yet another craftsman was D. F. Summerford of Bexar on Route 78 near the Mississippi line. He made Bristol-glazed stoneware, marked D.F.SUMMERFORD/BEXAR,ALA., from 1890 into the early years of this century.

Peter Cribbs's brother, Daniel, established what was probably the most important pottery in western Alabama when, in 1829, he opened a shop near Tuscaloosa. His salt-glazed vessels, stamped DAN'L CRIBBS/TUSCALOOSA, are highly prized. By 1860 this manufactory could boast of an output of 60,000 gallons per year. Daniel's son, Harvey H., became county sheriff and managed the family business until the early 1900s. Another Tuscaloosa maker was Charles K. Oliver (1855–80), who produced both salt- and alkaline-glazed wares. His mark was C.K.OLIVER.

There were potters active in other areas of the state as well. Joel E. Falkner, from Georgia, opened a business near Sterrett in Shelby County, a few miles east of Birmingham in the 1850s. His incised mark, J.E.FALKNER, is rare; after his death in 1864, his son, W. Hilliard, maintained the shop through the 1880s. The Falkners' lime-glazed grave markers were ad-vertised through local newspapers. A later manufacturer (1900–20) in the vicinity was Albert A. Bruner; while Evan Presley had a substantial shop in Autauga County near Montgomery during the mid-nineteenth century. The 1850 census credits him with a yearly output of 15,000 gallons.

There were many other potters in Alabama, but reluctance to mark their wares makes them hard to trace. However, they had good reasons for this lack of individual identification. When asked about it, a twentieth-century representative of the craft, Jerry Brown, simply replied, "I'll always know if I made it by looking at it" (quoted in *The Traditional Pottery of Alabama*, Montgomery Museum of Fine Arts, 1983).

## FLORIDA

Though there were good clay sources, particularly in the western part of the state, Florida never developed a stoneware industry. At present only a single pottery is known, which existed for a brief period at Knox Hill in Walton County, some eighty miles east of the Mobile Bay area. In the collection of the Florida State Museum is a large alkaline-glazed jar with lug handles attributed to M. M. Odom and Robert Turnlee, 1850–59. Shards of similar pieces have been recovered at the pottery site, but nothing else is known of this venture.

## MISSISSIPPI

Mississippi, Alabama's neighbor to the west, inherited a substantial number of alkaline-glaze specialists from that state and from South Carolina. However, the most important center, in northern Marshall County, was primarily given over to potters, many from neighboring Tennessee, who worked in salt glaze or, later, Albany and Bristol slips.

The Holly Springs area of Marshall County contains rich banks of stoneware clay, and by 1870 an active community of potters had arrived to take advantage of this resource. Among the better known are C. Joseph Herr who made salt-glazed wares stamped C.J. HERR/HOLLY SPRINGS, MISS., 1870–80; H. W. Steinbliss, another German craftsman, whose wares were stenciled H.W.STEINBLISS & CO./HOLLY SPRINGS, MISS.; and the later Allison Pottery, which remained in business from 1890 until well into this century. In nearby Jackson was the shop of yet another immigrant, Anton Schaab (1870–80), whose stoneware was impressed A.SCHAAB.

One of the earliest Alabama practitioners of the salt-glazing method was Peter Cribbs from Ohio, who settled in Monroe County southeast of Holly Springs in 1829. Though he moved across the line to Lamar County, Alabama, in 1841, he left behind a legacy of stoneware form and decoration.

The best-known craftsman from adjoining Itawamba County was John C. Humphries, who made salt- and Bristol-glazed stoneware with cobalt blue decoration from 1875 until 1900. Among his products were grave markers. The business passed to his son, E. J. Humphries, still working around 1920.

However, not all the potters in the east used a salt glaze. The Kentucky-bred William B. Brush, who established himself in Tippah County adjacent to Marshall around 1850, produced alkaline-glazed wares; as did Holland Leopard, a native son of South Carolina, who moved to Winston County, Mississippi, around 1850 after working in Georgia. His son, Thad, maintained the family manufactory until 1900. Well-formed pieces impressed TL are attributed to him.

Water Valley in Yalobusha County, some forty miles south of Holly Springs, was home to one of Mississippi's last alkaline-glaze potters. Benjamin Franklin Ussery, an itinerant who had worked in North Carolina, Tennessee, Georgia, and Alabama, finally settled down there around 1875. During the next decade he turned out a variety of wares impressed B.F. USSERY/WATER VALLEY, MISS.; early examples bore an alkaline finish, but after 1880 he turned to powdered Albany slip.

Much farther south is Jones County and the community of Laurel, a bit more than twenty miles north of Hattiesburg. The Rushton family, who had come from North Carolina and worked in Alabama, owned a pottery here before 1860. Most involved were B. J. Rushton (1860–70) and O. E. Rushton. Their alkaline-glazed vessels appear to have been unmarked. The site of their kiln has been excavated disclosing numerous shards with a dark alkaline glaze.

Central Mississippi had only a few potteries. One of these was at Canton in Madison County north of Jackson. The proprietor was L. P. Hossley, in business 1890–1905. His Bristol-glazed pots were often stenciled L.P.HOSSLEY/AT WOLNER'S CORNER/CANTON MISS.

Two manufactories on the western border, along the Mississippi River, are known. C. J. Miller of Vicksburg began the production of Bristol-glazed stoneware around 1890. His son, W.F., continued the business from 1910 until 1930. Their stenciled marks are C.J.MILLER/VICKSBURG,MISS. and W.F.MILLER/VICKSBURG, MISS. Downriver, at Natchez, was the shop of another maker of Bristol-glazed wares, A. J. Smith. He had been born in Illinois but by 1880 was running a pottery on Franklin Street, which he continued until late in the century. His products were stenciled A.J.SMITH/604 FRANKLIN ST./NATCHEZ, MISS.

## TENNESSEE

As with neighboring Mississippi, most of Tennessee's important stoneware-making establishments date to the second half of the nineteenth century. Craftsmen from the Midwest, Virginia, and North Carolina, accustomed to salt glazing, moved into the state and established a widespread craft of which at present little is known.

One of the earliest centers was at Baxter in Putnam County about fifty miles east of Nashville. The LaFever family (thought to be related to potters of the same name who worked in Lincoln County, North Carolina, and Mobile County, Alabama) established a kiln around 1840. Eli LaFever, a descendant of the founders, was still working here 1900–25.

There was apparently enough business to support more than one shop, as at least two other potters practiced independently during the 1800s. These were William Hedicaugh (1870–1900) and Monroe Vickers (1880–1900).

Northeastern Tennessee, bordering Virginia, was closely allied in technique to the practices of the Germanic potters who worked in the Shenandoah Valley and along the Great Road south from Pennsylvania. Best known of these craftsmen is Charles Decker. After employment in Philadelphia at the Remmey factory and later in Abingdon, Virginia, he settled in 1872 near Johnson City, Washington County, where he worked until 1906. He brought to the isolated Nolichucky River Valley the turning and decorating skills of a metropolitan craftsman, and turned out wares, such as cobalt-decorated inkwells, banks, sugar bowls, gatepost ornaments, and massive garden urns not typical of local potters. He also made a more traditional Southern form, the grave marker, and an unusual salt-glazed hunting horn.

Decker had four sons, all of whom practiced his trade and, at times, up to twenty-five employees. His Keystone Pottery, as shown in an 1895 photograph, was a sizable structure. Most wares, however, were unmarked or simply impressed with a "D." An unusual lawn ornament, shaped by his eldest son, is stamped MADE BY/CHARLES F. DECKER, JR./KEYSTONE POTTERY/CHUCKY VALLEY, TENN./JAN. 15, 1885.

William Grindstaff, who worked 1870–1900 in Blount and Knox counties to the west, produced both redware and stoneware, including an Albany-slip-glazed face jug. He is also the maker of the only other known stoneware hunting horn, a salt-glazed specimen impressed W. GRINSTAFF 1871. Rivals in the Happy Valley area were J. D. Garner, 1888–96, and William Wolfe, who ran a kiln at Blountville, 1848–56, before moving to Wise County, Virginia.

Most of Tennessee's large cities had at least one stoneware kiln. Among those presently known are that of the Montague family in Chattanooga 1875–1900; the Harley Pottery in Nashville, which opened for business in 1870 and continued through 1905; and Richard B. Keller, who made salt- and Albany-slip-glazed vessels impressed R. B. KELLER at Memphis from 1890 until 1916.

Earlier potteries were usually located in smaller communities such as Grand Junction in Hardeman County, east of Memphis and close to the Mississippi border. The itinerant craftsman B. F. Ussery settled here in 1860 and continued to produce utilitarian salt-glazed vessels stamped BFU until 1875 when he moved south to Yalobusha County, Mississippi. His replacement may have been Samuel Smyth, who came up from Marshall County in that state to run his own shop 1887–91 at Grand Junction. Another small concern was run by P. Harmon, who was located in Greene County in northeastern Tennessee. His shop in the Appalachian foothills lasted a long time, from 1855 until 1890. Other relatively isolated stoneware makers were Adam Cable of Sulphur Fork (1869–75); C. L. Krager, a German potter who worked at Daisey from 1870 until 1900; and the Russell family, whose kiln in Paris, Henry County, up near the Kentucky border produced salt-glazed wares from 1855 until 1900.

# 14

## OHIO

AS WITH PENNSYLVANIA, the sheer magnitude of the Ohio pottery industry has discouraged a statewide study. Over a thousand potters worked here, and dozens of individual shops flourished during the course of a century.

Stoneware kilns were scattered throughout the state, located in most cases adjacent to rich veins of suitable clay which were plentiful within its borders. Zanesville, on the Muskingum River in the county of the same name, was the first important center. Samuel Sullivan built a small shop here in 1808, and the Connecticut craftsman Solomon Purdy had arrived by 1812; they were closely followed by Jacob Rosier, whose business at nearby Jonathan Creek was active by 1814. Earlier than all these may have been the partnership that left behind the ware stamped SMITH & JONES/SLAGO POTTERY, dated by some to 1804.

In any case, by 1840 there were twenty-two potteries in Muskingum County; and their products were shipped via the Muskingum,

Ohio, and Mississippi rivers as far south as New Orleans. Among these firms were Howson & Hallam (1840–50); A. B. Lake, whose impression, A.B. LAKE/MANUFACTURER OF/STONEWARE is dated 1830–50; the Star Pottery, active into the late nineteenth century; and the Zanesville Stoneware Company established in 1887 and continuing into this century.

Included in the earlier marked wares is a cooler incised Oliver Dubois/Zanesville, Ohio/ Sept 11th 1821/Price $2.00. Like much Ohio ware of this period, it resembles pottery being made at the same time in New York, New England, and Pennslyvania. And well it might, for it was from these states that many pioneer Ohio craftsmen came.

Even more important as a pottery center was Summit County in northern Ohio, which is well covered in C. Dean Blair's *The Potters and Potteries of Summit County, 1828–1915*. The focus of the trade was Akron and the impetus a canal dug in 1827 between there and Cleveland on

Lake Erie. With clay, transportation, and a ready market, potters could not be far behind. The little-known firm of Fisk & Smith opened its doors at nearby Ellet in 1828, and before the year was out Solomon Purdy arrived from Zanesville. Another Connecticut potter, Edwin H. Merrill, came down from Painesville northeast of Cleveland to work for Fisk & Smith. He bought them out in 1833, establishing a family firm that continued through 1900. Known marks include E. H. MERRILL & SON, E.H. MERRILL CO./AKRON, OHIO, and C.J. MERRILL/AKRON, OH.

Initially, most of the shops were located at Mogadore, some five miles southeast of Akron center and where the Purdy family relocated in the early 1830s. They were soon joined by others. Eight different manufactories were in competition there by 1841, and the numerous employees became at times so boisterous that the Justice of the Peace was required to build the community's first jail. Appropriately enough, the cost of construction was levied upon the pottery workers!

Besides the Purdys, the important early makers were Isaac M. Mead and Franklin L. Sheldon. The former was active 1840–60, leaving behind a substantial quantity of ware impressed MEAD/OHIO, I.M. MEAD/MOGADORE, OHIO, and I.M. MEAD CO. The latter was a Massachusetts potter who had worked in Jordan, New York, 1840–45. He established himself at Mogadore in the latter year and maintained his business until 1878. Though his New York ware was marked, he seems to have left no signed Ohio examples. Solomon Purdy's shop was continued after 1840 by his son, Henry (1840–50), whose ware was impressed H. PURDY/OHIO or H.E. PURDY. The earlier ware, stamped S. PURDY, might be attributed either to Zanesville or Mogadore.

Other Mogadore craftsmen include R. S. Baird (1845–55); J. S. Monroe & Sons (1845–85); Hill, Foster & Co. (1849–51, continued by E. H. Hill until 1892); Myers and Hall (1866–96); S. L. Stoll (1864–73); Nicholas Fosbinder

*Blue-decorated, salt-glazed churn marked* I.M. MEAD/ MOGADORE, OHIO. *Made by Isaac M. Mead, Mogadore, Ohio, 1840–60.*

*Blue-decorated, salt-glazed jug stamped* H. PURDY/OHIO *and manufactured at Mogadore, Ohio, 1840–50 by Henry Purdy.*

(1860–85); and Martin & Hall (1866–68, continued as Martin Brothers until 1884). Few of these manufacturers marked their ware.

During a single year, December 1843 to November 1844, teamsters hauled 659,000 pounds of Mogadore ware to the canal at Akron. This transportation cost represented a substantial burden to the pottery owners. The first to opt for a location closer to the canal were the Merrills who, in 1847, relocated to Middlebury (now East Akron). Others quickly followed. During the period 1850–1920 some two dozen stoneware potteries operated in Akron (known as "Stoneware City") and its suburbs. Among the longer lasting were Alexander J. Park (1862–85); Johnson & Dewey (1860–73), continued from 1873 until 1884 as Johnson and Baldwin; F. J. Knapp & Co. (1860–89); Shenkle Bros. & Mann (1865–71), succeeded by W. M. Shenkle & Co., 1871–80; Spafford & Richards (1865–76), then Spafford & Miner until 1880; The Akron Stoneware Company (1879–1900); Cook, Fairbanks & Co. (1877–98), continued 1898–1912 as William Fairbanks & Son; The Ohio Stoneware Company (1881–1912); and Weeks, Cook & Weeks (1883–88), which was Weeks Brothers (Arthur and Frederick) from 1888 until 1891 and F. H. Weeks during the period 1891–1910.

Oddly enough, many of these often large manufactories appear not to have marked their ware. Weeks was an exception, leaving behind examples impressed WEEKS BROS./AKRON and F.H.WEEKS/AKRON,O. Other known marks are JOHNSON & BALDWIN/AKRON,OHIO (1873–84); WM.ROWLEY,MANUFACTURER/MIDDLEBURY (1875–83); H. RHODENBAUGH (1860–70); BOSS BROS./MIDDLEBURY,O. (1860–65); CHAPMAN, UPSON/AND WRIGHT/MANUFACTURERS/MIDDLEBURY,OHIO (1850–60); VIALL & MARKLE (1860–80), and U.S.-STONEWARE CO./AKRON,OHIO (1889–1915). The last stamp appeared often on sponge-decorated, molded stoneware, a popular item at the turn of the century.

One of the best-known Akron manufactories

was established in 1900 when the venerable E. H. Merrill Company combined with Whitmore, Robinson & Co. (founded 1862) to form the Robinson Clay Products Company whose mark, R.C.P. CO./AKRON,O. or ROBINSON CLAY PRODUCTS CO./AKRON/OHIO, graced richly decorated molded stoneware through 1915.

Despite early successes the Akron factories, like others throughout the country, fell upon hard times at the end of the nineteenth century. In an effort to curb rampant competition, seven of the firms formed the Akron Pottery Company in 1896. Though this association lasted but four years, it left behind some interesting marked wares, including Bristol-glazed, brown-spotted Staffordshire-type dogs marked AKRON POTTERY CO.

*Molded stoneware watercooler with cobalt highlights on a Bristol-slip ground. Manufactured 1900–15 by the Robinson Clay Products Company of Akron, Ohio. The firm's stenciled mark appears on the base.*

*Molded stoneware dog with brown mineral slip spots on a Bristol-slip finish. Made by the Akron Pottery Company, Akron, Ohio, 1896–1900.*

Other communities in what is now greater Akron that had pottery operations include Tallmadge, Cuyahoga Falls, and Portage Lakes. Tom Cave, working about 1840, is said to have been the first craftsman at Tallmadge, followed by Clark & Fenn (1845–50); Thomas H. Fenton & Co. (1850–75); Alvin S. Moore (1850–70); Thomas Harris (1863–80), whose ware, stamped T.HARRIS, is eagerly sought after, and Haynes & Felix (1872–80).

J. R. Thomas established the first stoneware works at Cuyahoga Falls in 1857, continuing it until 1887; while Jacob Welsh, who had previously worked in Mogadore, removed to Barberton (formerly New Portage) in 1850, remaining active until 1862 despite the fact that the pottery was twice burned out. His ware is impressed WELSH POTTERY/NEW PORTAGE, OHIO. Doylestown, three miles southwest of Barberton, had an earlier kiln, built in 1835 and operated until around 1845 by Samuel Routson. Soon after this he moved his business south-

west to Wooster, where he was active into the 1850s. The impressed mark, S.ROUTSON, is usually found on brown-glazed or lightly decorated wares, though an early salt-glazed example is stamped ROUGH & READY/S. ROUTSON/ DOYLESTON, O.

Both Canton and Massillon, which lie about twenty miles south of Akron and are five miles apart, had stoneware shops. The Massillon Stoneware Company was in business 1882–1900, while Canton's Shorb family, Adam A. and Adam L., made salt-glazed wares from about 1842 until 1850. A nearby competitor was the Navarre Stoneware Company (1880–90), only a few miles south of Massillon.

There was also a small but important kiln at Atwater in Portage County some fifteen miles east of Akron. Gordon Purdy, son of Solomon of Zanesville and Mogadore, established himself there around 1855. During the decade or so he worked in Atwater, Purdy turned out some remarkable decorated wares, including a large double-handled watercooler embellished with a human figure, American flags, and an overflowing cornucopia, all in a rich, cobalt blue. The mark G.PURDY/ATWATER,O. distinguishes these choice examples. A second Portage County potter, Jacob Bennage, was trained at Mogadore and left behind a few 1836–40 pots impressed J.BENNAGE/PORTAGE CO. OHIO before migrating to Parke County, Indiana.

To the north, on Lake Erie, there were several pottery operations. The Merrill family was making stoneware at Painesville, twenty-five miles northeast of Cleveland, before 1830; they transferred their operations to Summit County in 1833. Cleveland had several stoneware manufacturers, among them Daniel Fisk (1835–37), who marked his bulbous wares D.FISK, and A. D. Higgins, who was in business from 1837 until 1850.

Nor was Zanesville the only center in central and southern Ohio. One of Ohio's most creative and interesting potters was E. Hall, who worked in Muskingum and Tuscarawas counties in the 1850s. In 1856 he made and signed a large double-handled watercooler, intended as an ad-vertising piece for a firm of retail stoneware dealers, which was covered with decorative elements: an applied heart and floral motifs, impressed stamping, and an unusual towerlike stopper as well as the impression MADE BY E.HALL/OF NEWTON TOWNSHIP/MUSKINGUM CO. OHIO/AT W.P.HARRISES FACTORY. Two years later he was in Tuscarawas County south of Canton where he produced stoneware impressed

*Blue-decorated, salt-glazed stoneware jug marked
J. BENNAGE/1837 and made in Portage County, Ohio,
by Jacob Bennage, a potter who later worked in Indiana.*

*Blue-decorated, salt-glazed stoneware jar marked D.FISK
for Daniel Fisk who worked in Cleveland, 1835–37,
as well as in Cuyahoga County and the Akron area.*

*Small "patent" jug with wire bale handle with incised and cobalt slip decoration on a Bristol-slip ground. The name, Joseph Patton, is not that of a known potter; and Copley, Ohio, did not have a stoneware manufactory. The piece was probably produced 1900–10 as a gift.*

E. HALL/TUSCARARAS CTY. OHIO and E. HALL/OHIO. He is believed to have worked here until about 1860.

The southwestern quarter of the state had a substantial number of shops, though many of them remain relatively unexplored. Amon Jenkins built a kiln on Front Street in Columbus about 1840, managing it until 1864 when a son, William, took charge. He continued until 1868. Chillicothe, thirty-five miles to the south, was home to the firm of George L. Wolfe and B. Howson from 1860 until 1870, while there had been much earlier stoneware makers at Hillsboro and Mount Sterling. Richard Illif is said to have been producing salt-glazed wares at Hillsboro, thirty miles west of Chillicothe, before 1820; while Lazier Burley was active about 1825 at Mount Sterling, a small community twenty miles southwest of Columbus. Little is known of either potter.

Cincinnati, on the Ohio River, was an important manufacturing and transportation center with numerous potteries making redware, stoneware, and yellowwares. Uriah Kendall, who established a business there about 1830, made salt-glazed pieces, marked U. KENDALL/FACTORY/CIN., until 1840 when his sons took over. They converted the plant to a yellowware manufactory. Much the same was true of the English potter George Scott. His shop,

built to make stoneware around 1840, was turning out fancier items by mid-century. Among the potters who worked here was the well-known Illinois craftsman Cornwall Kirkpatrick, who ran the so-called "Fulton Pottery" from 1853 until 1857.

Kirkpatrick was even more involved in a stoneware manufactory at Point Pleasant on the Ohio about twenty-five miles southeast of Cincinnati. This business had been started about 1838 by William P. Lakin and was sold in 1849 to Cornwall Kirkpatrick, who operated it until 1856. Nathan Davis, the new owner, continued until his death in 1874, then George, Henry, and James Peterson kept the shop active through 1890. It was one of the larger potteries in southern Ohio, producing 35,000 gallons in 1850. Like most later Ohio stoneware, Point Pleasant ware was unmarked.

# 15

# INDIANA AND ILLINOIS

THE STATES OF Indiana and Illinois underwent major population expansion in the second quarter of the nineteenth century; among the arriving settlers were potters, most of whom had previously worked in New York, Pennsylvania, Ohio, or Virginia. They brought with them a variety of styles and techniques, ranging from ovoid, blue-decorated jugs of the sort usually associated with early New York and New England to plain cylindrical vessels dipped in solid brown glazes not unlike those seen on Southern wares.

## INDIANA

The Indiana industry was centered in the western part of the state, primarily in Clay, Parke, and Putnam counties where rich deposits of stoneware clay were found. There were other important locations, particularly along the Ohio River which forms the state's southern boundary.

Longest lasting of the Indiana sites is that at Clay City, a little over ten miles southeast of Terre Haute. A New York craftsman, Truman Smith, built a stoneware shop here around 1845. His salt-glazed ovoid wares, impressed TRUMAN SMITH, are similar to examples then being made in the Empire State.

Smith died in 1861, and a son, Ralph D., who had worked with him, conveyed the business to John Everhart in 1867. Everhart leased the kiln to various potters until 1881 when he sold the site. Four years later it came into the hands of Beryl Griffith, a potter from Vermillion, Illinois. He ran the pottery until 1911 when he turned it over to his son, Clyde, who, in turn, passed it on to his son, Lloyd, in 1938. Lloyd Griffith's daughter, Cheryl, continues the Clay City Pottery to this day.

Clay County was home to over twenty different potteries during the nineteenth and early twentieth centuries, more than twice the number to be found in any other Indiana county. Among the earlier manufacturers was John B.

Ziegler who, though he was active here for only a few months in 1853, left behind quite a few blue-decorated semiovoid pieces impressed J.B. ZIEGLER. By 1867 he was in Kansas, where he practiced his trade until at least 1870.

Another important potter in the vicinity was Francis Nolen (1850–54) of Cloverland, ten miles east of Terre Haute who turned out a churn with blue-filled scratch work of a leafy plant, the only known piece of Indiana stoneware with incised decoration. Nolen's pottery at Cloverland had been established in 1847 by Jacob Bennage, another Ohio potter, whose bulbous jugs were impressed J. BENNAGE and lightly touched with cobalt. Nolen bought the works in 1851, but sold out in 1854 to the Pennsylvania craftsman Henry Flowers who, with his brother Lewis, continued until at least 1870.

Other Clay County shops included those of Neal Vestel (1843–51), a Virginia native who later moved to Kansas, and Hezekiah Perry

(1851–71) who were located just north of Brazil; Levi Brackney (1856–61), succeeded by Cyrus Rinehart (1861–69), also of Brazil Township; and George Husher, whose shop was a mile west of the community center. Husher was from Ohio and had worked in Illinois, but by 1856 he was in Clay County where he opened a kiln prior to 1860. His impressed mark, GEO. HUSHER/BRAZIL, IND., is found on a substantial quantity of ware, for he remained active until 1877 when he went bankrupt. Though Husher's home was sold to pay his debts, his old log potter's shop still stands. While much of Hush-

*Stoneware pudding crock with a brown mineral slip glaze made 1856–61 by Levi Brackney of Brazil Township, Indiana.*

er's ware was salt glazed he produced some pieces that appear to be ash glazed in the Southern manner.

Clay County's most important factories were located in and around Brazil, a sizable community fifteen miles northeast of Terre Haute. The Delaware craftsman William R. Torbert opened a pottery at Walnut Street and Railroad in 1859. His straight-sided vessels were usually brown-slip glazed and stamped W.R. TORBERT. By 1859 George Baker had joined the firm which remained active until 1899. Pieces marked TORBERT & BAKER are usually salt glazed and often decorated with a stenciled cobalt wreath surrounding the gallon capacity number.

Nearby, on Murphy Avenue, was another long-lived operation, that of Isaac Cordery, a New Jersey native who had worked in Ohio and had in 1856 purchased his own kiln site in Brazil. By 1869 he was producing 50,000 gallons of stoneware each year (which sold for eight cents per gallon delivered).

In 1873, Isaac's son, William, in partnership with David D., George, and Silivin Weaver, converted the works to the manufacture of stoneware water pumps, a specialization as profitable as it was unique; for the business continued until around 1910. The salt-glazed pumps were made in press molds and proved both durable and sanitary. They are, however, seldom seen today.

Brazil's last and greatest enterprise was the Standard Pottery erected in 1903, a mile southwest of the city center. Designed on a large scale and intended for mass production, it turned out Bristol-glazed wares decorated only with a stenciled circle within which appeared the logo STANDARD POTTERY BRAZIL, IND. Stoneware's time had passed, though, and the factory shut down in 1908.

Putnamville, in Putnam County to the northeast of Clay County, was the home of one of Indiana's earliest stoneware makers, John S. Perry. His classic ovoid wares reflect an Eastern background, and he may well be related to the Sanford S. Perry who worked in New York and Virginia.

Perry started making stoneware in Putnam County in 1831; in 1864 he was succeeded by a son, Isaac S. Perry, who had been running his own business in Madison County northeast of Indianapolis since 1853. A second son, Hezekiah H. Perry, had been active in Clay County since 1851. He too returned to Putnam County in 1871, and the manufactory remained in the family at least through 1879. By far the most common ware is that impressed, simply, J.S.PERRY.

The Perrys' major competitor for the Putnam County stoneware trade was Amos W. Welker, who was active in Warren Township from 1864 through 1879. He, too, made the usual utilitarian household vessels.

Parke County's first works was at Annapolis about twenty-five miles north of Terre Haute, where three Ohio potters, David L. Atcheson, David Huggins, and Jacob Bennage, fired their initial kiln in 1841. Early ovoid wares are usually marked D.L.ATCHESON/ANNAPOLIS,IA. or D.F. HUGGINS.

Various partners came and went, but the Atcheson family persevered in Annapolis. A grandson was still the owner in 1904 when Bristol-slip-glazed wares bore the stenciled logo H.R.ATCHESON POTTERY/ANNAPOLIS,IND.

Strong competition, though, came from Samuel N. Baker of Rockville five miles to the south. Lacking knowledge of stoneware production he employed Atcheson's erstwhile partner, Jacob Bennage; and by 1848 was making an excellent product. The firm was Baker & Son in 1872 when it was producing 25,000 gallons of ware annually. The most often seen mark is SN BAKER/ROCKVILLE IA.

Other stoneware works in western Indiana included an as yet unidentified shop in Attica, Fountain County, fifteen miles southwest of Lafayette which about 1870 produced wares stamped ATTICA; and the pottery of Thomas

*Salt-glazed stoneware jar marked D.L. ATCHESON/ ANNAPOLIS,IA and made at Annapolis, Indiana, 1841–50.*

employment at the Anna, Illinois, pottery run by the Kirkpatrick brothers, who were famous for their eccentric ceramics. This Loogootee pottery was continued until 1892.

The community of Shoals, five miles east of Loogootee, had a stoneware factory 1870–92. The first proprietors were Benjamin P. Devol and A. M. Catterson; by 1887 William James was in charge.

At Huntingburg in Dubois County, another twenty miles to the south, was the 1880–90 pottery of Vital Walz, a German potter who came to the United States in 1854 and worked in several locations before settling in Indiana.

Reed near Worthington in Greene County. Reed had been active in Tuscarawas County, Ohio, 1846–65; and he made stoneware in Indiana from the latter year until 1880. His stoneware, impressed T.REED, sometimes bore blue slip decoration in the Pennsylvania or New York manner.

About twenty-five miles south of Worthington is Loogootee in Martin County where Martin T. Stuckey established a stoneware shop in the 1844–48 period. It was continued into the 1880s by his son, whose wares were blue stenciled in the manner of Pennsylvania and West Virginia and marked MANUFACTURED/BY/UPTON STUCKEY. Another firm, started by Charles and John Folks in the 1870s, made not only utilitarian stoneware but also novelty items such as frog cups; these innovations reflected John's prior

*Blue-decorated, salt-glazed stoneware preserve jar impressed T.REED and made in Greene County, Indiana, 1865–85 by Thomas Reed. Reed previously worked (1846–65) in Tuscarawas County, Ohio.*

*Salt-glazed stoneware jar with stenciled mark, MANU-FACTURED/BY/UPTON STUCKEY. Made by Upton Stuckey at Loogootee, Indiana, 1875–85.*

*Albany-slip-glazed stoneware mugs incised Trinity/Springs/Ind. and made at the Loogootee, Indiana, Pottery, 1885–1900. One of the firm's partners, John Folks, had worked at the Kirkpatrick Pottery in Anna, Illinois, where similar pieces were produced.*

The Ohio River was the other important area in Indiana's stoneware trade. Rich clay deposits were found along its banks, and its broad waters provided ready transportation for both raw materials and processed ware.

Westernmost of the pottery towns was Evansville, where German craftsmen August and Louis Uhl founded a family business in 1854. Louis bought out his brother's interest in 1879 and in 1891 transferred the shop, now known as the Uhl Pottery Co., to Huntingburg, the site of clay deposits, where it was operated into the twentieth century. The most frequently encountered impression is UHL POTTERY WORKS/EVANSVILLE, IND. Erstwhile competitors in Evansville had included L. Daum & Sons (1864–66) and A. M. Beck (1882–84).

Cannelton, some thirty-five miles to the east, had a stoneware works that shipped its wares downriver as far as New Orleans. The shop, founded in 1862 for the sale of clay products, began to produce stoneware in 1872, continuing into the nineties. Later wares, covered with a brown Albany-slip finish, bore the stenciled logo CANNELTON STONEWARE CO./CANNELTON, IND.

Easternmost of the Ohio River kilns were those located in Jeffersonville and New Albany across the water from Louisville, Kentucky. The earliest recorded stoneware makers at Jeffersonville were Pile and Dustin (c. 1850), while George Unser ran a successful business there during the 1870s and 1880s. His stamp, G. UNSER/JEFFERSONVILLE/IND., is frequently encountered by collectors.

New Albany had a kiln for a brief period in

the 1860s. Its proprietor, William Keller, announced himself as a "Manufacturer of Stoneware Fruit Jars, Flower Pots and Stone Water Pipes" in the *Indiana State Gazetteer* for 1865. Keller's shop was located at Seventh and Water streets, but little else is known of its history.

## ILLINOIS

Illinois too had a large number of stoneware potteries. One of them, at Anna, produced wares that have developed a national following among collectors.

The earliest center was at Ripley, in Brown County twenty-five miles east of Quincy. According to local legend an odd coincidence led to the establishment of the first works. In 1836 the Huntingdon County, Pennsylvania, craftsman John N. Ebey, traveling west with a load of ware for sale, spent the night at the home of a local farmer. During the evening, as Ebey was describing the sort of clay necessary to produce stoneware, a neighbor remarked that he had seen similar soil caught in the roots of a fallen tree. A trip to the site convinced Ebey that the clay was suitable, and by the end of the year he had moved to Ripley and fired his first kiln of salt-glazed ware.

However, the Ripley veins were too rich to be kept secret, and within a few years Ebey had competition. L. D. Stofer from Summit County, Ohio, built two kilns in 1847, which were maintained until his death in 1891. At times their total annual production reached 250,000 gallons.

A third works, erected in 1848 by the Kentucky craftsman Francis Marion Stout, was carried on by the founder until his son Isaac Newton Stout joined the firm in 1878. After his father's retirement, Isaac maintained the business at least until 1887. His stenciled mark, I.N.STOUT, is often seen on local stoneware.

By 1870 the *Illinois State Geological Survey* re-

ported that "about a dozen potteries have been established in Ripley, and this number may be increased indefinitely as the wants of the community shall require, as the supply of raw material is abundant."

Among the firms known to have been active are Charles W. Keith (1849–69); Adam E. Martin (1852–64); Harvey Irwin (1875–82); Stofer & Leach (1870–85); W. A. Canada (1880–85); Dennis & Elett (1880–90); E. Warren (1880–86); Crawford and Sons (1880–90); and B. C. Vincent and Company, (1890–1900). The last of these companies went out of business around 1913.

Most Ripley vessels appear to have been utilitarian in nature and were characteristically given a dark brown Albany-slip glaze. However, the Stout firm produced some elaborate crock-type cookie jars with applied braided handles, embossed geometric decoration, and covers surmounted by bird-form finials.

At the end of the nineteenth century the Ripley shops were superseded by larger and more modern facilities erected at Monmouth and Macomb. The former is some thirty-five miles north of Ripley and located on the same clay belt. In 1893 William Hanna, a local banker, with several associates established the Monmouth Pottery Company with an annual capacity of 6 million gallons of stoneware.

Despite fires in 1897 and 1905, the company prospered until 1906 when it was merged into the even larger Western Stoneware Company, a corporation that remains in business today. Monmouth stoneware is straight sided, salt glazed, or slipped in Albany or Bristol finishes and decorated only with stenciled capacity numbers within a circular motif. Most common among the several marks is MONMOUTH POTTERY CO./MONMOUTH,ILL.

Not all Monmouth Pottery ware was plain. Marked examples of blue spongeware watercoolers, crocks, and pitchers are seen, as are a variety of miniatures: crocks and jugs, pigs, dogs, cows, and chickens. Some of these small pieces are Bristol glazed, others dipped in Albany slip or sponged in cobalt blue.

A formidable rival to the Monmouth Pottery emerged in 1899 when William S. Weir, another local banker and Hanna's former business associate, incorporated the Weir Pottery Company. Though its founder died in 1901 and this plant, too, was sold to the Western Stoneware Company in 1905, the Weir Pottery has left an important mark in American potting history.

In 1903 it was awarded a contract to produce the various cast stoneware mugs, pitchers, vases, bowls, and butter crocks given away as premiums by the Sleepy Eye Milling Company of Sleepy Eye, Minnesota. These vessels, glazed in Flemish blue and gray, were marked "Old Sleepy Eye" and featured the bust of a Sioux Indian chief whose people once lived in the area of the flour mill. The order was for 500,000 pieces, and many of these have survived to become one of today's most popular pottery collectibles.

The factory also filled an order in 1903 from the H. J. Heinz Company for one million of the patented Weir Stone Fruit Jars, conical vessels with bail tops which for a time competed with the more popular and practical glass mason jar. The lids of these jars are often embossed THE WEIR PAT' MAR 1ST 1892, while the usual company logo was WEIR POTTERY CO. stamped within a circle.

Macomb, fifteen miles south of Monmouth, had two late stoneware manufactories. The Macomb Pottery Company on North Lafayette Street was established in 1880 and a second plant was later built on Piper Street. From at least 1901 until the merger with the Western Stoneware Company in 1906, the company president was a woman, Carrie Fisher.

Macomb products were the usual mass-produced Bristol- or Albany-slip-glazed wares typical of the area. Not everything was jiggered or molded, however; for one employee, "Big Bill" Thompson, was capable of hand turning

*A group of Midwestern stoneware: bean pot, miniature jug, and canning jar, in the brown-and-white finish (Albany slip and Bristol slip) popular at the turn of the century. The preserve or fruit jar lid bears the embossed mark of the Weir Pottery Company, active 1899–1905 at Monmouth, Illinois.*

30-gallon jars! The company mark, stenciled or embossed, was MACOMB POTTERY CO./MACOMB, ILL.

A local rival was the Macomb Stoneware Company, which was incorporated in 1889 and operated successfully until 1906 when it too became part of Western Stoneware. Situated on North Campbell Street, the factory was never a large one; but it was busy enough that white- and brown-glazed stoneware bearing the impressed mark MACOMB STONEWARE CO./MACOMB, ILL. appears frequently in the area.

Other, smaller, factories in western Illinois included the Alexis Pottery Company at the town of the same name, about eleven miles northeast of Monmouth, which was active from 1892 until it burned in 1900; and the D. Culbertson Stoneware Company (1895–1905) at White Hall, twenty-five miles south of Ripley. It also became a part of the Western Stoneware conglomerate. Other earlier shops at White Hall included those of Michael Baker (1858–65); W.W. Hubbs (1868–75); George Hill & Co. (1875–94); M.C. Purdy & Co. (1870–91). A.D. Ruckel, a former partner of Purdy's, established in 1883 White Hall's long-lasting pottery. This remained active until 1951. Early ware is slipped in brown and stamped A. D. RUCKEL & SON/WHITE HALL, ILL. Later examples are stenciled WHITE HALL POTTERY WORKS.

In April 1906 the Western Stoneware Company was formed, incorporating firms in Illinois as well as manufactories in Iowa and Missouri. This company remains in business today, producing a wide variety of stone and earthenware. The stenciled logo, a maple leaf within which appears WESTERN/STONEWARE/CO. and sometimes the number of the producing plant, is common.

There were several stoneware establishments in north-central Illinois. Andrew Kirkpatrick, an Ohio potter whose sons were later active at Anna, Illinois, ran a pottery in Vermilionville, LaSalle County, from 1836 until 1857; continued by his son John (whose ware was impressed J. KIRKPATRICK & CO.) until 1867, and by another son, Murray, until 1871. Another important LaSalle County works was the Lowell Pottery Company at Lowell. Established in 1884 by Alfred R. Stoffer it continued until 1932 under various names and managements. Among the Bristol-glazed wares made here and stenciled LOWELL POTTERY CO./TONICA, ILL., is a jar decorated in cobalt with a picture of the pottery buildings. Peoria on the Illinois River was the site of an important works operated by Joseph Jager from 1864 until 1889. The Peoria Pottery's (1863–1902) familiar brown-glazed wares were carried by riverboat, wagon, and railway throughout the West. Examples bearing the mark PEORIA POTTERY or PEORIA/ILLINOIS have shown up in Colorado, Oregon, and even northern Mexico.

The most important factory in southern Illinois was that run at Anna by the brothers Cornwall and W. Wallace Kirkpatrick. Both had learned the trade at their father's Ohio and northern Illinois potteries and had then struck out on their own.

In 1857, Cornwall, who had been working in Cincinnati, built a pottery in Mound City near Cairo, Illinois, but this venture appears to have failed by 1859; that year he joined his brother, Wallace, in the tiny town of Anna about fifteen miles north of Mound City. There they found suitable clay and inexpensive transportation via the Illinois Central Railroad. Success came quickly. By 1860 the works already employed five potters other than family members and was producing 80,000 gallons annually.

The brothers continued to run the pottery until Cornwall's death in 1890. Wallace maintained the business, part of the time in partnership with James Toler, until his own death in 1896. His widow sold the factory in 1900.

It appears that the Kirkpatricks' production wares were both ordinary and generally unmarked. However, they made many special

*Blue-decorated, salt-glazed stoneware miniature flask in the form of a pig bearing an incised map of the Illinois railway system. Made at the Kirkpatrick Pottery, Anna, Illinois, 1870–80.*

order items, some of which bear the incised inscription, KIRKPATRICK POTTERY/ANNA, ILLINOIS, and these are eagerly sought after by collectors. Among the best-known types are small stoneware flasks in the form of pigs, which have incised upon them (usually through an Albany-slip glaze) a map of the Illinois railway system and such quaint phrases as "Latest and Most Reliable Railroad and River Guide."

Less often found are grotesque jugs with applied decoration in the form of encircling snakes and human busts and figures, often protruding from the surface of the vessel. Usually in a salt glaze with rich blue highlights, these are believed to have been presentation pieces, though they convey a strong teetotalist message.

There were also mugs with frogs in the bottom (a popular English form), miniature jugs and log cabins, owl form whistles, shell-shaped inkwells, figures of dogs in the Staffordshire manner, and other unusual objects. Some of these were incised with salutations, including the name of the pottery and, sometimes, illustrations of the pottery, making them the only identifiable wares from the Anna shop.

*Salt-glazed stoneware temperance jug with partial mineral slip, manufactured by the Anna, Illinois, pottery of Cornwall and W. Wallace Kirkpatrick, 1870–90. Though these graphic jugs were often gift pieces, they also carried a strong temperance message.*

# 16

# MISSOURI

DESPITE THE EFFORTS OF local historians and of Charles Van Ravensway, author of *The Arts and Architecture of German Settlements in Missouri*, the fascinating history of Missouri stoneware production remains largely unknown to collectors outside the state. Yet Missouri was the westernmost outpost of traditional Eastern stoneware manufacture. The craft flourished here from at least 1839 until 1942 when a kiln owned by the Evans family at Dexter in Stoddard County (which had been established in 1850) finally was shut down. Moreover, the number of potters (who came not only from the East but also from the South) ranges into the hundreds and the number of documented shops into the dozens. But the limited number of marked pieces makes it difficult to fully evaluate the output of these kilns.

One thing is clear: the state's excellent system of waterways encouraged the trade. The earliest potteries were located on or near the Mississippi. Then, early in the nineteenth century, kilns spread up the Missouri River, along which flat boats could carry ware west into the developing territories. Latest to develop (after the Civil War) were isolated rural shops serving the hill farms of central and southwestern Missouri.

It is generally believed that the state's first stoneware kiln was built in 1839 by the firm of A. A. Austin & Company at Commerce on the Mississippi, near the point where Illinois, Kentucky, and Missouri come together. By 1850 the works were owned by C. C. Bowen, and it appears that he passed them to Peter Rhodenbaugh, who arrived from Parke County, Indiana, in the 1860s. Rhodenbaugh's son and grandson continued the business into the 1880s. Documented pieces include examples impressed A. A. AUSTIN & CO./COMMERCE, MO.

Active competition was provided by Charles Koch, a potter from Santa Fe, Illinois. Koch settled at the tiny Scott County community of New York in 1863 and later moved to Commerce where he remained in business until his

death in 1878. He employed cobalt blue floral decoration applied with a slip cup, much in the manner of Pennsylvania and New York potters.

There is also some indication that Thomas H. and Newton G. Caldwell were making similar salt-glazed wares in New Bloomfield, Callaway County, as early as 1826 (with the business remaining active until around 1890). Moreover, the many French and German potters working in St. Louis from late in the eighteenth century may also have initiated production of stoneware before 1850.

Another early producer was Frederick Woolford of Calcedonia in Washington County. He was making stoneware at Farmington in neighboring St. Francois County around 1840. A few years later he moved twenty miles west to Calcedonia where, after his Washington Stoneware Manufactory produced traditional wares for a few years, he embarked in 1848 on the manufacture of Queensware. By 1852 he was in Kaolin, Missouri, in partnership with Elihu Shepard, and he does not appear to have resumed stoneware manufacture.

John Cranson established himself at Rocheport on the Missouri River, ten miles west of Columbia, in 1844. The business he founded remained active until the late 1880s. He was but one of many who flourished in the Boone, Cooper, Moniteau, and Howard County area during the second half of the nineteenth century.

At California, Moniteau County, twenty miles west of Jefferson City, Albert Hoberecht and Joseph Gertz were active around 1875, being succeeded in the early 1890s by the Blanck family, August and Francis Xavier, who had had a pottery at nearby Boonville 1880–90. Among the identified examples from the hand of August Blanck is a salt-glazed "snake jug" similar to those made at Anna, Illinois. Jugs of this sort were produced in quantity at several sites in Missouri.

Boonville, on the Missouri River in Cooper County, was the most important manufacturing center in central Missouri for over half a century. Marcus Williams was making stoneware here in 1839 and possibly as early as 1834, while his son, Marcus, Jr., carried on the trade from 1849 into the early 1860s. Other, later Boonville potters included George and Michael Volrath (1860–70), purchasers from Williams who sold out to Nicholas Lauer (1870–75); the Blanck family and, most important of all, John M. Jegglin (Gegglin) whose shop remained in business from 1867 until around 1880. That year it was leased to the Blancks by John's son, E. A. Jegglin, who returned later to operate the kiln until about 1894.

Pieces bearing the stenciled mark of the Jegglin family demonstrate that they, too, produced salt-glazed snake jugs as well as a large quantity of utilitarian wares. Charles Weyrich, who worked in Boonville 1860–80, is also thought to have made some stoneware as well as the redware that was his specialty.

Potteries in the vicinity of Boonville included that of Caldwell & McCumber at Arrow Rock, some fifteen miles to the northwest (in business 1850–60), and the Pilot Grove pottery of Jacob Huffman and his sons, Philip and Christopher (1880–90), ten miles south. Another twenty miles southwest of Pilot Grove was the Florence, Morgan County, manufactory of John M. Hummel and his son, active 1860–90.

The heart of the Eastern trade was St. Louis, where numerous potters toiled for, perhaps, one hundred and fifty years. City directories are filled with the names of craftsmen and manu-facturers; yet many of these made earthenware, and there is no firm indication of stoneware production prior to 1850. Among the many known proprietors active during the second half of the nineteenth century are H. M. Thompson & Co., 1855–59; Jacob Broun & Company (Broun & Zimmerman), 1860–69; Michael Roth, 1858–67; Joseph Hirn & Company, 1860–70; the Excelsior Stoneware Works, 1870–75; and George Heffner, in business around 1860. Many of these firms seemed to be concentrated on the water-front, in and around Dock Street.

Washington, on the Missouri River forty miles west of St. Louis, had its own stoneware factory. Located at the corner of Main and Jackson, it was managed during the 1860s by the firm of Baudissin & Buix. Also active in the community (1870–73) was Glassir & Company. By 1875, the proprietor was Joseph Bayer. He continued for a decade, leaving behind stoneware marked JOS. BAYER/WASHINGTON, MO.

In west-central Missouri there was an important complex of shops centering on the Calhoun–Clinton area in Henry County. During the 1880s they turned out 65 percent of the

*Stoneware from Boonville, Missouri: left to right, crock marked F.BLANCK & BRO./ BOONVILLE, MO., 1880–90; preserve jar by John M. Jegglin, 1867–80; jug by Charles Weyrich, 1860–80; miniature bank and jug both by the firm of Blanck & Jegglin, 1880–1900, and crock by John M. Jegglin, 1867–80. The large crocks are salt glazed, the other pieces Albany-slip glazed.*

*Stoneware preserve jars: one in salt glaze with blue slip decoration in the Eastern manner, remainder in various mineral slips. Piece at far right was made and marked by the Huffman family of Pilot Grove, Missouri, 1880–90. The other jars are attributed to Caldwell & McCumber, Arrow Rock, Missouri, 1850–60.*

stoneware made in Missouri. The Calhoun Pottery, in business 1871–91, served as an umbrella for various partnerships, including Robbins & Son (1875–80), Dawson & Son (1872–74), Darby & Sons (1878–89), Reeves & Kirkpatrick (1883–86), and Damron & Miller (1878–80). Best known of these craftsmen was G. A. Jegglin, son of the Boonville potter John M. Jegglin. He settled in Calhoun around 1880 and remained until 1893.

While most of the vessels made at Calhoun were purely utilitarian in nature, some interesting offhand pieces have also survived. The firm of Edwards & Minish, active 1890–92, turned out some rather crude snake jugs, including an example marked EDWARDS & MINISH/ CALHOUN, MO. which is adorned with two lizards and a turtle as well as the obligatory pair of snakes! H. J. Underwood & Son, in business from 1883 until 1891, made more sophisticated

wares including marked cast cobalt-glazed stoneware dogs in the manner of Staffordshire figures.

Clinton, ten miles northeast, had its own works, the Clinton Pottery Company, which was chartered in 1889 and grew out of the efforts of several earlier proprietors including Onwider & Carr (about 1886). The goal of the Clinton Pottery Company was to dominate the Western trade, and in 1891 alone it shipped one million gallons of stoneware, one-third of the state's en-

*Stoneware from the Calhoun, Missouri, factory: left to right, salt-glazed, blue-decorated preserve jar attributed to A. Rabine, 1871–75; fruit jug and small pitcher by G. A. Jegglin, 1880–93; salt-glazed churn stenciled DAWSON & SON/CALHOUN, MO ., 1872–74, and unmarked salt-glazed jug from the 1870s.*

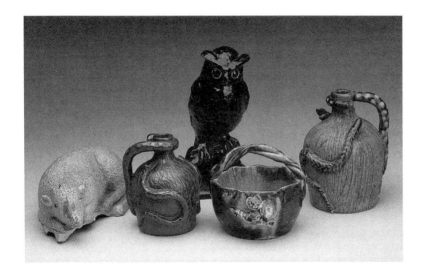

*Missouri potters produced a variety of figural pieces.* Left to right: *a lamb from the Clinton Pottery, a snake jug made by August Blanck at California, an owl and a "pretzel" basket from Calhoun, and a snake jug by G. A. Jegglin of Boonville. The pieces show various mineral glazes and date 1880–1900.*

tire output. Ware, typically Albany-slip glazed, was stenciled MANUFACTURED/BY/CLINTON POTTERY CO./CLINTON, MO.

Apparently, there were not enough buyers for all this stoneware, for in 1897, the firm's assets were seized by creditors. The property was bought at auction by a group of investors who incorporated as the Clinton Stoneware Company. This, in turn, was merged into the Illinois-based Western Stoneware Company conglomerate in 1906. Production was discontinued four years later.

Though the Clinton factory turned out a huge quantity of mass-produced stoneware, unusual pieces made here include a crock converted into a penny bank that bears the potter's name and a date, both incised through the Albany-slip glaze to the stoneware base, in much the same way Pennsylvania potters made sgraffito ware. Staffordshire-type slip-cast dogs, similar to those produced at Calhoun, were also among the output.

Kansas City had a late shop, the Kansas City Pottery, working 1881–91, but the most interesting location was St. Joseph at the Kansas border. The Pennsylvania craftsman Charles McChesney in partnership with William Bloomfield built a kiln on Charles Street in the early 1860s where he turned out salt-glazed ves-

sels decorated with cobalt flowers. The mark, BLOOMFIELD & MC CHESNEY/ST.JOE,MO., has been found on several such pieces. The firm probably did not survive much beyond 1875. An unsuccessful rival was C. E. Kemp, whose pottery on Felix Street opened in 1866 and closed a year or two later. Two pieces marked C.E.KEMP/ST. JOE,MO. are known.

Directly east across the state is the hamlet of Lakenan on the North Fork of the Salt River. Here another migrant found a home. In 1853 the Ohio potter David F. Huggins left Clay County, Indiana, where he had worked since 1850 (he had previously been in Parke County, Indiana, since 1841). After practicing his trade for a few years in Brown County, Illinois, Huggins reached Lakenan in the late 1850s. There, he continued to throw the same beautifully proportioned ovoid crocks and jugs he had made in Indiana, impressing them D.F.HUGGINS/LAKENAN. The business lasted into the 1860s with later wares being stenciled HUGGINS & SON/LAKENAN, MO.

There were also a few small enterprises in the southwestern part of the state. Most significant among these were the kilns at Deerfield, just across the line from Fort Scott, Kansas, and Lamar in Barton County, about twenty-five miles southeast of Deerfield. Abraham Redfield is the first known stoneware maker in Deerfield. His business, established around 1871, had passed to the firm of Martin and Sons by 1880; they remained in business for the rest of the decade. Murphy & Curry were working at Lamar 1880–85, and a later owner was N. F. Fancher, in business as early as 1888 and continuing until at least 1891.

This review represents but a small portion of the stoneware workers who were once active in the state of Missouri, hopefully future research will reveal both more craftsmen and more sites.

# 17

## MINNESOTA, WISCONSIN, AND MICHIGAN

THE STONEWARE MARKET in Minnesota and Wisconsin was initially dominated by goods shipped north from potteries in Ohio. However, following the exploitation of important clay banks in southern Minnesota, large pottery complexes developed in both states. One, in Red Wing, Minnesota, had, by 1900, become the most important American producer of utilitarian stoneware. Michigan, however, never developed an important industry.

### MINNESOTA

The four sites at which Minnesota stoneware was manufactured, New Ulm, Mankato, Owatonna, and Red Wing, lie in an arc across the southeastern corner of the state, below Minneapolis. Charles C. Cornell, in business at Owatonna from 1863 until 1871, appears to have been the first to make stoneware in the state. However, the honor may actually belong to Henry B. Kauffer and Theodore Fittler, whose plant at Fourth and Warren streets in Mankato was in operation around 1860. Like Cornell, they initially produced redware, but before 1870 they were turning salt-glazed wares. Their business continued through the decade. By 1875 a second stoneware factory had appeared in Mankato, this one owned initially by Andrew Gaptor. He sold out around 1880 to John A. Sanborn who, in 1882, entered into a partnership with John A. and Myron G. Willard. They acquired Sanborn's interest the following year, and continued the business for a year or two more. The New Ulm works was opened around 1870 by Christian Dauffenbach, John Steckert, and Franklin Friedman; it probably operated for only a few years.

Red Wing, on the Mississippi southeast of St. Paul, was destined to have a much longer future. There had been earthenware potters here since the 1860s, and in 1876, one of them, David Hallem, attempted the manufacture of stoneware.

Within a year he had failed, not through lack of skill or raw materials, but because the Ohio potteries who supplied the area responded by cutting their prices in half!

However, it was a short-lived triumph. The abundant stoneware clay beds in Goodhue County near Red Wing and the emerging market stretching from Wisconsin (which had no stoneware clays) north to Canada and west into the Dakotas had attracted the attention of some wealthy local businessmen. Capital, which the previous Minnesota craftsmen had always lacked, became available.

In February 1877, the Red Wing Stoneware Company was organized. Hallem's small shop was purchased, and he was employed to make molds and assist in experimental work. In January 1878 the first building of what was to be the largest pottery complex in the upper Midwest was built.

Within a few years, the firm found itself barely able to keep up with orders. However, others were eager to enter the field. In 1883 the Minnesota Stoneware Company, a formidable competitor, appeared on the scene; in 1892, the North Star Stoneware Company was established. Total industrial capacity exceeded the demand, and the rivals soon found it necessary to form a selling consortium, the Union Stoneware Company, to control supply and regulate prices.

Despite this, North Star failed in 1896. The two remaining firms continued until 1906 when they joined forces as the Red Wing Union Stoneware Company, a title which was changed to Red Wing Potteries in 1936. After a series of business reverses and a prolonged strike, business was terminated in 1967.

Due both to the variety of the items produced and to the fact that all three original potteries as well as the consolidated company regularly marked their vast output, stoneware from Red Wing is among the most popular and collectible of Midwestern wares.

It is also possible to see in vessels made by the Red Wing Stoneware Company and the Minnesota Stoneware Company the transition from hand thrown to molded and mass-produced wares. Early examples are salt glazed and decorated in cobalt, including a few with freehand birds and flowers. Later jugs and crocks are finished in Bristol or Albany slip or the popular combination of the two. After 1900 the stoneware body was used to produce a vast array of kitchen and storage items (bowls, pitchers, cookie jars, hanging saltboxes, mugs, canister sets, and casseroles) which were sponge decorated in blue, green, red, and brown or combinations thereof. So many were stenciled with the names of grocers and other merchants who used them as promotional items that they form the basis of an entirely separate area of collectibles.

Marks found on Red Wing stoneware are placed either on the base or on the side of the vessel. The base is usually preferred for table and kitchen wares, and most such marks are impressed or embossed. On the other hand, with the exception of some early pieces, most crocks, jugs, churns, and similar vessels are marked with a stencil. More common among the great variety of ciphers are:

North Star Stoneware Company: NORTH/ figure of a five-pointed star/RED WING/MINN.; N O R T H within the arms of a five-pointed star; NORTH STAR/STONEWARE/COMPANY

Minnesota Stoneware Company: MINNESOTA/ STONEWARE CO./RED WING; MADE BY/MINN. S.W. CO./RED WING; MINN. S.W. CO.; M.S. CO./RED WING MINN.

Red Wing Stoneware Company: RED WING STONEWARE CO.; R.W.S.W.; RED WING CO.; RED-WING/STONEWARE/CO.

Red Wing Union Stoneware Company: RED WING/UNION/STONEWARE CO./RED WING/MINN.; UNION STONEWARE/RED WING MINN.; MADE IN/RED/WING.

Red Wing Potteries: RED WING/USA

Both the Red Wing Stoneware Company and

the Minnesota Stoneware Company often marked their wares with a stenciled logo: the former, a bird's wing in red; the latter, a pair of birch leaves in black—a cipher also adopted by the Red Wing Union Stoneware Company.

## WISCONSIN

Wisconsin lacks clays suitable for the manufacture of stoneware. However, unlike neighboring Michigan where this appears to have prevented development of a significant native industry, potters in the state were able to build up a substantial trade.

The craft was centered upon Milwaukee and Sheboygan some fifty miles to the north. Both were located on Lake Michigan, across whose waters Ohio clay was initially shipped. However, by the 1870s it became possible to obtain cheaper clay by rail from the great beds at Red Wing, Minnesota.

Earliest known of the Milwaukee stoneware makers was Isaac P. Brazelton (probably from Ohio) who operated a pottery in conjunction with his grocery store on Chestnut Street from 1844 until 1855 when he moved to Sheboygan. Nothing is known of his subsequent history. In 1854 the *City Directory* reported that stoneware valued at $2,100 had been produced in the city the previous year, and this may be attributed to Brazelton.

The Hermann family, makers of redware, were in the city as early as 1847, and in 1856, Charles Hermann established what was to be Wisconsin's most important stoneware manufactory on Johnson Street near the Milwaukee River. Various partners were involved in the business which, for most of its life, was denominated Chas. Hermann & Co. Among the early associates were Charles and Weymer Remy; in 1882 a stepson, Louis P. Pierron, was admitted to partnership. He became sole proprietor of the Pierron Pottery in 1886, continuing it until 1935.

By 1892 this company employed twenty-five workers and turned out over 600,000 gallons of stoneware each year. The mark customarily employed was some variation of C. HERMANN & CO./ MILWAUKEE, WISC. There are also pieces (miniature souvenir flasks) marked COMPLI-MENTS OF/ THE/PIERRON/POTTERY CO., but these are identical to forms made at the Red Wing, Minnesota, pottery and are thought to have been made there for Pierron who also used the brand MANUFAC-TURED/BY/L.M. PIERRON/MILWAUKEE, WIS.

The 1857 *Milwaukee Directory* indicates the presence of yet another stoneware maker, John B. Maxfield, located at the corner of West Water and Clybourne streets. He and his brother Amos were active from 1854 until 1858. Their ware, impressed J.B. & A. MAXFIELD/MILWAUKEE, was of ovoid form and decorated with blue flowers. The kiln used by the Maxfields had been built in 1851 by Oscar F. Baker whose stoneware, marked O.B. BAKER & CO/MILWAUKEE, is similar to that of the brothers to whom he sold the shop in 1854.

In 1868 Charles Hermann found his first serious local opposition in the form of the partners Caspar Hennecke and Nicholas Wagner, who opened a stoneware shop on Buffalo Street. Confining themselves primarily to ornamental stoneware (vases and garden statuary), they prospered. The business was incorporated in 1888 and continued until 1905, though stoneware manufacture was discontinued in 1899.

The stoneware manufacturer Isaac P. Brazelton left Milwaukee for Sheboygan in 1855. It is not known if he made ware there; the first recorded manufacturer is Theodore Gunther who, in 1862, in partnership with Peter Berns founded on Wisconsin between 5th and 7th streets what was to become the Eastern Stoneware Factory. Their ware, which was sometimes blue decorated, bore the mark T.H. GUNTHER & BERNS, SHEBOYGAN. In 1887 this company was succeeded by Mies, Diedrich & Company, a firm that produced stoneware until 1893.

There was also a pottery in Menasha. Carlton Bachelder, a New Hampshire craftsman, made stoneware on Water Street and west of Tayco from 1855 until 1868. His blue-decorated, salt-glazed wares were impressed OHIO STONE/ MANUFACTURED BY/C. BACHELDER/MENASHA, WIS. Examples are not common.

## MICHIGAN

The only presently documented Michigan stoneware pottery was located at Grand Ledge, a small community on the Grand River just northeast of Lansing. The 1860 federal census lists the potter George Loveless as active here. It is likely that he was succeeded by Louis Harrington, who had a shop in the 1860s on West Jefferson Street, near where a large sewer tile manufactory was later located.

Both Loveless and Harrington are thought by local historians to have made stoneware, and a few unmarked churns, jugs, and crocks found in the area are attributed to them. These pieces are either salt or Albany-slip glazed and of a form that might have been made almost anywhere in the Midwest.

# 18

## OTHER MIDWESTERN POTTERIES

THERE WERE important stoneware manufactories in other Midwestern states. Kentucky had numerous kilns, some of them quite early, while Iowa had a widespread industry in the second half of the nineteenth century. Shops in other states within this geographical area tended to be both scattered and late.

### KENTUCKY

Louisville, on the Indiana border, was the most important center of Kentucky stoneware manufacture. Potters from New England, Virginia, and Ohio converged here, and their products were shipped up and down the Ohio River.

John and Frederick Hancock, English potters via East Liverpool, Ohio, were active about 1840 (the business possibly continued into the 1850s). George W. Doane, also from Ohio, competed with the Hancocks from 1838 until around 1860, leaving behind one of the state's

most artistic pieces of ware, a large churn impressed GEO W. DOANE/LOUISVILLE KY and decorated with an incised sailing ship and the phrase "Homeward/Bound."

The city's largest, most lasting manufactory was the Louisville Pottery, established in 1845 and continued until 1922 by the German craftsman Henry Melcher and his descendants. Other immigrant potters with a similar background included William Frost (1836–46), George Hettinger (1832–40), Abraham Dover (1843–48), Anton Sauer (1865–69), and John Bauer & Company (1887–1905).

Though redware was made at Lexington, Kentucky, as early as 1796, the first documented stoneware kiln was that of the Cornelison family at Bybee or Portland in nearby Madison County. Founded in 1809, it has persisted into the present century. Waco, a small community about thirty miles southeast of Lexington, was likewise an active center. D. Zittel and Company was in business here 1870–1905, and they were succeeded by Grimstead and Stone, still making ware in 1922. Stoneware produced was either salt glazed or finished with Albany slip, sometimes combined with a lead glaze.

Jeffersonville, in Montgomery County, some thirty-five miles east of Lexington, was home to another craftsman of Germanic extraction, George Unser. He made salt-glazed wares here from 1865 until about 1869.

There were various other stoneware manufacturing centers. Maysville, on the river bordering Ohio, had the shop of Isaac Thomas (1837–60), whose products, including a churn inscribed Kentucky/1837, were stamped I. THOMAS, while the Kirkpatricks of Ohio and Illinois were active in Covington, another river town, directly across from Cincinnati, Ohio. Cornwall E. Kirkpatrick bought an existent pottery here in 1839 and operated it until 1848, producing such wares as preserve jars and salt-glazed smoking pipes. His successors remained in business until at least 1851 when it was reported that the pottery had been burned to the ground by "an incindiary." Owensboro, much farther down the Ohio River, had a small kiln in the 1850s and early 1860s. Its proprietor was J. A. Scott.

Shops in western Kentucky included that of W. P. Bonner in Eddyville near the present Kentucky Lake (1856–59), and the small kiln of August Keppner at Wickliffe on the Missouri River. This was in operation from 1880 until 1900. About twenty miles downstream, the firm of Schenck & Rocker at Columbus manufactured Albany-slip-glazed wares from 1870 until around 1900.

The most important center in this area was Graves County, which had four separate hamlets where stoneware was made. Most important of these was Bell City, near the Calloway County line, where W. B. Howard & Son were active 1870–90. Their kiln was continued by W. D. Russell's Bell City Pottery, in business

until 1922. J. W. Pittman made brown-glazed stoneware at Lynville, five miles to the northwest, from 1870 through 1900 and the Water Valley Pottery Company (1875–90) was located in the community of the same name about twenty miles farther west. At Mayfield, some twenty miles northwest of Water Valley, was a shop run 1890–1900 by Morris Cooley and Robert A. Hale.

Calloway County, which adjoins Graves on the southeast, had a much earlier kiln about which little is known. A "Captain" Bonner is said to have made salt-glazed stoneware here during the 1850s. Another western site was the city of Paducah on the Illinois border. A. J. Bauer, a name well known in the annals of American pottery, established himself here in 1860. The business remained active until the turn of the century.

## IOWA

Many of the major Iowa potteries tended to cluster about population centers such as Fort Dodge, Sioux City, Davenport, and Des Moines. One of the largest was the Fort Dodge Stoneware Company, which grew out of a shop established in the 1870s by an immigrant potter, Martin White. His mark was WHITE'S POTTERY WORKS/ FORT DODGE, IOWA. Following his death, his sons, W. G. and A. M. White, along with others, incorporated in 1892 as the Fort Dodge Stoneware Company. Ware, including churns, jugs, crocks, and flowerpots, was finished in Bristol or Albany slip; special pieces, such as miniatures, were sponged in blue. Several marks were employed, including impressed FORT DODGE/STONEWARE/CO. or FORT DODGE STONE- WARE CO./FORT DODGE, IOWA, and the stencil FORT DODGE STONEWARE CO./MANUFACTURERS/ FORT DODGE, IOWA. In 1906 this firm merged into the expanding Western Stoneware Company of

Monmouth, Illinois. This proved a short-lived association, however, as the plant burned to the ground ten months later and was not rebuilt.

James Toler, who had been employee and partner in the Anna, Illinois, pottery, established an independent business at Sioux City, Iowa, in 1896. The location, straddling the South Dakota and Nebraska borders, should have been ideal, but by 1900 he had returned to Illinois. At the opposite end of the state in the city of the same name, was the Davenport Pottery, which operated from about 1880 until 1887. The capital city, Des Moines, had a business, active during the 1880s, which was owned by E. L. and J. L. Weeks, probably members of the Akron, Ohio, family of craftsmen. Des Moines also had kilns operated in suburban Carlisle during the 1870s and 1880s by Matthew Farley and the firm of McBurney & Franklin. Ohnhause and Baker made salt-glazed wares in Iowa City, 1860–75. Cedar Rapids, twenty-five miles to the north, had its own pottery, this one owned during the 1860s by Francisco Smith.

There were also rural kilns. Typical was that owned near Coalport by William Welch, a North Carolina craftsman who began to practice his trade in the 1820s. In 1836 he built, somewhere in Van Buren County, the first pottery in the Nebraska Territory. From there he moved to Fairfield and by 1845 he was at Pella, Marion County, west of Des Moines, before finally settling in Coalport, where he fired his first stoneware in 1847. By 1860 he had leased the business to Thomas H. Smith and his son, Cass, who carried on into the 1880s. Their ware was stamped T. H. SMITH. The Iowa Historical Society owns several miniature Albany-slip-glazed pieces turned by Cass Smith.

A later pottery near Pella was that of Silas and John King at Knoxville, about fifteen miles to the southwest. They were in business from 1880 until 1909 and their ware was impressed KING & CO./KNOXVILLE, IOWA.

Other small shops were located at Vernon in western Crawford County (Robert M. Dickson, 1865–87); Red Oak, Montgomery County, southeast of Council Bluffs (W. H. Close, 1880–90); Eldora, Hardin County, where Henry Tolman (1865–67) was replaced by H. C. Sweet, active into the 1880s; and Attica, where Joseph J. Jennings and Ira Kendrick turned ware during the 1870s.

The Mississippi River, forming the state's eastern border, offered attractive transportation possibilities, and the pottery at Davenport was joined by others at Fairport, at Bellevue, southeast of Dubuque, and at Burlington in southeastern Iowa. Fairport, near Davenport, had a half-dozen shops in the 1860s, two of which still survived twenty years later. Among the early proprietors were William Lee and Daniel Russell, Eli Brunson, John Fenstel, and the firm of John Sparks and David Morris. The Bellevue kiln operated only for a short time in the 1880s and 1890s but has left behind some ware impressed BELLVUE POTTERY/BELLVUE, IOWA. The entrepreneurs at Burlington, in the southeast corner of the state, were the Turley Brothers, in business from 1870 into the 1890s.

The Melcher family, another prolific group of Germanic artisans active in the Midwest, had potteries in two Iowa communities, Lowell and Parrish. In 1848 the brothers David and Dennis Melcher established a stoneware shop at Lowell, sometimes known as "Jugtown," on the Skunk River, twenty miles west of Burlington. The business was successful enough to be continued into the 1870s by the founders' sons. Edward was running it in 1870 when it was illustrated in the *Henry County, Iowa, Atlas*. The factory appears as several frame buildings surrounding a large, upright kiln. Rows of stoneware vessels line the grounds.

Late in the 1870s a potter named Gerber, who had been employed by the Melchers, opened his own competing works known as the Lowell

Pottery. This remained in business until the close of the century. Ware was often marked LOWELL POTTERY/LOWELL, IOWA.

Some members of the Melcher family (or relatives by marriage) appear to have also had a hand in the establishment, about 1875, of a stoneware business in neighboring Parrish. This was later run by the firm of Beck & Beck.

Another important focus of the trade was Ottumwa in Wapello County. The Indiana potter Leander T. Stuart went there in 1847, and potters from Germany and Scotland (as well as Kentucky) were active in the area about 1880. Among the known owners was John P. Williams, whose manufactory was busy during the 1860s and 1870s.

## KANSAS

The few known Kansas stoneware manufactories were clustered along the eastern border. Though the potter Neal Vestel left Clay County, Indiana, in 1851 to set up a business in the Kansas Territory, the earliest known works are those of Gottlieb Epple (1860–68) at Eudora, just east of Lawrence, and Julius Keller, who, with a partner named Hoffman, established a shop at Leavenworth which was maintained from 1860 until 1863. There was also a kiln producing brown-slip stoneware at Fort Scott from 1890 until around 1900.

In north-central Kansas the focus of production was Clyde in Cloud County. Truellis Stevens and Jacob Sohlinger, who had been working in Missouri, built their own pottery here in 1869. After Stevens left the business four years later, Sohlinger remained active until 1882. His place was taken by W. B. Mosier, who lasted but a few years more. Both were done in by the cost of fuel for their coal-burning kilns and competition from larger, more efficient manufactories to the east.

## NEBRASKA

In 1853 the Clay County potter John B. Ziegler left Indiana for "the West." He may have tarried in Iowa or Missouri, but by 1859 he was in Dakota City, Nebraska, just across the river from Sioux City, Iowa, where, in partnership with another German craftsman, Charles F. Eckhart, he was running the state's first stoneware factory. The rare impression DAKOTA CITY/ N.T. is attributed to this firm. The 1860 federal census credited the kiln with five employees and an annual output worth $5,000. Ziegler left town sometime after a disastrous fire in March 1861 and Eckhart continued the business until at least 1867 though another potter, P. Neff, was active a year earlier.

Ziegler appears to have taken up residence (1862–65) at Bellevue, another Iowa River town just below Omaha. A single stoneware jar, stamped J.B. ZIEGLER/BELLVUE, N.T. remains to mark his passing.

During the 1860s and 1870s there were other attempts at pottery making in Nebraska, but it was not until the 1880s that large-scale manufactories appeared. The biggest and longest lived of these was the Lincoln Pottery Works at the corner of First and H streets in Lincoln. Established in 1880 by Webster and O. V. Eaton of Rochester, New York, the firm was incorporated in 1888 and remained in business until 1903. Its mark was LINCOLN/POTTERY/LINCOLN, NEB.

By 1893 this kiln was turning out 300,000 pieces of stoneware each year, including milk pans, cuspidors, jars, jugs, pots, churns, beer mugs, bean pots, flowerpots, and various ornamental wares such as urns, vases, and hanging baskets. And as Lloyd Shaw noted in his *Lincoln: Early History* (1900), "(t)he Lincoln Pottery Company is purely a Nebraska Institution, and they want the Nebraska trade, and hope and expect to get it if good goods and low prices count for anything." The company donated prizes in the name of public relations to the Nebraska State Fair: 100 gallons of assorted stoneware for the best dairy exhibit and one pair of lawn vases plus assorted vases and flowerpots to the person showing the best floral display.

There was another important factory, the Louisville Stoneware Manufacturing Company, in the community of the same name midway between Lincoln and Omaha. The firm, established in 1878, had an initial capacity of 7,000 pieces per month. It appears to have become the Louisville Pottery Works by 1884 and the Western Pottery thereafter, remaining in business until at least 1894 when it was again termed The Louisville Pottery and Stoneware Manufacturing Company.

A third major firm, the Omaha Pottery Company, was incorporated in 1884 and remained active through at least 1907. Though initially designed as a center for the production of brick and terra-cotta, it is believed that this shop turned out some stoneware around the turn of the century.

# 19

# WESTERN POTTERIES

WHILE BOTH Texas and Arkansas had important stoneware manufactories and California could boast of several sizable kilns that were active during the second half of the nineteenth century, most Western states produced little stoneware. It is possible, though, that future research will reveal more craftsmen who were employed in the trade.

## TEXAS

Stoneware makers established themselves in Texas soon after statehood was achieved in 1846. The first to arrive favored alkaline finishes, but by the 1870s salt glazing became dominant, and at the end of the century the preferred surfaces were Albany and Bristol slips.

Many of the pioneer craftsmen had worked in South Carolina or been trained by others from that area, and they frequently had spent time in Alabama, Georgia, or Mississippi on the way

west. As a consequence, identifiable early Texas wares often resemble, in both form and finish, earlier examples from the Southern states.

Rusk County, near the eastern border with Louisiana, was the destination of several early arrivals. The 1850 federal census listed two kilns here, one run by James Prothro, the other by Cyrus Cogburn. Both produced alkaline-glazed wares. Prothro, who had come from Alabama, was in Rusk County by 1846. His son, Newton, who made crude tablewares during the Civil War period, continued the business into the 1870s. Cyrus Cogburn's shop was near the present-day community of Mt. Enterprise. It had ceased to function before 1860.

A third Rusk County kiln was owned by a Georgian, Taylor Brown, who bought land there in 1837. There is, however, no evidence that he made stoneware before 1870. The business was still active in the late 1880s. An important rival was John D. Leopard who had worked in South Carolina, Georgia, and Ala-

*Bristol-glazed stoneware watercooler with decoration in cobalt blue, Texas, 1900–20.*

bama and had probably been employed in the 1850s by James Prothro. By 1864 he had his own establishment near Henderson, Rusk County, where he worked into the 1880s. Joseph C. Rushton, from Alabama, came to Henderson soon after the Civil War. Following employment with Taylor Brown he ran his own shop (1880–1900). Known examples are marked J.R.

A later Rusk County manufacturer about whom little is known is John F. Hunt (1890–1900), whose business was continued by T. L. Hunt until about 1910. During the period 1900–09, competition was provided by the Russell Pottery of Henderson, which specialized in giant, slab-formed watering tanks for ranch and industrial use. Pieces impressed HENDERSON POT-TERY/HENDERSON/TEXAS may be associated with this latter firm.

West of Henderson is Athens, Texas, where Levi Cogburn, probably a son of Cyrus, settled before 1860. Although he died during the 1860s, the business may have continued to operate

under the guidance of a black potter, Joseph Cogburn (slaves were often given a master's name), who was living at the site in 1870. A later pottery run by the Liebrich family (1900–10) was located at Tyler, thirty miles northeast of Athens. In Winnsboro, north of Tyler, was the Winnsboro Pottery, 1900–15.

There were other East Texas potteries. Near Mims Chapel in the border county of Marion there was a kiln run (1850–67) by Jefferson S. Nash from Edgefield, South Carolina. Two alkaline-glazed vessels impressed with his mark, J.S.NASH, are known as well as similarly stamped shards from the site. It is thought that some of his ware was made by a black craftsman, Milliken Frazier. Also, John S. Brown, of the well-known Atlanta, Georgia, family of potters, turned out alkaline-glazed stoneware at Gray Rock in northeastern Titus County during the 1870s. The state's earliest known stoneware maker, J. R. Tanner, made salt-glazed vessels at Marshall in Harrison County during the 1840s. Interestingly enough, the only stoneware factory still operating in Texas is the Marshall Pottery at Marshall.

In southeastern Texas there was a small factory in Montgomery County. James Kirbee, from Talbot County in Georgia, and his sons, Louis and Jefferson M., were established in Montgomery just north of Houston by 1850. Despite a lack of suitable local clay they persisted through the 1860s. Shards excavated at the site of their kiln sometimes bear impressed decoration identical to that used at the Landrum Pottery in Edgefield, South Carolina.

Southwest of Houston, in Jackson County, was the shop of Abraham Babcock, a New Jersey redware maker who settled along the Mustang River in 1852. He was still working in the

1860s and, by then, had supplemented his output with stoneware.

Some of the most important Texas manufactories were located in the counties around San Antonio. The Reverend John M. Wilson built his Guadalupe Pottery in the county of the same name in 1857. The location on Salt Creek was just east of the city. A rare example, impressed H. WILSON & CO., probably reflects management by Wilson's son. Though the first ware was salt glazed, by 1866 an alkaline finish was being used. In 1869 an employee, M. J. Durham, took over the works, operating it until 1903. During this latter period, pots again bore a salt glaze.

Associated with this firm around 1870 was Isaac Suttles, from Ohio, who by 1872 had his own shop at nearby La Vernia. During the following decade he made a substantial quantity of ware, much of it impressed I.SUTTLES/LAVERNIA/TEX. The Littel Pottery, active 1905–08, may have marked a continuation of Suttles's business. Another member of the family, George W. Suttles, had his own pottery 1870–1900 in adjoining Wilson County. Among other items, he made unglazed stoneware birdhouses and a charming Albany-slip-glazed jug incised with a figure of a man in obvious distress and the words, "Got a bad Cold." Incised or otherwise decorated ware is rare in Texas.

Germanic potters moved into the area during the 1870s, and one of the first to own his own shop was William Saenger of St. Hedwig, a community just a few miles northwest of La Vernia. After working there 1880–85, he moved to Elmendorf in Bexar County northwest of San Antonio where activity continued until around 1920. The products consisted of salt- and Albany-slip-glazed stoneware, and storage vessels, some with a capacity of fifty gallons—large even for Texas! Several marks, including WM.SAENGER/ELMENDORF/TEXAS, are known.

In 1888 Ernest Richter, a former employee in the Saenger shop, established his own business at Elmendorf. He sold out in 1905 to the firm of Newton, Weller & Wagner which became the Star Pottery Works in 1909. This continued until 1915, producing a variety of Bristol-glazed stoneware, including an unusual ceramic and cast-iron patent churn. The most common mark is STAR POTTERY WORKS/ELMENDORF,TEXAS.

William Meyer, another German, came to Bexar County in 1887. The business he founded with Frank Schulz remained active until the 1940s. Meyer is particularly remembered for his use of a natural glaze, Leon slip, which came from nearby Leon Creek and fired to a wide range of colors from brown to yellow to green. His wares, sometimes stamped MFG.BY/MEYER POTTERY/ATASCOSA,TEXAS, are considered highly collectible.

There were also potteries in the Austin area. Matthew Duncan, yet another craftsman trained at Edgefield, South Carolina, was in Shelby County, Texas, by 1846. Eight years later he was in Bastrop, Texas, about twenty-five miles east of Austin, where he and his brother, George, made alkaline-glaze stoneware. A son, George II, continued the business into the 1880s, manufacturing salt-glazed vessels.

Matthew Duncan's son-in-law, James W. Allen, had his own kiln at Yegua Creeks in northern Bastrop County during the 1850s and 1860s where, among other things, he made stoneware pipe bowls. An interesting, though late, effort in the same area was the McDade Pottery in the community of the same name, just inside the northern Bastrop County line. Here, 1910–30, press-molded animals, Bristol glazed and modeled on Staffordshire forms, were made.

Between Austin and Dallas there were a few firms including the Baker Pottery in Marlin, active 1890–95 and a kiln in Limestone County to the northeast, which was owned by W. C. Knox, who made salt-glazed wares during the 1870s.

Denton, northwest of Dallas, had several shops which supplied that metropolitan area. Earliest by far was J. C. Lambert, who was working there in the 1860s. His seldom seen mark is J.C.LAMBERT. At the turn of the century the following firms were in business: J. Sublitz (1900–10); D. B. Dougherty (1900–08); and A. H. Moss (1905–10). R. Melcher at Weatherford, west of Fort Worth, was making both redware and salt-glazed stoneware during the same period.

## ARKANSAS

Though Arkansas had fewer potteries than its neighboring state of Texas, the industry here was substantial. Potters came from Missouri and the Midwest as well as from Southern states producing a range of finishes, from salt glazing through Albany and Bristol slips to alkaline glazes, though the latter were relatively uncommon.

The earliest documented craftsmen were the Bird brothers, William, Joseph, and Nathaniel, who in 1843 built a "groundhog" kiln near Princeton where they manufactured salt-glazed wares. In 1862, the business passed into the hands of John Welch, who continued it until 1874.

Lafayette Glass, a wandering potter from Tennessee, was making stoneware in Mansfield some twenty-five miles south of Fort Smith in 1858. Apparently things did not go well, because by 1860 he was in Murfreesboro, Pike County, north of Texarkana. He remained here until 1868 when he relocated at Benton, twenty miles southwest of Little Rock. The location was a good one: adjacent both to the state capital and to the developing resort area about Hot Springs. Though Glass left in 1879 (by the following year he was working in Marshall County, Mississippi), his was the first of numerous stoneware potteries in the area.

Between 1869 and 1900, nine different kilns operated in or around Benton. Among the better-known manufacturers were the Hyten Brothers (1895–1912), who continued a business established in 1881 by their father, John F. Hyten. Among the interesting examples from this kiln is a wall sconce in the form of the American shield and glazed in white Bristol slip highlighted with cobalt. Among the few potters to mark their wares was W. H. Bennett (1890–1905), whose Bristol-slip-glazed crocks and jugs bore the stenciled logo, BENTON BRICK/AND/POTTERY COMPANY/BENTON, ARKANSAS.

Other Benton firms, about which little is presently known, include F. W. Bush (1879–81); Samuel Henderson (1884–96); E. L. Herrick (1891–97); Charles and H. A. Rhodenbaugh (1886–1900); Tyler and Shanks (1879–81); A. E. Wilbur (1876–87); and Frank Woolsey (1882–95). Another member of the Wilbur family, J. D., had his own shop at Boonesboro, Arkansas, 1880–85.

Malverne, about twenty miles southwest of Benton, also had a share of this industry. First on the scene was E. A. Nunn & Company, active 1874–92. Competition was offered by O.C. & T. N. Atcheson (1888–98), thought to be members of the well-known family of potters from Parke County, Indiana.

Texarkana, on the Texas border in southwest Arkansas, had at least one manufactory, this operated by D. S. Collins & Company, 1888–92. An Albany-slip-glazed whiskey taster in the form of a pig (similar to Anna, Illinois, examples), which is incised "Texarkana Pottery," may have been made at Collins's shop or that of a predecessor.

In the northeast corner of the state, near Missouri, there were potteries at Paragould and at Rector, twenty miles to the northeast. The partnership of Black and Simmemon operated in the former community 1897–1903; Garner & Grubbs made stoneware in Rector from 1895 until 1900. Another late manufactory was that owned by J. S. Robertson (probably one of the Robertsons who made stoneware in Barrow County, Georgia) at Story, Arkansas, around 1898–1900.

## CALIFORNIA

Given both its burgeoning population and its geographic remoteness from other stoneware manufacturing sites, California must have appeared most attractive to migrant potters. The cost of shipping ceramics in bulk either by sea or, later, by rail was high, and stoneware clays were available in both the San Francisco and Los Angeles areas. Moreover, there was even a brownish slip clay, similar to that known in New York, Texas, and Michigan, which could be used for glazing.

Among the first to take advantage of this situation was J. W. Orr, who established himself in the Michigan Bar area in 1859. With various partners, he continued until 1896. Clay from the rich beds at Michigan Bar was also shipped to Oakland, where it served as raw material for two larger manufactories. One of these, the Pioneer Pottery opened in 1856 by Daniel Brannon, operated until 1887, manufacturing not only stoneware but also yellowware and Rockingham. A rare example of early marked California stoneware, a churn impressed D.BRANNAN/SAN ANTONIO, is at the Smithsonian Institution in Washington, D.C. Also active 1872–84 was Henry Bundock's East Oakland Pottery, a sizable establishment producing both utilitarian storage vessels and flowerpots.

Sacramento, northeast of Oakland, had what may be the state's earliest stoneware works. It was built in 1854 by the firm of Baker and Gasser and passed into the hands of G. D. Clark in 1860. It was still operating as N. Clark & Sons (a name peculiarly reminiscent of the Athens, New York, firm) as late as 1887.

The major producer in Los Angeles was J.A. Bauer & Company (1890–1958), which included salt-glazed wares in its varied selection of ceramics. The Charles W. Bowers Memorial Museum in Santa Ana has one of the few public collections of California stoneware, including among its holdings large crocks impressed BAUER or J.A. BAUER/POTTERY CO./LOS ANGELES, which were used to cure olives.

During the period 1900–03, a competitor, the Los Angeles Stoneware Company, attempted to enter the field. Though a few examples impressed with the company name may be found, it would appear that there was room for only one stoneware works in Los Angeles.

The Los Angeles potteries decorated their products with stencils of oranges, olives, peaches, and other fruits and associated leaves appropriate to the farms and gardens of the area.

## OREGON

Oregon was the only other West Coast state that had a significant early stoneware industry. Barnet Ramsey, a vision-impaired Illinois craftsman, built a kiln at Springfield, now a suburb of Eugene, in 1853. Around 1862 he moved some forty miles north to Albany, where he was in partnership with William Pollock until 1864 when he settled in Halsey twenty miles down the road to Eugene. He continued there until 1868. Examples of his ware at the Oregon Historical Society appear to have a brown slip glaze.

A relative, William Ramsey, Jr., took over a redware pottery in Eola in 1869. After a year, though, he moved to Buena Vista, just north of Albany, where the state's largest stoneware shop was located. Ramsey and his partner, a man named Miller, manufactured stoneware until 1875. Their competition was formidable. In 1865 the family firm of Freeman Smith & Sons had built a sizable factory at Buena Vista, an important Willamette River landing that allowed shipment north and south through central Oregon. Three years later this was the largest stoneware manufactory in the state, producing wares described locally as of "a density and fineness that cannot be excelled." Known as the Oregon Pottery Company, the business continued until around 1890.

In the meantime the Smiths established a second pottery at Portland, where it might serve Washington as well as Oregon. This branch was in business from 1885 until 1896, gradually losing ground during later years to the rival Pacific Stoneware Company, which entered the lists in 1892 and persisted until the 1950s.

# GLOSSARY

AS WE ARE all aware, knowledge is power; and vocabulary is often the standard by which others define us. These commonly used ceramic terms are designed to allow the collector to understand the language of the field and to use it in such a way as to let dealers, collectors, and auction house personnel know that he/she is a sophisticated participant.

*Albany Slip:* A rich brown slip formed by mixing water with a fine brown clay, first found at Albany, New York, but also mined in California, Michigan, Indiana, and other states. Widely used to glaze stoneware

*Alkaline Glaze:* A stoneware glaze employed in the South consisting of wood ash, clay, and sand to which individual potters might add such things as slaked lime or iron foundry cinders; colors ranged from off-whites, browns, and blacks through yellows and greens and were often streaked

*Applied Decoration:* Pottery decoration that is separately molded or hand formed and then attached, using slip, to a ceramic body prior to firing

*Bisque:* Or biscuit, a ceramic body which has been fired once but not yet glazed

*Body:* A technical term for the combination of clays used in producing a piece of pottery

*Bristol Glaze:* An opaque white feldspathic slip with zinc oxide base maturing at 1,150–1,200 degrees Centigrade

*Burning:* The process of firing pottery in a kiln

*Ceramic:* A mineral-based substance, such as earthenware or stoneware, that is fired at a high temperature to a hard state

*Clay:* An earth or soil that becomes malleable when wet and hard after firing

*Cobalt Oxide:* Or "cobalt," a compound that when mixed with silica and potash produces a blue glaze generally used to decorate stone-ware

*Cockspur:* A usually small, three-cornered piece of baked clay used to separate items which are to be fired in a kiln

*Coggle Wheel:* A small wooden or metal wheel with shaped rim and handle which is used to make decorative impressions in soft, unbaked clay

*Coleslaw Decoration:* Applied decoration consisting of many tiny convoluted strands of clay that resemble wood shavings: rarely found on stoneware

*Collar:* A thick, raised band encircling the neck of a crock or jar

*Crazing:* Tiny cracks in ceramic glazes produced by the differing rates at which the body and glaze contract in firing or through age; also termed spidering

*Drape Molding:* The process of shaping a ceramic body by laying unfired clay over a form, pressing it down, and then trimming off the excess, much as in making a pie crust: occasionally used in the manufacture of stoneware plates and shallow bowls

*Earthenware:* Slightly porous pottery that is fired at a relatively low temperature, usually below 1100 degrees Centigrade

*Embossing:* Raised decoration formed by molding or hand shaping; not separately made and then applied

*Extruder:* A device, usually of wood, through which clay is forced to give it shape; typically used to make the ridged handles of pre-1840 stoneware jugs

*Ferruginous:* Material containing red oxide of iron

*Finial:* A molded or hand-shaped knob or protrusion that serves as the lift or handle on a lid

*Firing:* Heating a ceramic body to the desired hardness in a kiln

*Frog-Skin Glaze:* A greenish yellow colored stoneware glaze employed primarily in North Carolina: produced by throwing salt into a hot kiln of ware previously glazed with Albany slip

*Glaze:* A mixture of clay, water, and sand along with various metallic oxides or alkalies that is applied to a ceramic body before firing: it vitrifies during the firing process, producing a water-resistant surface

*Glaze Mill:* A device used to grind glaze ingredients to a fine powder before use and consisting of two stones, the smaller top one rotating against the stationary bottom one

*Greenware:* Unfired pottery

*Impressed Decoration:* Ceramic decoration created by pressing a shaped wood or metal stamp into the soft clay surface before firing; see Coggle Wheel

*Incised Decoration:* Ceramic decoration created through use of a sharp pointed instrument to scratch designs into the soft clay body prior to firing: best seen in early Northeastern stoneware

*Jigger:* See Jolly

*Jolly:* A device in which plastic clay is shaped in a turning mold, often mounted on a potter's wheel; the mold forms exterior of vessel, while a template cuts interior contour

*Kaolin:* A fine clay that fires to a pure white; often employed for teeth or eyes in Southern face jugs

*Kiln:* A stone or brick oven or furnace in which ceramic products are baked or fired

*Kiln Furniture:* pieces of previously baked clay used in stacking and separating pottery in a kiln; includes rings, cockspurs, and variously shaped blocks of clay

*Lead Glaze:* A redware glaze consisting of a mixture of lead oxide, water, and clay that fires to a shiny, glasslike surface; rarely employed on stoneware

*Leather Hard:* A term applied to greenware which is still wet but no longer plastic or flexible. Also termed "rubber hard"

*Lug Handle:* Term for the semicircular handles attached horizontally to sides of stoneware pots, crocks, and jars

*Manganese Oxide:* A metallic oxide used in ceramic glazes that fires from purplish brown to black; sometimes employed in stoneware decoration

*Mark:* The name and sometimes address of a potter embossed, impressed, incised, or ink stamped on his wares

*Modeling:* Shaping a soft clay body by hand and with hand-held tools

*Mold:* A plaster of Paris, wood, metal, or ceramic form made of one or more parts, often hinged, and used in shaping ceramics

*Molding:* The process of shaping pottery, either by pouring liquid clay or pressing soft clay into a mold and allowing it to harden there; once removed from the form the piece retains its configuration; see also Press Molding

*Neck:* The narrow area between rim and shoulder of a piece of pottery

*Ocher:* A reddish brown, iron-bearing clay used to glaze (particularly interiors of) stoneware prior to widespread availability of Albany-slip clay; pieces so finished are usually about 1830 or before

*Orange Peel:* A collector's term for salt glaze, reflecting the characteristic rough, pebbled surface

*Overglaze Decoration:* Decoration applied after a piece has been once glazed and fired; a second firing at a lower temperature is usually employed to "set" this decoration; uncommon in stoneware

*Paste:* A term used to describe the clay body from which a piece of pottery is made; see also Body

*Pierced Decoration:* Decoration produced by cutting areas out of a clay body; sometimes encountered in Pennsylvania, Virginia, and certain Midwestern stoneware

*Pipe Clay:* See Kaolin

*Plasticity:* That property of a clay body that allows it to be changed in form by pressure without cracking, and to retain a new shape when the pressure is removed

*Potter's Wheel:* A machine on which ceramic objects are shaped; the simplest consists of two disks joined by a shaft and set in a wooden frame; as the lower is turned, often by the foot, the upper, upon which the clay body rests, rotates

*Pottery:* Ceramics made from a clay or a mixture of clays; also the shop or factory where ceramics are manufactured

*Presentation Pieces:* Pottery intended as a gift or to commemorate a special occasion; often ornate, one-of-a-kind, and sometimes with date, name, or initials of recipient

*Press Molding:* The process of shaping pottery bodies in which plastic clay slabs are pressed by hand or a mechanical plunger into plaster or clay molds; see also Molding

*Production Pieces:* Standard wares made by most stoneware potteries such as jugs, jars, pots, and churns

*Pug Mill:* A machine for mixing and compressing plastic clays consisting of a large cylinder within which a bladed central shaft rotates

*Ribs:* Pieces of shaped metal or wood used by the potter in forming ware as it turns on the wheel

*Rim:* The upper edge of a piece of ceramic ware, also termed the lip

*Rouletting:* Banded decoration produced by a coggle wheel; see also Coggle Wheel

*Rubber Hard:* See Leather Hard

*Salt Glaze:* A shiny, glasslike, impermeable glaze usually employed on stoneware; produced by throwing salt into a hot kiln, where vaporized sodium in salt combines with silica in ceramic body

*Sgraffito:* A decorative technique, occasionally employed on stoneware, in which a potter covers the ceramic body with an opaque slip (usually Albany slip) and then scratches designs through it, partially revealing the underlying clay body

*Shard:* Or sherd, a term used for fragments of broken, usually antique, pottery

*Shoulder:* That part of a ceramic body between waist and neck

*Slip:* A suspension of ceramic materials in water

*Slip Casting:* Creation of a ceramic body by pouring slip into an absorbent (typically plaster of Paris) mold

*Slip Cup:* A small clay cup open at the top and having one or more small openings in side of base: Goose quills were inserted in these and slip, usually cobalt or kaolin, was trailed through them to create designs on a stoneware body

*Slip Decoration:* Stoneware decoration that is composed of colored slip and may be applied with slip cup or brush

*Slip Script:* Slip decoration in the form of initials, names, or expressions

*Sponged Decoration:* Stoneware decoration that consists of colored slip applied at random or in a pattern and with sponge or cloth: most typical is that found on late molded wares such as those from Red Wing, Minnesota

*Sprigging:* The application to a leather hard ceramic body of separately molded decorative elements such as handles or masks

*Stoneware:* A vitrified ceramic body ranging in color from shades of brown through gray to near white and fired at above 1200 degrees Centigrade

*Throwing:* The process of forming vessels on the potter's wheel; also referred to as turning

*Turning:* See Throwing

*Underglaze Decoration:* Decoration applied to a bisque ceramic body before the application of a glaze

*Waist:* The widest part of a ceramic body

*Wheel-thrown:* Shaped by hand on a potter's wheel

# BIBLIOGRAPHY

THE FOLLOWING BOOKS, museum catalogs, and articles have been selected as helpful to the student of American stoneware. Some are most valuable for their text, others for the photographs they contain. Many are out of print but can be located through used book dealers. As is the case with every area of antiques and collectibles, a good reference library is often the key to success.

Adamson, Jack E. *Illustrated Handbook of Ohio Sewer Pipe Folk Art*. Zoar, Ohio: privately printed, 1973.

Baldwin, Cindi. *Edgefield Face Vessels: African-American Contributions to American Folk Art,* in *American Visions,* August 1990.

Barber, Edwin A. *Marks of American Potters*. Philadelphia: Patterson & White Co.; reprinted, Southampton, New York: The Cracker Barrel Press, 1972.

————. *The Pottery and Porcelain of the United States: An Historical Review of American Ceramic Art From the Earliest Times to the Present Day*. New York and London: Putnam's Sons, 1893. Combined with *Marks of American Potters* and reprinted, New York: Feingold & Lewis, 1976.

Barka, Norman F. and Chris Sheridan. *The Yorktown Pottery Industry, Yorktown, Virginia,* in *Northeast Historical Archaeology*, Vol. 6, Nos. 1–2, Spring 1977.

Barons, Richard I. *18th and 19th Century American Folk Pottery*. Exhibition catalog. New Paltz, New York: State University of New York at New Paltz, 1969.

Barret, Richard C. *Bennington Pottery and Porcelain*. New York: Bonanza Books, 1958.

Bensch, Christopher, ed. *The Blue and the Gray: Oneida County Stoneware*. Exhibition catalog. Utica, New York: Munson-Williams-Proctor Institute, 1987.

Bivins, John, Jr. *The Moravian Potters in North Car-*

*olina*. Chapel Hill, North Carolina: The University of North Carolina Press, 1972.

Blair, C. Dean. *The Potters and Potteries of Summit County, 1828–1915*. Akron, Ohio: Summit County Historical Society, 1965.

Branin, M. Lelyn. *The Early Potters and Potteries of Maine*. Middletown, Connecticut: Wesleyan University Press, 1978.

———. *The Early Makers of Handcrafted Earthenware and Stoneware in Central and Southern New Jersey*. Rutherford, New Jersey: Fairleigh Dickinson University Press, 1988.

Bridges, Daisy Wade, ed. *Potters of the Catawba Valley*, in *Journal of Studies, Ceramic Circle of Charlotte* (North Carolina), Vol. IV, 1980.

Broderick, Warren. A *Survey of the Pottery Industry of Fort Edward and Sandy Hill*, in *The Hudson Valley Regional Review*, Vol. 8, No. 1, March 1991.

Burbage, Beverly S. *The Remarkable Pottery of Charles Decker and His Sons*, in *The Tennessee Conservationist*, Vol. XXXVII, No. 11, 1971.

Burrison, John A. *Georgia Jug Makers: A History of Southern Folk Pottery*. Ann Arbor, Michigan: University Microfilms International, 1973.

———. *The Meaders Family of Mossy Creek: Eighty Years of North Georgia Folk Pottery*. Exhibition catalog. Atlanta, Georgia: Georgia State University, 1976.

Clement, Arthur W. *Our Pioneer Potters*. Brooklyn, New York, Maple Press, 1947.

Conway, Bob and Gilreath, eds. *Traditional Pottery in North Carolina*. Waynesville, North Carolina: The Mountaineer, 1974.

Corbett, Cynthia Arps. *Useful Art: Long Island Pottery*. Setauket, Long Island, New York: Society for the Preservation of Long Island Antiquities, 1985.

Corrigan, David J. *The F.B. Norton Pottery: Stoneware of Every Description*. Exhibition catalog. Worcester, Massachusetts: Worcester Historical Museum, 1980.

Cueller, Robert. *Shenandoah Pottery Highlights Zigler Estate Auction,* in *Antiques and the Arts Weekly,* September 14, 1990.

Cullity, Brian. *Face-to-Face: Figurative American Sculpture,* in *Antiques Journal,* November 1990.

Davies, Mel. *Clay County Indiana Traditional Potters and Their Wares*. Exhibition catalog. Columbus, Indiana: Ad Craft Printing, 1981.

Dearolf, Kenneth. *Wisconsin Folk Pottery*. Kenosha, Wisconsin: Kenosha Public Museum, 1986.

Denker, Ellen Paul. *The Kirkpatricks' Pottery, Anna, Illinois*, in *Northeast Historical Archaeology*, Vols. 7, 8, 9, 1978–1980.

DePasquale, Dan and Gail and Larry Peterson. *Red Wing Stoneware*. Paducah, Kentucky: Collector Books, 1983.

———. *Red Wing Collectibles*. Paducah, Kentucky: Collector Books, 1985.

Dewhurst, C. Kurt and Marsha MacDowell. *Cast in Clay: The Folk Pottery of Grand Ledge, Michigan*. Lansing, Michigan: Michigan State Folk Culture Series, Vol. I, No. 2.

Ferrell, Stephen T. and T. M. Ferrell. *Early Decorated Stoneware of the Edgefield District, South Carolina*. Exhibition catalog. Greenville, South Carolina: Greenville County Museum of Art, 1976.

Giannini, Robert L., III. *Anthony Duche, Sr.: Potter and Merchant of Philadelphia,* in *The Magazine Antiques,* January 1981.

Greer, Georgeanna H. *American Stonewares: The Art and Craft of Utilitarian Potters*. Exton, Pennsylvania: Schiffer Publishing Ltd., 1981.

——— and Harding Black. *The Meyer Family: Master Potters in Texas*. San Antonio, Texas: Trinity University Press, 1971.

Guilland, Harold F. *Early American Folk Pottery*. Philadelphia, Chilton Books, 1971.

Harrison, James M. and Louis S. Meyer. *Nineteenth Century Erie County Stoneware,* in *The Journal of Erie Studies*, Vol. 18, No. 1, Spring 1989.

Hillier, Bevis. *Pottery and Porcelain 1700–1914*. Des Moines, Iowa, and New York: Meredith Press, 1968.

Horne, Catherine Wilson, ed. *Crossroads of Clay: The Southern Alkaline-Glazed Stoneware Tradition*. Columbia, South Carolina: The University of South Carolina, 1990.

James, Arthur E. *The Potters and Potteries of Chester County, Pennsylvania*. West Chester, Pennsylvania, Chester County Historical Society, 1945; second edition, Exton, Pennsylvania: Schiffer Publishing Ltd., 1978.

Ketchum, William C., Jr. *Early Potters and Potteries of New York State*. New York: Funk & Wagnalls, 1970; revised second edition, titled *Potters and Potteries of New York State, 1650–1900*. Syracuse, New York: Syracuse University Press, 1987.

———. *The Pottery and Porcelain Collector's Handbook*. New York: Funk & Wagnalls, 1971.

———. *The Knopf Collectors' Guides to American Antiques: Pottery and Porcelain*. New York, Alfred A. Knopf, 1983.

———. *The Pottery of the State*. Exhibition catalog. New York: Museum of American Folk Art, 1974.

Lasansky, Jeanette: *Made of Mud: Stoneware Potteries of Central Pennsylvania 1831–1929*. University Park, Pennsylvania: The Pennsylvania State University Press, 1979.

Leder, Steven B., ed., *Stoneware Collectors Journal,* Vols. 1–5, Hamden, Connecticut: privately printed, 1984–1988.

Loar, Peggy A. *Indiana Stoneware*. Exhibition catalog. Indianapolis, Indiana: Indianapolis Museum of Art, 1974.

Locker, Paul. *The Late, Great S. Routson and His Pottery*. Wooster, Ohio: privately printed, 1983.

Madden, Betty. *Arts, Crafts and Architecture in Illinois*. Urbana, Illinois: University of Illinois Press, 1974.

Martin, Jim and Bette Cooper. *Monmouth Western Stoneware*. Des Moines, Iowa: Wallace-Homestead Book Company, 1983.

McCormick, Tamsie. *William Keller: Tale of a Midwest Potter,* in *The Tri-State Trader,* Vol. 12, No. 17, August 1979.

Michael, Ronald L. *Stoneware from Fayette, Greene and Washington Counties, Pennsylvania,* in *Northeast Historical Archaeology,* Vol. 6, Nos. 1–2, Spring 1977.

Mississippi State Historical Museum. *Made by Hand*. Exhibition catalog. Jackson, Mississippi: Department of Archives and History, 1980.

Mounce, Eva Dodge. *Checklist of Illinois Potters and Potteries*. Springfield, Illinois: Foundation for Historical Research of Illinois Potteries, 1989.

Museum of Our National Heritage. *Unearthing New England's Past: The Ceramic Evidence*. Lexington, Massachusetts: Scottish Rite Museum and Library, Inc., 1984.

Myers, Susan H. *Handcraft to Industry: Philadelphia Ceramics in the First Half of the Nineteenth Century*. Washington, D.C.: Smithsonian Institution Press, 1980.

Newark Museum. *The Pottery and Porcelain of New Jersey: 1688–1900*. Newark, New Jersey, 1947.

New Jersey State Museum. *Early Arts of New Jersey: The Potter's Art c. 1680–1900*. Trenton, New Jersey: New Jersey State Museum, 1956.

Noel Hume, Ivor. *Pottery and Porcelain in Colonial Williamsburg's Archaeological Collections*. Williamsburg, Virginia: Colonial Williamsburg Foundation, 1969.

Osgood, Cornelius. *The Jug and Related Stoneware of Bennington*. Rutland, Vermont: Charles E. Tuttle Company, 1971.

Perry, Barbara, ed. *American Ceramics: The Collection of the Everson Museum of Art*. New York: Rizzoli International Publications, 1989.

Powell, Elizabeth A. *Pennsylvania Pottery, Tools and Processes*. Doylestown, Pennsylvania: The Bucks County Historical Society, 1972.

Quimby, Ian M. G., ed. *Ceramics in America.* Charlottesville, Virginia: The University of Virginia Press, 1973.

Ramsay, John. *American Potters and Pottery.* Boston: Hale, Cushman & Flint, 1939; reprinted, New York: Tudor Publishing Co., 1947.

Rauschenberg, Bradford L. *B. DuVal & Co./Richmond: A Newly Discovered Pottery,* in *Journal of Early Southern Decorative Arts,* May 1978.

Rice, A. H. and John Baer Stoudt. *The Shenandoah Pottery.* Strasburg, Virginia: Shenandoah Publishing House, Inc., 1929.

Rochester Museum and Science Center. *Clay in the Hands of the Potter.* Rochester, New York: Rochester House of Printing, 1974.

Russ, Kurt C. and John M. McDaniel. *The Traditional Pottery Manufacturing Industry in Virginia: Examples from Botecourt and Rockbridge Counties, 1785–1894,* in *Proceedings of the Rockbridge Historical Society,* Volume X, 1987.

Scarborough, Quincy. *Connecticut Influence on North Carolina Stoneware: The Webster School of Potters,* in *MESDA Journal,* May 1984.

Schaltenbrand, Phil. *New Geneva and Its Stoneware Production,* in *The Antiques Journal,* December 1978.

———. *Old Pots: Salt Glazed Stoneware of the Greensboro–New Geneva Region.* Hanover, Pennsylvania: Everybody's Press, 1977.

Schwartz, Marvin D. *Collector's Guide to Antique American Ceramics.* Garden City, New York: Doubleday & Co., Inc., 1969.

Smith, Elmer L. *Pottery: A Utilitarian Folk Craft.* Lebanon, Pennsylvania: Applied Arts Publishers, 1973.

Smith, Howard. *Index of Southern Potters.* Mayodan, North Carolina: The Old America Company, 1982.

Smith, Joseph J., with introduction by William C. Ketchum, Jr. *Regional Aspects of American Folk Pottery.* Exhibition catalog. York, Pennsylvania: The Historical Society of York County, 1974.

Spargo, John. *Early American Pottery and China.* New York and London: The Century Co., 1926; reprinted, Rutland, Vermont: Charles E. Tuttle Co., 1974.

———. *The Potters and Potteries of Bennington.* Boston: Houghton Mifflin Co., 1926; reprinted, New York: Dover Publications, Inc., 1972.

Stevens, Bob and Kathy. *A Checklist of Missouri Potters,* in *Antique Review,* May 1985.

Stiles, Helen E. *Pottery in the United States.* New York: E. P. Dutton, 1921.

Stradling, Diana and J. Garrison, eds. *The Art of the Potter.* Antiques Magazine Library. New York: Universe Books, 1977.

Sudbury, Byron. *Historic Clay Tobacco Pipe Makers in the United States of America.* Oxford, England: BAR International Series, 1979.

Van Ravensway, Charles. *The Arts and Architecture of German Settlements in Missouri.* Columbia, Missouri: University of Missouri Press, 1977.

Viel, Lyndon C. *The Clay Giants: The Stoneware of Redwing, Goodhue County, Minnesota.* Des Moines, Iowa: Wallace-Homestead Book Company, 1977.

Vigo County Historical Society. *Function Follows Form: An Exhibit of Indiana Stoneware 1840–1900.* Exhibition catalog. Vigo County, Indiana: privately printed, 1987.

Watkins, Lura Woodside. *Early New England Potters and Their Wares.* Cambridge, Massachusetts: Harvard University Press, 1950; reprinted, Hamden, Connecticut: Archon Books, 1968.

Webster, Donald Blake. *Decorated Stoneware Pottery of North America.* Rutland, Vermont: Charles E. Tuttle Company, 1971.

Willett, E. Henry and Joey Brackner. *The Traditional Pottery of Alabama.* Exhibition catalog. Montgomery, Alabama: Montgomery Museum of Fine Arts, 1983.

Wiltshire, William E., III. *Folk Pottery of the Shenandoah Valley.* New York: E. P. Dutton, 1975.

Winburn, Hardy L., Jr. *Seventy Years of Saline County Pottery*. Benton, Arkansas: Niloak Pottery Company, 1938.

Winton, Andrew L. and Kate B. *Norwalk Potteries*. Canaan, New Hampshire: Phoenix Publishing, 1981.

Zug, Charles G. *The Alkaline Glazed Stoneware of North Carolina* in *Northeast Historical Archaeology*, Vols. 7, 8, 9, 1978–1980.

———. *The Traditional Pottery of North Carolina*. Exhibition catalog. Chapel Hill, North Carolina: University of North Carolina, 1981.

# INDEX

*Numbers in italics refer to an illustration and its caption*

# ACKNOWLEDGMENTS

*Among the many people who generously donated their time, knowledge, and photographs to this book, I particularly want to thank the following: Dr. Arthur Goldberg, Jack Hammann, Sue Hannum, Jim Harrison, Roy Stubbs, Sharon W. Joel, Steven B. Leder, and Bob Treichler.*

## PICTURE CREDITS

*Illustrations in this book are from the following collections: Jane and Jim Appuzzo, 19 (right); Author's Collection: 2, 3, 12, 19 (left), 20 (both), 21 (both), 27, 30 (top), 34, 39, 50, 99, 108 (both); Fran and Doug Faulkner, 38; Arthur Goldberg, iii, 7, 10, 11, 23, 41, 42, 43, 48, 51, 55, 77, 83 (bottom), 84, 87, 89, 103, 105, 111, 112, 114, 115, 118, 127, 138 (both); Jack and Sharon Hammann, 15, 31, Ken and Sue Hannum, 9 (top), 133 (bottom); James M. Harrison, 18 (top), 90, 92, 95 (both); A. Hodge, C. Miller, H. McDaniel, and Roy and Sue Stubbs, 142 (top); Sharon W. Joel, 17 (right); Candace and John King, 17 (left); Steven B. Leder, 7 (bottom), 18 (bottom), 28, 61, 64, 69, 70, 71, 72; Ed Miller, 126; Brian A. Moore, 131 (both), 134 (right); Dave Prime, 24; Private Collection, 5 (both), 6 (top), 8, 9 (bottom), 26, 29, 30 (bottom), 33, 49, 73, 75, 81, 100, 109, 120, 134 (left), 136, 151; David Roche, 4, 25; Marybeth Sollins, 59 (both), 60, 83 (top); Roy and Sue Stubbs, 14, 140, 141; Roy and Sue Stubbs, Johnson County Historical Society, and Mrs. Byron Stewart, 142 (bottom), 143; Nancy and Bob Treichler, 16 (both), 125 (both), 128(both), 129; Bill and Diana Zwerner, 133 (top).*